In this clear and often magical account of how David and Ellen helped
their kids find ways to take charge of their own education, a universal
lesson is written: real learning is much richer and more mysterious than
any school can encompass, and institutional habits, rules, and assumption
— which usually masquerade as scientific pedagogy — are an enormous
handicap to growing up whole. Albert's intense thoughtfulness about every
aspect of waking up to full humanity is a treat you should not miss.
— John Taylor Gatto, former New York State and 3-Time New York City
Teacher of the Year; author, *Dumbing Us Down: The Hidden Curriculum of
Compulsory Schooling*

An utterly fascinating critique of American education, as well as a joyous
celebration of the creative potential in every child.
— Anthony Manousas, *Friends Bulletin*

This invigorating adventure story is about more than homeschooling and
community-based education. It is about honoring our appetite for what is
real. It is about drawing out the innate creativity and brilliance of a child.
And that's good news for the child within each of us.
— Joanna Macy, author, *Coming Back to Life: Practices to Reconnect
Our Lives, Our World*

David Albert's *And the skylark sings with me* is a beautifully told story about how he and his wife are raising their daughters outside of conventional schooling, and the amazing results that they see unfolding before them. Albert's careful descriptions of what he and his wife do to nurture, support, and direct their children's learning will give heart to parents worried that before they can help their children learn about wolves, astronomy, biology, nature, math, and music — to name a few of the subjects covered — they must become certified teachers.

A joyous and memorable book!

— Pat Farenga, President, Holt Associates,
publisher, *Growing Without Schooling*

———◆———

We are tempted to say that *And the skylark sings with me* is of the greatest value to all homeschoolers. That would be a mistake. This articulate and moving description of care and love in education is of the greatest value to all parents and educators. May the inspiration in this book enter our hearts and minds as we honor children and life."

— Sambhava and Josette Luvmour, Encompass:
The Center for Natural Learning Rhythms, Nevada City, CA

And
the skylark
sings
with me

*A*nd the skylark sings with me

Adventures in Homeschooling and Community-Based Education

David H. Albert

NEW SOCIETY PUBLISHERS

Cataloging in Publication Data:
A catalog record for this publication is available from the National Library of Canada.

Cover design by Miriam MacPhail from an original painting by Soren Henrich.

Printed in Canada on acid-free, partially recycled (20 percent post-consumer) paper using soy-based inks by Transcontinental/Best Book Manufacturers.

Quotation from *Ravens in Winter*, by Bernd Heinrich (New York: Summit Books, 1989) used with gracious permission of the author.

Paperback ISBN: 0-86571-401-0

Published by New Society Publishers in cooperation with Holt Associates/*Growing Without Schooling*, 2380 Massachusetts Ave., Suite 104, Cambridge, MA 02140

New Society Publishers acknowledges the financial support of the Government of Canada through the Book Publishing Industry Development Program (BPIDP) for our publishing activities, and the assistance of the Province of British Columbia through the British Columbia Arts Council.

Inquiries regarding requests to reprint all or part of *And the skylark sings with me* should be addressed to New Society Publishers at the address below.

To order directly from the publishers, please add $4.00 shipping to the price of the first copy, and $1.00 for each additional copy (plus GST in Canada). Send check or money order to:

New Society Publishers
P.O. Box 189, Gabriola Island, BC V0R 1X0, Canada

Holt Associates publishes *Growing Without Schooling* magazine and other materials about how people learn outside of school. Our full list of books can be browsed at: www.holtgws.com

New Society Publishers aims to publish books for fundamental social change through non-violent action. We focus especially on sustainable living, progressive leadership, and educational and parenting resources. Our full list of books can be browsed on the worldwide web at: www.newsociety.com

NEW SOCIETY PUBLISHERS
Gabriola Island BC, Canada

To Patricia —
With all best wishes
for your family's learning
adventures!

David Albert

July 1, 2000

I love to rise in a summer morn
When the birds sing on every tree;
The distant huntsman winds his horn.
And the skylark sings with me.
O! what sweet company.

But to go to school in a summer morn,
O! it drives all joy away;
Under a cruel eye outworn,
The little ones spend the day
In sighing and dismay.

Ah! then at times I drooping sit,
And spend many an anxious hour,
Nor in my book can I take delight,
Nor sit in learning's bower,
Worn thro' with the dreary shower.

How can the bird that is born for joy
Sit in a cage and sing?
How can a child, when fears annoy,
But droop his tender wing,
And forget his youthful spring?

O! father & mother, if buds are nip'd
And blossoms blown away,
And if the tender plants are strip'd
Of their joy in the springing day,
By sorrow and care's dismay,

How shall the summer arise in joy,
Or the summer fruits appear?
Or how shall we gather what griefs destroy,
Or bless the mellowing year,
When the blasts of winter appear?

William Blake, "The School Boy"
from *Songs of Innocence*

This book is dedicated to
Krishnamal and S. Jagannathan,
and Jyoti and Malini Desai

And we are put on earth a little space,
That we may learn to bear the beams of love

William Blake, "The Little Black Boy"
from *Songs of Innocence*

Table of Contents

Foreword

Joseph Chilton Pearce

Here is a brilliant, insightful description of the challenges with which Nature confronts perceptive parents and a clear prescription for that mediated learning critically needed by a developing intelligence and spirit if a child is to actually embrace the world, rather than be intimidated by and retreat from it.

And the skylark sings with me should now be considered the definitive work on homeschooling, that reciprocal adventure between parent and child that allows true education to take place — for both of them. It is a journal describing what happens when parents joyously enter into their offspring's unfolding and find their own fulfillment thereby. This account of the nurturing of child genius strikes me as a superb model of what all parents can do to bring forth the best in their children, and to share in the joys and riches of doing so.

David Albert gives us, with unpretentious clarity and admirable economy, as profound an insight into the development of intelligence in children as is to be found in many a ponderous professional tome. I would go so far as to say that the perennial "nature versus nurture" debate must be seriously reappraised in the light of this book. DNA might carry essential blueprints for a range of intelligence, but the environment provides the raw materials through which these blueprints are actualized, as Ali and her adopted sister Meera demonstrate. All seeds contain life, but those dropped among rocks and thorns simply stand far less chance of expressing that life than those falling on fertile soil. When that environment provides the appropriate model-stimuli, the young spirit will flower. If environmental nurturing is not there, that same young spirit wilts.

This book stands as an urgent reminder that parents are the first and foremost environment, the fundamental determinant not just in conception and pregnancy, but through the developmental years. Meera and Ali's story is not just an account of exceptional precocity, but of exceptional parental support and guidance as well. As Albert so ably demonstrates, every child has his or her own particular genius, but it will manifest itself or not according to nurturing, the calling-forth of that genius. Here we see nature and nurture as an interdependent dynamic, rather as Meister Eckhart and the Sufi sage Ibn Arabi spoke of, creator and created "giving rise to each other."

Albert's description of the overwhelming failure of conventional schooling is unique and enlightening. Free of polemic, accusation, or casting of blame, his insightful, rather wistful perception of the tragedy schooling has inflicted upon childhood and society stands in stark contrast with the wondrous world his daughters reveal to us. To one well into the seventh decade of his journey to wherever, this marvelous magical tale brought poignant and disturbing reflections on my own childhood and semi-sleep-walk parenting, my sad witness to too many budding intelligences' failure to flower, too many promises broken. David Albert shows how it should have been for us readers, but, far more importantly, how it can be for our children, if we readers will accept the challenge presented. There are far too few Alis and Meeras — and Ellens and Davids — in our world, so take up the challenge and let there be more!

And the skylark sings with me is an intellectual tour de force that is a sheer delight to read, an elegant and graceful work of literary art; an exquisite portrait of the magical child's emergence into and embrace of the world as Great Nature intended. The text is multi-layered and filled with profound insights and discussions that will draw the perceptive reader back again and again, finding more every time. Accept then, this unique, delightful gift by reading with an open heart and mind, and share it with as many others as have ears to hear.

Saraswati

Piping down the valleys wild,
Piping songs of peasant glee,
On a cloud I saw a child
And he laughing said to me:
"Pipe a song about a Lamb!"
So I piped with merry chear,
"Piper, pipe that song again;"
So I piped, he wept to hear.

William Blake, "Introduction"
from *Songs of Innocence*

Saraswati had not prepared us for musicians. Serious musicians, two of them, each with very different and unique talents.

In Hindu mythology, Lord Shiva has two daughters: Lakshmi and Saraswati. A family can hope to win the blessing of one perhaps, but likely not both of at the same time. Lakshmi is the goddess of wealth and abundance. We have enough for our needs, praise be, but certainly not enough to cause much envy among our friends. But Saraswati — the goddess of memory and music — has blessed our household many times over.

And so we were caught almost totally unprepared. My partner Ellen had played the flute and oboe through junior high, could carry a tune, and enjoyed listening. Her musical tastes around the time of birth of our older daughter Ali leaned toward the political gospel of Sweet Honey and the Rock and the feminist folk-rock of Holly Near. I was a different story. Though without any childhood training to speak of, I had strong music and music history interests throughout my college years, sang in the college choir, and loved opera. I pursued virtually none of these interests for almost 15 years preceding Ali's birth, and had practically given up listening to classical music. Neither Ellen nor I had attended a classical music concert or an operatic performance in almost a decade, and counted no classical musicians, amateur or professional, among our friends.

There was the barest of threads. In my 30s, while in India, I had taken up the veena, the seven-stringed South Indian musical instrument made from the wood of the jackfruit tree. The veena is sacred to, and played by, the goddess Saraswati. I turned out to be quite good at it, for an American. The number of Americans who master the veena's intricacies beyond the beginner's level can be counted on two hands, with several fingers likely left over. I had played for religious rituals with up to 5,000 people in attendance in South India, a benefit concert in Sri Lanka, and at musical soirees in the U.S. At the time of Ali's birth, I hadn't studied the veena in several years, and rarely practiced.

Not a particularly propitious beginning for musical children, I would have thought. Ali played happily to the sounds of the Beach Boys during her first year or so, and Ellen and I were working so hard we scarcely gave music a second thought.

The fateful turn of events occurred at a Handel's *Messiah* Sing-and-Play-In held in July. Yes, July. Santa Cruz, California, possessed the unusual distinction of holding its yearly participatory celebration of Handel's great oratorio shortly after its annual July 4th "Anarchist-Socialist Softball Game," which now must be approaching its 25th year. And I, for reasons having nothing to do with religion, musical upbringing, or tradition, somehow decided I had to attend. Ellen also thought this would be a fun outing and decided to bring 20-month-old Ali along.

We arrived early and Ellen, trying to amuse the already-squirming toddler, decided to lead her by the hand up to the makeshift stage to look at the instruments, none of which Ali had ever encountered live before. To Ellen's astonishment, Ali knew their names — flute, cello, trumpet, clarinet ... We don't know from where — we didn't teach her. We've assumed she must have picked up this information from an episode of *Sesame Street* when we weren't looking, but honestly we just don't know. (It would be years yet before Ellen and I would have a serious "kids and TV" discussion.)

We had explained to Ali that we were going to sing the "Hallelujah Chorus." I have no idea why we thought this might be a useful explanation, as Ali had never heard the Hallelujah Chorus! After examining the instruments, Ali turned around to face the gathering singers, and in her high-pitched toddler's voice urged, "Now let's all sing together," and launched into her version of "Michael Row Your Boat Ashore," the only song she knew with "hallelujah" in it.

Ellen hustled Ali off the stage and, to keep her occupied, asked whether she'd like to learn to play any of those instruments some day. Ali replied, "The violin. I want to learn to play the violin. *Now!*" Ellen assured her that someday she might learn to play. The rest of the evening was uneventful; I don't even remember whether we stayed late enough to sing the "Hallelujah Chorus."

Nothing would have come of this except that every day, sometimes twice a day, for the next three months, Ali demanded that she wanted to learn to play the violin. This sounded absolutely crazy to us. Did they make violins that small? Could a teacher be found who would be willing to teach a toddler still in diapers? Would a bad experience turn her off from music-making for life? Would she learn anything that would be of value?

The answers to the foregoing questions are: Yes, Yes, No, and emphatically Yes. Ali's first violin was 14 inches long (a "1/64th" as it's called), and currently sits atop our piano. A local teacher versed in the Suzuki method found the idea of teaching an under-two-year-old somewhat amusing, and Ali was pretty determined. Ali had now given us two of our most important homeschooling lessons, both of which carried over into all aspects of our learning adventures: first, that we weren't going to be able to do everything ourselves, and hence would have to learn how to find other resources; and second, that we were going to be experimental in approach rather than be governed by someone else's narrow conception of "age-appropriateness."

We learned another lesson, too, which led me to risk beginning this book with our family's musical adventures. I am aware of course that music is not every child's cup of tea, and our experience around it might be sufficiently foreign as to make it difficult for some readers to relate to easily. But the point is that music turned out to be, regardless of our own expectations, something both of our children are passionate about, something intimately entwined in their earliest notions of their unique identities. Our kids taught us that our task is to seek avenues for whatever inward leadings they exhibit to blossom, and to find ways for our children to become who they already are, or were meant to be.

Anyway, the story is supposed to go like this: "Ali picked up the violin and bow and within seconds was playing Bach and sounding like Yehudi Menuhin, today her favorite violinist." Nothing could be further from the truth. Parenthetically, it should be noted that Menuhin, upon demanding a violin for his fourth birthday, was given a metal one which he promptly broke in frustration. Menuhin, by the way, along with Isaac Stern and the sensational young violinist Hilary Hahn, is one of the world's most famous contemporary products of homeschooling, having lasted in first grade precisely one day. Fourteen-inch violins played by a virtuoso might sound like a cat in heat; played by Ali it was more like chalk upon easel. Still, she got the general idea that four left-hand fingers could be set down upon four variously tuned strings at dozens of different points, and that only one spot at a time would be correct. At her first public appearance, she walked onto the stage, announced she would play "Mary had a Little Lamb," brought the violin to her chin, strummed the strings twice, and proceeded to *sing* it, to great applause.

Seeing and hearing Ali and our younger daughter Meera today, parents often ask our opinion of the Suzuki method. This is despite the fact that neither of our children learned by utilizing it. But for what it's worth, from what we know, we look upon Suzuki quite favorably. Firstly, it must be said that Suzuki is single-handedly responsible for hundreds or even thousands of string programs springing up in elementary and middle schools across the country, which, for some children, is the best experience they will ever have in school. When Ellen and I were growing up, the violin was thought to be simply too difficult for all but the most talented children. Band instruments, pianos, or even, perish the thought, accordions (I too have my own prejudices) were the recommended choices for pre-teens. Now we know, thanks to Suzuki, that stringed instruments can be taught effectively to children at an early age. Furthermore, recent brain research suggests that for a string player to have any real hopes of succeeding, instruction should commence before age 12 (and preferably much earlier) to reinforce brain/fine-motor skill interactions. I would note, however, that my own experience and that of the late John Holt, a founder of the modern homeschooling movement who successfully took up the cello after age 40, are firm reminders that our early childhoods do not have to be the sole determinants of our musical destinies.

Secondly, Suzuki insists on substantial parental involvement, more than just driving one's child to and from lessons. In some larger Suzuki schools including most of those in Japan, parents are required to attend their own classes while their children are learning. That level of parental commitment is sure to redound to the child's benefit, as is the creation of a musical community.

Thirdly, the early stages of Suzuki teaching focus on repetitive motion training. It's rather like learning to throw a baseball the right way — you're more likely to get it if you do it a couple of thousand times. Repetitive motion training is particularly useful for the majority of children who are reasonably physically coordinated, have moderately good musical ears, but may not yet be ready to tackle complex symbol systems.

Fourthly, the selections included in the well-edited Suzuki music books are meticulously chosen to allow a child to progress and gain technical proficiency. The accompanying music tapes provide an aural crutch and standard by which students can chart their own progress.

Lastly, while there have been some notable exceptions, Suzuki was under no illusion that he was going to produce a bumper crop of virtuosi, though he surely had his share. His goal was to create a climate in which music could be better appreciated by young and old, and to raise the general benchmark levels of musical performance. The major growth of community youth symphonies around the U.S. and the rest of the world, even at a time when general understanding and appreciation of classical music is on the decline, in part attests to Suzuki's success. If today I have a single quibble with the application of Suzuki's work, it is with some Suzuki teachers who, at some remove from the master, elevate technique over musicianship, control and method over total involvement and the free flight of the child's imagination. But then I wouldn't only say that about Suzuki teachers!

Regardless of our thoughts about Suzuki, after six months of sawing, Ali told us and her music teacher in no uncertain terms that *she wanted to read the notes*. Out went Suzuki and in came Leopold Mozart, scales, and later, the progressively more difficult exercise books. In hindsight it is plain that two-and-a-half-year-old Ali knew herself well and had better sense than we, the one saving grace being that we listened. Ali has always possessed good fine-motor skills, but her gross-motor skills tend toward clumsy. Her ear is better than average and has now been trained for a long time, but all in all we knew from very early on that she lacked the magical concatenation of natural talents that marks a true virtuoso. But what she has, and what others besides her parents recognize, is an abundance of intellectual curiosity. With Ali reading the notes, recognizing their relationships in sound, and understanding their physical demands upon her playing, the intellectual puzzle posed by the music itself became the motivating force behind her growth as a musician.

Early on, Ellen and I agreed on some ground rules for our children's musical education. The cardinal and inviolate rule is that music is to be its own reward. From age five on, Ali and Meera came to understand that learning an instrument assumes daily practice, seven days a week, with inevitable and not-infrequent exceptions. There are no external rewards for practice: the reward for practice is more lessons, and more opportunities to make beautiful music. They do not have to practice, and they do not have to take lessons; this is totally their choice. Of course, we have our share of squabbles, and there have been those terrible practice days, and *dry* periods (adults experience them, so why shouldn't kids), but Ali and Meera always know what our expectations, and their responsibilities, are. We have explained to surprised and bemused teachers that we don't approve of them giving gold stars or reward stickers for practice, only for progress (and after the fact), and never as prizes.

If this seems a bit harsh in theory, in practice it has served both of our children extremely well. Several of their music teachers have remarked that our rapport with our children around music is unique among the families they serve. We keep Ali and Meera motivated by making them aware and excited about the musical universe the future holds in store for them if they apply themselves. For Meera, this takes the form of classical compact discs, mostly of famous pianists. For Ali, it's usually new sheet music.

We often celebrate their small triumphs — performances and student recitals — with commemorative gifts, usually music-oriented: books, compact discs, musical-note jewelry, etc. When possible, I date the object with a note, so they can look back at the gift and be reminded of how far they've come since then. I try to make sure these gifts are offered as surprises and are given regardless of how well their actual performances went.

Our move to Olympia, Washington, was somewhat disruptive to all of our lives. Ali gave up the violin for the following year. We then found her another teacher, but both temperamentally and musically, it wasn't a perfect match. When her teacher announced a year later that she wanted to devote herself totally to country fiddle-playing and limit to her teaching to that, six-and-a-half-year-old Ali tearfully insisted that she only wanted to study classical music. It was time to look for a new teacher.

Ali and we quickly narrowed down the field of new violin teachers to two fine candidates. The deciding factor was remarks each teacher made to Ali following her auditions. Upon hearing Ali attempt pieces that were perhaps somewhat above her technical abilities, the first teacher complimented her profusely and stated it was now time to go back to simpler music and concentrate on polishing up her technique, fixing her bow hold, etc., to make the music sound even more beautiful. The second teacher, noting similar deficiencies, suggested she would start with yet more difficult music to challenge Ali's imagination. They would work on technique, but slowly, over time. We wouldn't have had a clue as to which was the correct approach (assuming there is one), but Ali had absolutely no uncertainty — she chose the latter.

After three years, Ali's relationship with Phyllis — who is primarily a viola player and a member of the local symphony and chamber orchestra —

is complex and a thing of beauty. At times, the learning process is barely perceptible — work on an alternative fingering here, a rhythmic correction there. Exercises, selected pieces, and compositions of Ali's own choosing make up a steady and ever-changing diet. Ali enjoys seeing Phyllis perform in symphony and chamber music concerts, and at other local cultural events. We are especially pleased that our children encounter their teachers in other than instructional settings.

Just before she turned seven, we signed Ali up to participate in our local public school's second-year strings program, as we wanted her (and she wanted) to have the opportunity to play in a group. While the other students were fifth graders, Ali more than held her own. An experience in the music program reminded us of the fascinating gaps that occur in our children's general knowledge as a result of homeschooling. Ali got to class early one morning and excitedly told her teacher about her birthday present from her grandmother — a tape of Sibelius' Second Symphony performed by the Philadelphia Orchestra — which she had requested. She also played a portion of a new composition she was writing. When the other children arrived, the music teacher placed new sheet music on each of their music stands. All of the other children broke out in song, "Frosty the Snowman/Was a very jolly soul..." Ali, normally quite reserved, anxiously looked around, plaintively inquiring, "Who is Frosty the Snowman?"

The following summer, Ali auditioned for and was accepted into the Capital Area Youth Symphony as their second youngest member. The Olympia area, with a metropolitan population of around 70,000, on a per capita basis has one of the largest youth symphony associations in the United States, with well over 400 members. Ellen has since joined its board, with a special interest in increasing young musicians' attendance at area music events. Ali regularly attends and even has her own season tickets to various local music groups, and we've kept our family expenses down by becoming ushers at the local performing arts center and distributing publicity posters in exchange for free admission. Ali's progress has been steady, with her greatest initial problem being that in her orchestral chair, her feet had difficulty reaching the floor. She continues to be creative. Ellen and I rarely attend rehearsals, but at a recent dress rehearsal, I noted her bowing was going in an entirely different direction from the second violinists around her. "What happened?" I asked. "Well," she replied, "my music stand partner wasn't turning the pages quickly enough, so I decided to play along with the firsts, who have the melody." The "creativity problem" was cleared up before the performance. Ali does not seem to mind competitive auditions for chairs. She can be a perfectionist at times, but her perfectionism is inner-directed rather than competitively motivated. Given that she is much younger than most of her fellow violinists, she doesn't feel much pressure. In one audition, she jumped from tenth chair to third. "How did you do it?" I asked. She grinned, "Well, it turns out I practiced the wrong passage. So I played the required one that I didn't practice, and then asked to play what I'd practiced. They seemed to like them both."

Ali moved from violin size to violin size, each increase improving her tonal quality. When reaching the "3/4" size, she was pleased to have us purchase her own instrument, since she would have it for a while. We were satisfied since it was cheaper than renting, and we could resell it when Ali grew into her next one. Actually, *she* purchased the instrument, paid for with funds earned from selling six of the mutated cornsnakes she had bred that summer. The violin cost almost exactly what she received for the snakes, which pleased her immensely. When people would ask her what her violin cost, she would smile and sometimes reply, "Six snakes."

Her next violin purchase caught us unprepared. Ellen, Meera, and Ali went to Seattle to spend the day at the Northwest Folklife Festival, held each May. After looking at various craft activities, Ellen and Ali went to the large room where instruments consigned for the annual musical instrument auction could be inspected. The auction attracts musicians and dealers from the entire three-state region all the way up to Canada, and Ellen was hoping to find a reasonably priced oboe. While so engaged, Ellen suggested to Ali that she might enjoy looking at the violins. After trying out four or five, Ali ran back to Ellen with eyes aglow. "Look what I found!" She held an old, molasses-colored, full-size instrument that had clearly once had a large crack in it, and which a former owner obviously thought worthwhile to restore. She waxed rhapsodic about the tone and, to Ellen's unequivocally amateur ears, it sounded fine indeed. "Can we bid on it tomorrow?" she asked. Ellen told her she would have to consult with me, but suggested Ali could help pay for it herself. Ali had observed other youths playing on the walkways of the festival grounds, with passersby dropping coins into their instrument cases. Within minutes, Ali had retrieved her violin and was out there playing.

Ellen did consult with me that evening. I had misgivings. We knew next to nothing about selecting violins or assessing their relative value. Violins at the auction sold at anywhere from $50 to $5,000. Ali's teacher had not had the opportunity to try it out. And besides, Ali did not currently need a new violin; it would take more than a year to grow into the full-size.

But on the other hand, we could agree to set a bidding limit for ourselves. Ali would be needing a full-size instrument, and our limit would be lower than a decent instrument would likely cost locally. Ali could resell this one if she later decided she wanted a different violin. She was enthusiastic, as her playing the previous day had proven, and she'd have a good lesson in the value of money — she was already extremely frugal, but to date had shown little interest in worldly economics. What clinched it for me was that in undertaking to pay for it herself, Ali would find new opportunities to perform, and discover ways to connect her music to the world of listeners, something which to that point had for the most part eluded her, and for which she had had little occasion.

The next morning we went straight to the auction hall and got our bidder's number. The auctioneer was up to item #123; Ali's heart's desire was stringed instrument #359. We left the hall. Ali found herself a spot, set up her violin, and began to play. The previous evening she'd made herself a sign, printed in her eight-year-old's scrawl: "For My New Violin. Thanks! Ali." An hour later and some $50 richer, she returned to the hall. People were bidding on and buying instruments, sometimes three or four or more. Ali's teacher was there, having purchased a violin, a viola, and a box of bows.

At last #359 came on the block. Two minutes later, and after a round of spirited bidding, Ali owned her violin, purchased for $446, our winning bid having been right at our price limit. I was reassured to meet our main competitor, a Portland, Oregon, violin teacher who purchased quality violins at the auction to resell to her better students. Ali beamed with her new instrument in hand.

Meera and Ali performing at a wedding, 1996

Within 31 days, she paid off "Violetta," as the violin had now been named. Ali performed at a local college outdoor festival, earning $186 in two and a half hours, the bag of coins and bills being too heavy for her to carry. During the summer, she performed regularly at the local farmer's market, delighting in being paid in fresh vegetables by the grocer whose stand she graced, thus helping to attract customers. We happily chaperoned, and enjoyed conversations we had with other parents and the occasional musician as they passed by. Ali played at Pike Place Market in Seattle, before and after Shakespeare theatrical performances in the park, and in front of her favorite nature store during our local community "Art Walk." We helped her develop her repertoire to include music passersby would be likely to recognize, all within the limits of her playing ability. This included a mix of popular favorites and well-known classical pieces: Brahms' *Hungarian Dance no.5*, Dvorak's *Humoresque*, pieces from Bach's *Orchestral Suite no.3*, "La Donne é Mobile" from *Rigoletto* (those who are not opera aficionados might recognize this as the theme from the Spattini Spaghetti Sauce commercial), "Somewhere Over the Rainbow," the theme from *Fiddler on the Roof*, "Oh Wouldn't It Be Loverly" from *My Fair Lady*, "My Favorite Things," "Lonely Goatherd," and "Edelweiss" from *The Sound of Music*, and "Greensleeves." The quality of her playing would not have marked her as some kind of child prodigy, but her enthusiasm more than made up for whatever musical deficiencies there might be. She showed and shared her violin with other children, and took delight in the occasional foreign coin, polished rock, or apple dropped into her violin case.

Over the course of the summer, Ali earned $1,300, approximately $55 per hour. Together we constructed a bar graph for her to keep track of her earnings, which she was required to count and take to the bank, and taught her how to do percentages so she could calculate how close she was to her goal. We reached an understanding that funds were to be restricted to jointly agreed-upon educational uses. After paying off the violin, Ali used some of the funds to enroll in a telescope-making workshop that winter. More significantly, you could detect a marked improvement in Ali's playing. Her hands and fingers got stronger, her bowing more precise, and her sense of self-assurance strengthened.

Hahn, Hilary, *Hilary Hahn Plays Bach* (audio compact disc). New York, NY: Sony Music Entertainment, Inc., 1997. The extraordinary debut recording by the phenomenal teenage homeschooled violinist, containing the fiendishly difficult last three Bach "Partitas and Sonatas for Solo Violin," recorded when she was 17. The story goes that Hahn took up the instrument at the Peabody Conservatory before age four after walking through downtown Baltimore with her dad and coming upon a sign offering free violin lessons. At age 16, she completed her B.A. in Music from the prestigious Curtis Institute of Music in Philadelphia through a homestudy program. Asked whether she believes she is gifted, Hahn replies, "I wouldn't call it a gift, just hard work." She reports that once, at age six, she asked her teacher whether she really needed to practice every day. "No, dear," the teacher responded, "you only have to practice on days you eat." A great gift for the budding homeschooled musician, or just for yourself!

Holt, John, *Never Too Late: My Musical Life Story*. Reading, MA: Addison-Wesley, 1991. All of Holt's books have been an inspiration to homeschooling families for more than a generation. This is my personal favorite, a friendly reminder that serious learning, and the love of it, do not have to be reserved to the young. Holt's legacy lives on in the best of the homeschooling newsletters: "Growing Without Schooling." Write for a sample: GWS, 2380 Massachusetts Avenue, Suite 104, Cambridge, MA 02140; or check out their website: www.holtgws.com

Menuhin, Yehudi, *Unfinished Journey: Twenty Years Later*. New York, NY: Fromm International, 1996. Among the most engaging and well-written of musical autobiographies. After reading it, one could only wish his parents had written a book about their family's unique homeschooling experiences. Menuhin writes that his first-generation immigrant parents used to smuggle him at age two into the balcony for matinee concerts of the San Francisco Symphony Orchestra. Asked about it later, his mother said they did so because they couldn't afford a babysitter. Hmmm. Menuhin at four chose his own future teacher by insistently pointing at Louis Persinger, the SFSO's concertmaster. Persinger, who at the time did not even teach children, soon found himself giving Menuhin lessons five days a week. How his parents managed to break down Persinger's barriers to get him to teach a raw five-year-old who, up to that point, was without any special display of talent, remains a mystery. We've lost a good story.

Suzuki, Shinichi, *Nurtured By Love: A New Approach to Education*, translated by Waltraud Suzuki. New York, NY: Exposition Press, 1969.

ON CHOOSING A MUSIC TEACHER

Parents often ask us for advice on how to select a music teacher. We have quite a bit of experience in this regard and strong opinions which, to date, have stood us in good stead.

We've learned most critically that the selection of a music teacher should not be taken lightly, especially for the beginning student. You are choosing what will hopefully blossom into a long-term relationship for your child, one that might last for many years or even a lifetime. In the best of circumstances, music teachers become like cherished members of the family. Be prepared to invest at least as much time and energy as you would in buying a new car — the relationship may last longer.

We suggest you start with a minimum of three to five good candidates. Don't make a decision until you've met and done due diligence on all of them. Ask friends, musicians, church music directors, or music stores for recommendations. Some music stores will have annotated lists of teachers.

Before making a single appointment, make a list of questions you want answered. Questions we've asked have included:

- How many other students does the teacher have, for what duration, and over what range of age and ability? This can be important, as serious students will want to see others more adept than themselves, whose progress they can use as benchmarks.
- Does the teacher specialize in a particular type of music or teach using a particular technique or method? Is this flexible? The best method in the world will fail if it does not meet the specific needs of an individual child.

- How often are lessons held, and for how long? Can lessons be scheduled at a time when you can conveniently attend with your child, if necessary, and at a time when your child's attention is likely to be optimal?
- Does the teacher ever hold group lessons or master classes, and are all students expected to participate? When is the next one and, if soon, can your child sit in?
- How often are student recitals held?
- Is the teacher an active member of a local music teachers' association or guild? This can be invaluable because there will often be joint recitals involving students with several different teachers, graded competitions, and joint master classes, sometimes with special guest instructors. You will, however, have to be prepared to figure out how you want to deal with the competitions which, in our experience, can cause music-making to uncomfortably resemble a sporting event.
- Does the teacher perform locally as part of a musical group? This can provide opportunities to meet other musicians.
- Will music theory be part of the lesson, or will theory assignments be made between lessons?
- For piano students: will lessons be held at a studio or at your home? There are good arguments for either approach. If at a studio, will the instrument used for lessons be an electric piano, an acoustic upright, or a grand? More advanced students will likely want to learn on an acoustic instrument; there are advantages for the teaching piano to be similar to the one your child will practice upon.
- How far away from your home is the studio?
- What will the lessons cost, and is tuition charged by the lesson or by the month? Are there opportunities to barter?
- Are there other families you can call for references?

Don't expect to have all your questions answered on your visit. Indeed, having made this long list of questions, I can assure you that the answers to all of them combined are not as important as the rapport — the emotional chemistry — between the teacher and your child. Good chemistry may lead to a lifetime of musical fulfillment; poor rapport, especially for the beginner, can lead to grave frustration and disappointment.

Unfortunately, just as your meeting with the car salesman may be among the worst ways to evaluate an automobile purchase, your interview of the music teacher may not be conducive to getting a feel for the potential rapport. The teacher is in an awkward position, focusing on you as the purchaser, even though your child is the consumer of the service. We watch carefully to discern how the initial interaction goes. If you respond favorably to the answers given most of your questions, but are unsure about the chemistry, ask the teacher for several trial lessons (for which you should pay). Above all, explain to your child what the process is and how she is included in the decision-making.

Hares With Shells
on Their Backs

And because I am happy & dance & sing,
They think they have done me no injury,
And are gone to praise God & his Priest & King,
Who make up a heaven of our misery.

William Blake, "The Chimney Sweeper"
from *Songs of Experience*

People often ask me why I am such an ardent proponent of homeschooling. They may have met my two daughters — Aliyah Meena — (who just turned ten and who goes by Ali) and Meera Behn (now seven and Meera for short) — and discover they have never attended a full day of school. They may recognize my name from letters to the editor in the local newspaper defending homeschooling, or know that I have testified before legislative committees and supported the interests of homeschoolers before our local school board, some of whose members I count as friends.

If truth be told, it has never been my aspiration to be a champion of homeschooling. What I aspire to be is the strongest possible advocate *for my children* and for ensuring their learning needs are met in the best possible fashion. For our family, both in the past and currently, that has meant our own particular brand of homeschooling. I can imagine circumstances where that could have been different, and can envision different possibilities in the future. But at least until now, homeschooling has provided the best available option for us.

As a citizen and as a taxpayer, I also consider myself a strong advocate for children in the public school system. This is not because I support the system's goals and objectives, methods of operation or instruction, or means of measuring success. Rather, I am acutely aware that many families do not have the physical or emotional energy, financial wherewithal, employment circumstances, or interest to pursue other avenues for their children's education. I recognize that the vast majority of children are attending and will continue to attend public schools, and that I have a real stake in their future.

It is as an advocate of children — all children — and their families that I decided to write this book. The lessons our children have taught us are, I believe, not unique, even if our particular experiences are. Flexibility, options, and choices are our family's bywords, and just as we strive to ensure they are available for our kids, so we would like them to be there for other families as well. Whether this book is read by parents needing reassurance in considering homeschooling for the first time or by long-term homeschooling families, whether by parents seeking to enhance the learning process for their kids after school lets out (an early working title for this book was *Learning Without Recess*) or by teachers venturing to grasp why they find the system in which they work disheartening, whether by families and communities undertaking to build charter schools or by those rare school administrators open to revisiting or reevaluating their mission, my overarching goal is the same: to foster an understanding that our children — individually and one at a time — present us with new possibilities and new choices, and that real choices about our children's and our communities' future are truly ours to make.

For anyone who knows us well, the commitment my partner Ellen and I have made to homeschool our children might seem somewhat surprising. We are strong supporters of public and, especially, community institutions. It is a marvel of American democracy to observe citizens tax themselves to support safe and adequate water supplies, to build adequate roads and sidewalks, to construct adequate sewage disposal facilities, and to maintain an adequate public health infrastructure.

But education, we are persuaded, needs to be viewed differently. While the public school mission of an adequate education for all children in a democracy is a noble one, especially when we recognize how far we are as a society from achieving even this, from my perspective as a parent, the goal of an "adequate" education for my children is by definition "inadequate." Children are not the same as sidewalks; entrusted with the total development of human beings — each with their own personalities, gifts, capacities, and ever-changing learning needs — responsible adults could not but come, I believe, to the conclusion that "adequate" simply isn't good enough.

If we start from that premise, it soon becomes evident that what we have come to question about public education is not so much its actual practice, which varies quite widely from place to place and school to school, but its virtually universally accepted mission. This has little or nothing to do with "good" versus "bad" teachers (I've known plenty of good ones, in the conventional sense of the term, and, on balance, there are probably more who are well-intentioned than the other kind); educational "enrichment" (why would any parents suffer their children to undergo the "unenriched" variety?); curriculum reform (when hasn't there been curriculum reform?); or funding for schools, computers, or teacher salaries (show me well-funded schools and I'll show you kids whose parents at the very least feed them in the morning more often than not). If pressed, I'll indicate support for better teachers and better schools, educational enrichment, and curriculum reform. Certainly I support school breakfast programs, my only reservation being that it would be terrific if we could ensure kids got a decent breakfast at home! The funding question is a bit trickier, as it reveals our society's mindless, inexorable, and ultimately destructive tendency to conflate "more" with "better," the quantitative with the qualitative. But on the whole, from our perspective, these considerations are beside the point. In challenging public education's mission, at least for our children, we implicitly call into question the entire administrative structure of school buildings, scheduled school days and hours and vacations, age-bound grade bands, classrooms with prescribed numbers of children assigned, predetermined curricula, and arbitrary though strictly defined schedules for testing and evaluation. Taken together, these serve as the bureaucratic engine by which adequate educations are more or less efficiently produced; our experience indicates they have next to nothing to do with how children, how humans, optimally learn. Since "adequate" rather than "optimal" education is the public school mission, even given occasional protestations to the contrary, this shouldn't seem particularly surprising.

Our questioning also has little to do with the educational theory behind public schooling. In fact, I'd respectfully suggest there is precious little learning theory to be found in the operation of public schools, only administrative directive in disguise. This is disheartening. Collectively, we've discovered a lot in the twentieth century about how kids learn, as often from the cultural anthropologists, beginning with Margaret Mead, as from the education specialists. Most of it, however, as most any public school teacher with a long career can attest, simply becomes grist for the mill once it hits the educational combine.

The great anthropologist and philosopher Gregory Bateson once asked an educational behavioral psychologist who performed learning experiments on rats whether he ever did them at night, since rats are nocturnal. "No," said the psychologist, "They'd bite." "Oh," remarked Bateson, "so what you've been researching are the learning patterns of sleepy rats." Now one can raise the attainment levels of sleepy rats with the proper (I might have said "enriched") inputs, but they remain fundamentally rats, fundamentally sleepy and too docile to bite, and, most fundamentally of all, *caged*. For children in schools, the application of the rich discoveries regarding how humans learn is at once overgeneralized and then limited to what can be allowed to work within the narrow confines of the classroom and curriculum. It could hardly be otherwise within current cultural assumptions and administrative constraints. And those who show any real signs of being awake are just as likely to be punished as rewarded.

Perhaps a better metaphor would be to liken children in school to hares forced to bear the weight of the administrative machinery of public education on their backs as if they were tortoises. Some, the athletes of the public school world, bear it more gracefully than others and get used to the weight. Some become so weighed down they forget they are hares. Others chafe and rebel under the shell. Our family is part of a loose-knit non-sectarian homeschooling network — the Learning Web — and within it and elsewhere we have witnessed children, once unencumbered of the shells, experience an end to depression and discover a renewed vibrancy of spirit and a freedom to learn. Some, as if by magic, are cured of chronic conditions such as Attention Deficit Hyperactivity Disorder (ADHD), which formerly had been treated by the legal dispensing of mind-altering substances by secretaries in our "Zero Tolerance Drug-Free Schools." As many homeschooling families have experienced when taking their children out of public schools, the process of adjustment may take time, as the hares must relearn to stand up and straighten their backs before they can run again.

This book provides a narrative account of how our children have learned and, perhaps more critically, how, with our assistance, they have discovered ways to take charge of their own learning. I am sensitive to the weakness of this narrative approach. It is unscientific. It is impossible for us to know to what degree what some would consider the manifest precociousness of each of our children is due to our efforts, their genetic makeup (substantially different in the case of each of our children, as Meera is adopted), or other factors. We can't clone them to find out how they might have fared in a different environment, school or otherwise. I do not want to give the impression that my children's particular gifts, preoccupations, or foibles as detailed in this narrative are necessarily typical of the "homeschooled child." If there is a single underlying critique of public education that runs throughout this book, it is that there is no such thing as the typical child, homeschooled or otherwise, and that the working assumption that there is one is the single greatest cause of damage inflicted upon children in public schools. I would strongly suggest, however, that a prime lesson we have learned from our children is that there are no overachievers, only underestimators waiting to be proven wrong. I hope this account of my children's learning will be considered one slim volume in the library of human potential.

One of the reasons I have chosen to end work on this narrative at the turn of Ali's tenth birthday is to prevent our kids' future success (assuming they are "successful," whatever that might mean) from being the lens through which their education is perceived. I find there is something disempowering in the formulaic "My Homeschooled Kid Got into Yale ... And Yours Can Too!" genre, as it suggests that the learning experiences our children acquire today are intrinsically less valuable than those they might receive in the future at an institution more venerable than our backyard. We consider it important to resist the temptation to narrowly conceive of education as "preparation for life." Children are living, breathing, learning beings in the present moment, and satisfying their need to learn is critical to their current quality of life, which has its own inherent value, whatever tomorrow may bring. If there is anything typical of my kids, it is, as of all children — unless or until it is ground out of them — their delight in discovery.

What should be of some universal relevance is the intertwined record of what our children have taught us about helping them learn, utilizing the resources of our medium-size community of Olympia, Washington. I can say truthfully that we began our homeschooling adventures with little in the way of preconceived designs — certainly no master plan — and more often than not, what few plans we had turned out to be wrong-headed. Our children have taught us humility, and they've taught us respect. Experience has persuaded us that the bedrock of parental love and the foundation of any education worthy the name are one and the same, and that is learning to listen. Our education as parents/teachers is embedded in the episodic narrative, not because our children's education is necessarily so, but because these episodes have provided the openings for Ellen and me to revisit our own schooling and learning experiences and to reimagine them in the light of what our children have taught us.

Behind this anecdotal and highly personalized account of our children's teaching are the more general lessons which they have presented to us. From them, we have learned that

 A. Children understand and, given the opportunity, can articulate what they need to know at any particular point within the limits and natural round of their own individual and unique development;

 B. The primary job of the teacher (parent or otherwise) is not to teach but to provide the opportunities whereby these needs can be met;

C. These needs don't wait to be filled: if they aren't addressed adequately and in a timely manner, children become frustrated and will take out that frustration in aggressiveness, recalcitrance, or worst of all, passivity; and

D. No single individual can be expected to meet all of a child's learning needs at any particular point in time. It takes a community, with or without a school, to raise a child.

As our children have gotten older, their interests have deepened, and their studies have become more specialized. This is as it should be; therefore I have organized this book into rough subject areas to plot the development of their understandings. I am aware, however, that these subject divisions more closely parallel the way Ellen and I (and most adults) have been taught to think about education than our children's actual experience. A characteristic of Ali's and Meera's intellectual development has been the fluid, interpenetrating nature of insights gained. A quick scan of the text finds our kids making connections between evolutionary biology and opera and finance; astronomy and eighteenth century colonial history; music, religion, and mathematics; optics and trigonometry; sociobiology and ethics; and arithmetic, nutrition, and geography. Yet, to focus on the subject matter even in this manner is to miss the point. Our efforts as parents/teachers are not primarily directed at the mastery of science, mathematics, Latin, music, or Shakespeare. They are about the nurturing of citizens of the planet who, in abundant recompense, allow us to "borrow from eternity," for children provide us a glimpse of a future which, at least within the boundaries of our limited physical selves, we can never know.

The end I envision for my children's education is not the mastery of subject matter. It is perhaps here where, more than anywhere else, we part company with the practice of public education. For the end we envision lies not in the amassing of facts or concepts which, in itself, has little more intrinsic value than the accumulation of shoes, baseball cards, or sports cars, but in the responsible exercise of freedom — the freedom to learn, to create, to grow, *to be* — unfettered by prejudice, their own or that of others, unhampered to the highest degree possible by others' expectations and their own preconceptions, fears, and self-doubts, uninhibited by dependencies not freely chosen. These are high-sounding words and would not signify much if they did not inform our actual practice, as our learning adventures should illustrate.

The responsible exercise of freedom must start early if it is to flower. As learning is the primary means by which individuals and communities adapt, cultivating the freedom to learn is in my judgment among the best mechanisms to ensure both personal satisfaction and community and species survival. The joy and power of learning, freely exercised, is one of very few real alternatives to an ecologically devastating cult of consumerism — a fundamental belief that happiness or understanding can be purchased like a 4X4, whereby, as the television commercial promises, one is "free" to go where one pleases regardless of environmental consequences — and to equally destructive power relationships among individuals or among nations. The spontaneous desire to learn is given to us, I am absolutely convinced, by a Higher Power — whether God, Nature, or Reason — and failure to cultivate its free exercise cannot but result in the diminishment of the human spirit and the human heart.

The title of this book *And the skylark sings with me* is taken from the poem "The School Boy," one of William Blake's *Songs of Innocence and of Experience*. At once poet, illustrator, and visionary, Blake contemplated the processes of education as paralleling the dehumanization and destruction of community that marked the dawning of the industrial age. As the literary critic Alfred Kazin has stated, Blake would have seen in society's pedagogic carefulness the effort of caution to do the work of the imagination. "Under a cruel eye outworn," the child is driven from "learning's bower/Worn thro' with the dreary shower." In Blake's vision, the tragedy of childhood is that we inflict our civilization's lovelessness upon it: "How can the bird that is born for joy/Sit in a cage and sing?" Blake, as Kazin notes, considered the treatment afforded to and the experience of children as the nucleus of the entire human story. In that spirit, we offer our family's educational enterprise as an expression of an alternative story and a new song.

The sun does arise,
And make happy the skies;
The merry bells ring
To welcome the Spring;
The skylark and thrush,
The birds of the bush,
Sing louder around
To the bells' chearful sound,
While our sports shall be seen
On the Ecchoing Green.

William Blake, "The Ecchoing Green"
from *Songs of Experience*

In my ignorance, I would have thought we'd be prepared to deal with another musical child. We weren't. Saraswati's blessings are idiosyncratic, and are bestowed in ways I can't yet begin to truly fathom.

I have no explanation as to why virtuoso musicians (or artists of any kind for that matter) are born with their peculiar gifts. Is it built into their DNA, the curvature of the molecule capturing and crystallizing the musical energy of the universe? Is it unleashed by a particular kind of birth trauma, or is it such trauma which causes an individual to be born tone-deaf? To what degree is musicality inherited and, if so, does it skip a generation or two? Experience seems to range from there being dozens of musical Bachs throughout Germany during the seventeenth and eighteenth centuries, to a Yehudi Menuhin with two musically gifted sisters but entirely non-musical parents. Are there special floodgates that can be opened in children to allow such gifts to run free? Can they be turned on and off, like spigots? If so, where are the handles?

By the time Ali took up the violin a second time, three-year-old Meera, as outgoing as Ali is introspective, was already inviting herself to dinner at our next door neighbor's house. She was shrewd enough to compare menus first. In a stroke of irony, Ali — our California — born daughter-is close to being a vegetarian, nothing pleasing her more than a bowl of rice and very spicy lentil curry. Indian-born Meera will eat absolutely anything, so long as it nearly resembles a hamburger or hotdog.

Pretty soon, Meera was disappearing over to Evelyn's 10 or 15 minutes out of every two hours. We thought she was over there cadging snacks, as we knew Dick — Evelyn's husband and a retired state legislator — was a soft touch. She was there, but what we didn't know initially is that she was learning to play the piano!

Our next-door neighbor Evelyn, now in her late 70s, is a community treasure. Her open door has provided a welcome refuge for neighborhood children (and adults) for two decades. She also serves as county chair of one of the political parties and as long-time president of our neighborhood association. But maybe her most consequential function is as surrogate grandmother for a generation of children in our immediate area. So important to us are her extra pair of eyes and the attention she and Dick have lavished on both Ali and Meera that it would be difficult indeed for us to even consider moving.

Evelyn had introduced more than a dozen neighborhood children to the piano. But she quickly noted Meera was a bit different. Meera never went over to pound the keys, preferring instead to observe and listen — very striking behavior for her as she was, and is, almost always in perpetual motion. Tiny for her age, Meera would sit on Evelyn's lap watching as Evelyn played. Shortly, Meera carved out her own turf in the middle of the keyboard, doubling first Evelyn's right hand, then her left. Pretty soon Meera could tell, just by listening, whether a song was in the key of C, F, or G, and her ability to copy a rhythm was uncanny. These quickly became games to her, and she was (and remains) always excited by any opportunity to show off her new musical skills.

The neighborhood offered Meera her favorite song. During summer evenings, the ice cream truck would approach, announcing itself with Scott Joplin's "The Entertainer." It was not long before the "ice cream song," first in one hand, then in two, could be heard emanating from Evelyn's living room.

Ellen bartered massages for lessons with Glenna, a local piano teacher. Meera rapidly made her way through the first two Suzuki books, performing twice a year at a local nursing home, usually including a piece of her own devising along with the more normal fare, her signature song being "What

Shall We Do With the Drunken Sailor?" Her playing progressed so rapidly that by age five-and-a-half, her musical dexterity was equal to that of any of Glenna's students ranging in age up to 14, some of whom had been taking lessons for six years or more.

But there was a problem. Meera did not read music (she did not read words yet either), and watching other students bring their scores up to the piano to perform became upsetting for her. Meera told us and Glenna quite definitively that she *needed* to read music. Glenna tried some of the basic "big note" children's books, but Meera found them so musically underdeveloped that they could not hold her attention for long. It's hard to be forced to read one-finger versions of "Baa Baa Black Sheep" when you're playing full-fingered versions of Beethoven sonatinas or C.P.E. Bach's *Solfeggietto*.

Glenna had already succeeded in teaching Meera to name the notes on the keyboard, but suggested we visit another music teacher some 35 miles away. Mark had acquired a reputation for teaching reading to music prodigies, one of whom, several years older than Meera, had recently been featured on a regional television show. Mark listened to Meera play, tested some basic understandings and her sense of pitch, and asked us to trust him that in six months, with one half-hour lesson every other week and some pleasing work at home, Meera would be sight-reading.

Mark's method was not anything like we expected. For the first two months, Meera worked on nothing but hearing and playing chords in sequence, with letter names verbally attached to each. "She hears chords and chord relationships," Mark said, "so to confine her to individual notes is crippling." He noted that before the creation of "method books," which paralleled the development of the upright piano and hence the entrée of instruments into the parlors of middle-class homes in the late nineteenth century, people always learned this way. Following completion of these exercises, Mark would write down a series of letter names, again to be translated as chords in varying rhythms, in both left and right hands, rather than as individual notes. In the last three months, notes and chords began to appear on music paper. Mark was very particular not to attach names to the notes on the staff other than middle C. Only notes on the keyboard had names; the staff was to be recognized as symbolizing nothing more (and nothing less) than a vertical keyboard. "One symbol system at a time is enough," Mark said, "and the only one that counts is the one that results in the right sounds getting to her ear."

The method worked! Within three months of the end of Mark's tutelage, Meera could sight-read Bach and mastered several Bach *Inventions*, works of Kabalevsky, "The Entertainer" (this time, a fully realized version), Catherine Rollins' "Jazz Cats," Beethoven *Bagatelles*, Chopin *Waltzes* and, at her insistence, "Walking in a Winter Wonderland." Naming the notes on the page came almost without notice, moving from keyboard to the musical staff. Within six months she started performing as part of various adult recitals around town and decided to take up the clarinet as well.

Neither Ellen nor I had any experience with either violins or pianos prior to our kids taking them up, and so were ignorant of the specific demands learning them might entail. This made it especially engrossing for us to observe how different each child's approach to her instrument was and how temperamentally suited Ali and Meera were to their chosen musical media. As already noted, Ali is highly intellectually motivated and blessed with solid fine-motor skills. The violin provides great opportunity for the expression of these. From an intellectual point of view, the instrument offers multiple options for where any particular note is to be played on the fingerboard. These options are called "positions," and the skilled violinist is constantly required to make choices regarding where and how to play each note, taking into account timbre of sound, ease of fingering, and sequence of the note in relationship to those around it. It's rather like an evolving puzzle, with the student, over time and with more experience, taking increasing responsibility over possible solutions. At the same time, it should be understood that the violin, perhaps more than any other instrument, might be among the least likely to provide a child (or any beginning student for that matter) with instant gratification in terms of the quality of sound, as most parents who have lived with a child violinist will readily attest. This is also one of the reasons why Suzuki's approach, with its stress on repetitive motion training, is especially well-suited to the violin.

Meera is endowed with an unusually fine musical ear (she complains mightily when the piano is even slightly out of tune) and extraordinary physical prowess. The piano is a spacious extension of her physical self. We once

Meera, age seven, performing "Harlequin" by Amy Beach at
Seattle's Frye Art Museam

encouraged Meera to try the violin, and in the long run we believe she would
have succeeded if she'd really wanted to take it up, but even when she was
bringing the violin to her shoulder and raising the bow, one got the distinct
impression she felt like she was being confined to a cage. Meera is also more
likely to demand instant gratification than her sister, and the piano provides
it. Once one figures out the sequence of notes (or notes and chords),
whether it be "Twinkle, Twinkle, Little Star" or the *Moonlight Sonata*, the
music will provide its satisfactions to the ear every time. There are of course
fingering puzzles and hand crossings and the like required in learning to play
the piano too, but our impression is that many of these occur in later stages
of technique development. The earlier challenges are in understanding
chords and rhythmic patterns and in translating the much larger number of
notes on the page down to the keyboard. The upshot here is that the right
choice of instrument — one suited to the particular temperament and needs
of each individual child, regardless of a parent's own particular prejudices —

is critical, and probably receives less attention than it deserves. We were just lucky enough to have our kids find their own instruments before we had time to muck around in the process.

Projecting her musical future has become a game with Meera, who now has a sense of what kind of effort is necessary to master a substantial and unknown piece of music from beginning to end. Upon being given a book of the complete Mozart sonatas and fantasies for piano ("the biggest music book in the world!" she calls it, and at almost three inches thick, it sure feels that way), Meera asked how long it would take me to master everything in it. "About a hundred years," I replied, "if I practiced about six hours a day." "But you'll be dead by then," she noted. "That's right." "How long will it take me?" "Depends on how much you practice. If you work at it for two hours every day, I'd say about five years." "Really?" Meera was quiet for a few minutes. Then she said, "Can we set up a time when I can find out what it would be like to practice for two hours?" I am experiencing a mixture of pride and envy; Meera is enjoying all the attention, secure in the knowledge that with the requisite labor she can, even at age seven, surpass the musical achievement of most of the adults she knows. We now have a standing family joke: "Who is the best pianist — Horowitz, Rubinstein, or Meera?" "I am," Meera smiles. "The other two are dead."

Almond, Mark, *Piano for Quitters*. The instructor who taught Meera to read music now has a videotape program of his piano-learning techniques. Great for adults as well as children, as Mark has inspired many "piano quitters" (he had been one himself) to return to the instrument with the pleasure that may have eluded them in childhood. For more information about Mark's method, call 253-952-9226.

Ben-Tovim, Atarah and Douglas Boyd, *Choosing the Right Instrument for Your Child*. New York, NY: William Morrow Co., 1985. This is the result of a remarkable study undertaken by the Music Research Centre in northern England, based on interviews with several thousand children who had given up learning musical instruments, together with a control group who continued in their musical studies. There was no evidence that those who dropped out were any less musical than those who continued. In fact, it could not even be shown that those who eventually entered music conservatories were more musical than the music dropouts. By far the most common factor in musical failure was the wrong choice of instrument, not lack of musicality or musical potential. Such potential is much more likely to be realized when the chosen instrument poses no special physical, mental, or emotional problems for the child, and maximizes her own individual temperament.

Blake, William, *The Portable Blake*, edited by Alfred Kazin. New York, NY: Penguin Books, 1976.

Hallelujah! (Again)

"Drop thy pipe, thy happy pipe;
Sing the songs of happy chear:"
So I sung the same again,
While he wept with joy to hear.

William Blake, "Introduction"
from *Songs of Innocence*

It was Handel's *Messiah* again. This time it was in December in Olympia rather than in July in Santa Cruz, a Sing-In at the local Church of Latter-Day Saints. The crowd was rather different as well. Instead of casually dressed former hippies in jeans and cutoffs, men and women both sporting ponytails, there were women in champagne-, pink-, and lime-colored chiffon and silk dresses, men in well-pressed suits, and boys with crewcuts in white shirts and skinny black ties. Ali and I dressed for the occasion. After the second chorus, seven-year-old Ali timidly asked me if she could hold the vocal score. I gave it to her, and to my delight, she followed along quite easily. When we got to the choruses, she hit the alto entrances, not always with the right note, but virtually always at the right instant. "Pretty good," I thought, given she had no prior knowledge of the music, although her experience at her first *Messiah* Sing-In some five and a half years earlier had long become a treasured part of our family lore. Two weeks later, and now armed with her own score, Ali and I traveled up to Seattle to participate in a Sing- and Play-In at a large

33

Unitarian church. We both enjoyed ourselves immensely.

In early January, I saw a notice in the newspaper soliciting singers to participate in a performance of the Mozart *Requiem* to benefit local inter-faith AIDS ministries. I had not done anything like this in 25 years. Since Ali enjoyed the little Mozart she had heard, I offered to take her along, not to sing, but to sit next to me in the bass section during the half-hour rehearsals. For two weeks, she listened intently. The third week she asked if she could go sit with the altos. I told her that was fine with me, as long as she understood she would not be singing in the performance. Most of the singers — in our 40s, 50s, and 60s — enjoyed having Ali around and were pleased at how well she followed along. In the fourth week, after repeated lis-tening to a recording at home with the score in hand, she started correcting the Latin of the woman next to her.

By the time of the dress rehearsal, it was clear that Ali knew the piece and was singing at least as well as the local attorney in the bass section who was sitting next to me. The conductor thought she was performing, as did the altos around her. I wasn't about to argue. I drilled Ali in what I called the five rules of successful choral performance: 1) Have fun! 2) Don't rustle the pages of the score (not so easy when you have very small hands); 3) Watch the conductor; 4) Don't drop your score; and 5) Have fun! Given adequate preparation, which is the conductor's responsibility, everything else would take care of itself. And I knew Ali was prepared: we were used to hearing her sing the alto line of the famous "Lachrymosa" on car trips to the grocery store! Four-year-old Meera heard it so often, she began to sing along, too.

When Ali — all three feet eleven inches of her dressed in long black skirt, black shoes, and white blouse — walked through the nave of the church between two much taller altos with blue-rinsed hair to take her place in the front row of singers, there was quite a stir among the 400 people pre-sent. It was a bit nerve-wracking for me, standing in the back row and try-ing to sneak an anxious peek down to the front. People would observe her every move. She didn't disappoint. The performance was a tremendous suc-cess, with standing ovations, and Ali became a celebrity.

The very next morning we received a telephone call from the soprano soloist. Would we be willing to have Ali sing at New York's Carnegie Hall on the July 4th weekend? The Portland Children's Chorale was performing, but they were in desperate need of some additional singers who could learn new music quickly. We gasped, and said we couldn't afford the expensive trip. "Don't worry," Ruth said. "*We want her*, and we'll find a way." Ellen and I put together a fundraising letter to give to our friends and to Ali's fellow singers, naming one of her choir friends as our collection agent. We expected to receive small $5 or $10 donations. To our grateful surprise, an anonymous benefactor came forward with a blank check, offering to pay all costs beyond what was collected elsewhere.

Besides rehearsals, Ali spent the next two months perusing books from the local library about the geography and history of New York, and deciding what she wanted to visit while she was there. After the event, with some assistance from Ellen, Ali wrote the following article which appeared in a local magazine:

> The conductor raised his baton and the orchestra starting playing. I was watching and I was thinking, thinking about all the people who never have the opportunity to perform here, and all the great musicians who did — Milstein, Horowitz, Rubinstein, and my favorite, Yehudi Menuhin, the violinist.
>
> After the concert, my grandmother said that I did wonderfully at singing such hard stuff. I said that after doing Mozart's *Requiem*, this was easy. Last spring, I sang with a group of adults performing the Mozart *Requiem* in Olympia, and because of that I got invited to sing with the Portland Children's Chorale at Carnegie Hall on July 3rd.
>
> The pieces we were singing were *Three Dominican Folk Songs* by Francisco Nuñez, *Child's Dream* by Tomas Svoboda, and *We Return Thanks* by Scott Cohen. The conductor for the Children's Chorale was Dr. Jonathan Griffith. The Portland kids had been rehearsing since the fall, so we had to hurry up and learn the music. We had weekly rehearsals in Olympia and a bunch of

rehearsals in Portland. We also had to practice our music every day at home so we'd have it memorized by early June.

There were about 60 kids who went to New York, 5 of them from Olympia, including me. Most of the kids were 11 to 14, and I was the youngest, 7. Being the youngest wasn't a problem for me, once they remembered to put me in a place where I could see.

The Olympia kids had a fundraiser at the Farmers' Market at the end of June. Some of the kids who passed the audition but could not come to New York sang there too. We sang the Dominican folksongs and some other pieces we worked on together. I also played three pieces on my violin.

Most of the kids were going to New York on July 1st, but my family and I went a few days earlier to visit my grandparents who live there. I saw Shakespeare's *The Tempest* in Central Park, went to the Metropolitan Museum of Art, and to an Opera Gala to hear many young singers from around the country. I also saw Lincoln Center and ate in Chinatown.

We stayed in The Crowne Plaza Hotel right on Broadway. It was the biggest hotel I've ever stayed in. There were at least three other choirs from other parts of the country staying while we were there. We heard some of them perform the night before our concert. They were really good.

Most of the rehearsals in New York were in the hotel ballroom, except for one dress rehearsal in Carnegie Hall itself. The fun thing about the dress rehearsal was playing my violin in Carnegie Hall before the rehearsal started. Now I can say I've played Carnegie Hall, and I have a picture to prove it.

To my surprise, the stage was not at all as big as I thought it would be, but the acoustics were great. It produced a very full and beautiful tone. The orchestra came from Bialystok, Poland. My dad and I found it on the map. It was the first time I had sung with an orchestra that came from so far away. I got to give the second violinist a pin as a present. They were very good. After we were done singing, there was an intermission and we got to come out and listen to the rest of the concert.

We took a boat trip on the Hudson River after the concert. We got to see the Statue of Liberty, and many other interesting sights. It was beautiful. We got back to the hotel at 3:00 a.m.! …

Another immediate result of Ali's Mozart *Requiem* experience was her realization that she wanted to study music theory and composition. But we didn't own a piano, which would be essential. I prepared a flyer indicating we were looking to purchase a reasonably priced used upright. Ali passed them out to choir members following the *Requiem* performance. Ten minutes later, one of the sopranos approached Ali. "I have a piano that I don't play anymore," she said, "and I'd love for you to have it." Ali found me and I asked her friend how much she wanted for the instrument. "Oh, no," she replied, "I want to *give* it to her. You can just come and pick it up." The conductor of the *Requiem*, a music director of a large local church and now a good friend, agreed to teach Ali the piano and became her composition teacher. The match between them has turned out splendidly. Nathan is a composer of music for change-ringing bells and has spent much time perfecting a new bell notation system, which has in turn sparked Ali's intellectual imagination.

Ali sang for a year with a local children's choir newly formed by the same soprano who recruited her for the New York trip. But she wanted more substantive fare. She sang Gabriel Fauré's *Requiem* with us old folks again. This time choir members invited friends and families to bring their children to the concert, with Ali as the draw. But having heard the 90-plus member Tacoma Youth Chorus, she knew what she wanted next.

The audition instructions for the mixed-gender chorus, which advertised they were seeking singers ages 11-16, were that she was to prepare any song she wished. More than a year earlier, I had purchased an excellent recording of the mezzo soprano Cecilia Bartoli singing eighteenth-century Italian songs titled *Do You Love Me*. And in a secondhand bookshop, I found a printed edition of these same songs, which I had given to Ali following a musical performance. Here it was, a year later, and Ali decided to sing "Caro Mio Ben," a love song that she remembered from the recording. Beholding an eight-year-old sing such passionate fare was a bit incongruous. Judith, the music director, was momentarily nonplussed, but then proceeded with the audition. With 20 minutes of on-the-spot vocal training, Ali's voice rose five full tones, from alto to first soprano. Faced with the choice of a possibly returning to Carnegie Hall or joining the Tacoma group, Ali was adamant. "In my current choir I learn *what* to sing, but with the Tacoma Youth Chorus, I'll learn *how* to sing." Despite being more than four years younger than the average member, Ali has now become a choir mainstay and is likely to remain with them for years to come. In summers, we supplement this activity with trips to Seattle every Wednesday evening to attend "summer sings" sponsored by the Seattle Symphony Chorale. I've learned more choral music in the past two summers than I had in the previous 25 years; Ali's repertoire now ranges from Vivaldi to Poulenc, from Haydn to Duruflé.

I asked Ali which of her means of performing music she most preferred (knowing of course this could change over time). "Singing," she replied, to my surprise. "Why is that?" "Well, playing the piano," she explained, "is like pushing the button on a machine. You press the key, and it depresses a lever which presses a hammer which hits the strings. And there are dampers and pedals, too. It's very mechanical. The violin is closer. It rests on my shoulder, and I can feel the music in my fingers. But with singing, I am the instrument, and the music comes from the inside."

What pleases me most about what has happened during Ali's musical adventures is that she has remained fundamentally a child. I honestly don't believe this would have been possible had she been spending up to six hours a day, five days a week, in a traditional classroom, hounded by homework, and then tried to fit these other activities around the edges. As I write these

Ali, age eight, and friends performing the *Faure Requiem* in Olympia.

words, nine-year-old Ali is sitting on the floor of the family room, reading through the first draft of this chapter, querying individual word choices and syntax, and playing with blocks.

———◆◆◆———

Upon hearing of our children's early and deep involvement in music, friends and relatives, some of whom are or have been schoolteachers, often comment on how students who study music or who have arts programs in their schools score some number of points higher on the verbal and/or mathematics sections of the Scholastic Aptitude Test (SAT). And maybe they do, though I am very skeptical about what exactly this is supposed to suggest. First of all, if the tests truly measured aptitude rather than achievement, then previous instruction — in *any* subject — should have no effect. Recognizing this after so many decades, the educational bureaucrats at the Educational Testing Service have altered the name of the exam to the Scholastic

Assessment Test, without, however, changing its substance or, what they probably cared about more, its all-important acronym. Now, they are totally silent about whether the test reflects aptitude or achievement, or simply the ability to do well on the next test. Secondly, show me a public school district that still maintains significant music and arts programs, and I'll show you taxpayers and families wealthy enough and generous enough to support them. Thirdly, parents who take enough interest in their kids to make sure they have ongoing experience in music and the arts are also likely to care about their children's educational welfare generally, and the kids' test scores will be indicative of that care.

As an aware parent, I am acutely sensitive to the way test scores are utilized as a form of social screening. The comments we receive are intended as vague compliments on the commitment Ellen and I have made to our children's success. But also as a parent and as a citizen, whenever this factoid comes up in conversation, I wonder whether the little thinking behind it is backward, with profoundly negative implications for my community, whatever the validity of the tests. When they are 25, 40, 50, or 70, Ali may still be playing the violin or singing and Meera playing the piano, and I hope both will appreciate and actively contribute to their communities' cultural life. Will they still be taking multiple choice exams and suffer seemingly endless comparisons with people of exactly the same chronological age? Shouldn't we really be asking what these tests — and the huge effort that goes into training the kids to endure and perform on them — contribute to the ongoing life of our community? Might not the time, energy, and money expended by teachers and children and school district administrators and taxpayers be better spent on music lessons?

The eagle never lost so much time as when he
submitted to learn of the crow.

William Blake,
"The Marriage of Heaven and Hell"

Most families we know who undertake teaching their kids at home do
so because of problems they or their children discern or have, in fact, experienced in the public school system. The problems are varied and differ from
family to family. They include too much competitiveness; classes too large;
too much stress; too much reliance on standardized testing; a poor learning
environment; ill-equipped teachers; a poor social environment (violence,
consumerism, drugs, sex); a disagreement with teaching methods; a lack of
attention to religious values or a view of subjects (evolution, sex education)
as antithetical to those values or as usurping parental roles. Ellen and I agree
with some of these complaints, and disagree with others. We share our critique of public education throughout this book as the occasion invites and
as our experiences warrant.

Where we differ from some homeschooling families is that their main
objectives appear to be to protect their children by narrowing the range of
available experience. As parents, we too strive to protect our children, but
frankly we never apprehended the school system as a threat to our children's
innocence or understanding. If anything, we perceive the range of educational experience offered by schools — starting with the segregation of children into age-bound classes — as far, far too narrow. This is one of the main
problems our approach to homeschooling seeks to address.

We view our community as a flexible learning environment, as if
you'll permit the metaphor, our kids' "learning oyster." To a great extent, the
term "homeschooling" doesn't match our actual practice. Ali's and Meera's
education is "home-directed" and "home-evaluated." We do a minimal
amount of rote or semi-rote activities around the kitchen table or home
computer. But our particular success, tempered with knowledge of our false
starts and imperfections, is built upon utilizing, and teaching our children
to think of, our community and the larger world as classroom, teacher,

resource center, learning laboratory, and more. The early growth and experiences of Ali as a singer, supported in sundry ways by so many parts of the community — from local AIDS ministries to the farmers' market, from fellow choir members to an anonymous benefactor — provide an extended example of what can become possible utilizing this approach.

Our choice of homeschooling is driven at least in part by our vision of what learning could truly be like for our children. Our vision of the perfect learning environment is a library, but like none we have ever encountered. The library would have books and videos and tapes and computer linkups, but that would be just the beginning. There would be lots of librarians, or more accurately, "docents" — guides to the trails of knowledge. Primary docents would provide instruction in the technologies necessary to utilize the available resources. They would teach reading, but also computer literacy and other languages (including music, which is itself a language) necessary to exploit the power of information. There would be a vast learning exchange of skills, from basic mathematics to auto mechanics. There would be lending libraries of tools and materials, from carpenters' saws and hammers, to biologists' microscopes, to astronomers' telescopes. There would be organized classes, learning support groups, and lectures. Self-evaluation tools would be available for learners to measure their own progress.

There would be large gardens and orchards, staffed by botanists and farmers, where students could learn to grow fruits and vegetables, and home economists who could teach their preparation and storage. There would be apprenticeships for virtually every kind of employment the community requires.

There would be rites of passage and celebration of subject or skill mastery. There would be storytellers and community historians, drawn from the community's older members. Seniors would play a vital role in preparing young children to begin to make use of all the library has to offer.

The library would be the community's hub and its heart. It would be supported the usual ways we support schools, through public taxation, but all users, both children and adults, would be required to contribute time (not just tax dollars) to the library's success.

I could dress this vision up into something even more grandiose, or more detailed. But we are not naive. This vision is but a fantasy, and not one we are likely to see realized in our lifetime. But we're also aware that the current configuration of public education was only a dream in the early nineteenth century. It will change, and is changing, as the configuration no longer meets many of the needs of the surrounding society. As parents, however, we don't have time to wait for it to catch up.

Now that I've gotten that out of my system, I have a confession to make. Other than in my former career as a book publisher producing books which facilitated the growth of ideas like these, and in writing this book, we have not gone too far or been particularly successful in directly promoting the embryonic development of institutions in our own community to carry our vision forward. Like most families with younger children, we are busy people, with the usual excuse that home, work, and the essentials of family life lay claim to most of our energy and attention.

What brought us back to our vision was an absolute commitment to taking the interests and knowledge quests of our children seriously, coupled with an acute and awkward awareness of our own limited abilities to meet their expressed needs. I consider myself significantly more well-schooled than the average elementary schoolteacher, or at least have the graduate school years and degrees under my belt so indicating. However, a partial list of Ali's interests and my own initial ignorance, semi-ignorance, or lack of experience at the time these interests arose is telling. Here it is in no particular order:

- The violin, western music theory, and choral music: I'd never, in my entire life, touched a violin or viola or cello. I played the saxophone in elementary school. I hadn't sung in a choir in 25 years.
- Snakes and reptiles: I'd never touched a snake, though I'd seen some at the zoo. I once dissected a frog, and the sight of its intestines gave me bad dreams.
- Wolves and wildlife ecology: I grew up in New York City, so enough said.
- Botany: Ditto. I knew the difference between deciduous, evergreen, and palm trees? To this day I possess a white thumb: anything I plant is likely to turn to ash.
- Birdwatching and ornithology: I grew up among pigeons, robins,

starlings, sparrows, and an occasional bluejay, which were the extent of my personal observation catalog.

- Modern Darwinian genetics: I took biology 30 years ago, before the wide use of electron microscopes, and hadn't read anything since except in the course of my current employment in public health.

- Astronomy: I remember looking through a small telescope once when I was eight, and went to the planetarium when I was ten. I could find the Dippers and Orion's belt, and name the nine planets. I never encountered Tycho, Kepler, Huygens, Messier, or Herschel, even in college. I once saw a play about Galileo. What are "bosons"?

- Opera and the Italian language: I like opera, but hadn't attended one in over a decade, and did not listen to any. I once knew Latin...

- Shakespearean drama: I have lots of academic knowledge, no acting experience, and did not attend the theater.

- Mythology: I actually did some graduate work, but hadn't pursued anything in 20 years.

- Music composition: Zip.

- Weaving: I seem to remember making a potholder in first grade.

Meera adds two major items to the list:

- Piano playing: I have no experience whatsoever, and I'm envious.

- Gymnastics: Physical education is the only subject I ever got close to flunking in school.

Ellen and I are neither fools nor dunces, and I'm confident that our own general knowledge levels have increased in tandem with those of our children. And it is obvious that the odds of a child who develops one of these interests running up against a schoolteacher able to fulfill the child's needs at precisely the time it arises quickly approach zero. But we know our own limitations at least as well as we do those of the public schools. The constant challenge for us and for our children lay not in building the library of our dreams, but in finding new ways to access our community, its people, and its resources. In reality, the success of our approach to homeschooling is critically dependent upon it.

Actively accessing the community has taught Ali and Meera an important lesson directly contrary to that which they would have inferred from early years of most public school education. Schoolteachers are credentialed to be experts in *teaching*. They may have limited knowledge about, and little or no real interest in, the content of the bulk of their lessons beyond what is necessary to communicate this content to their charges. This is not to say schoolteachers do not have their own peculiar obsessions, of which children, if they are lucky (or especially favored), may catch a glimpse. Some few of us have the fondest memories of teachers who were painters, restored old cars, played sousaphones, kept aquariums of exotic fish, wrote poetry, or raised horses. But this expertise is, or is expected to be, peripheral to their teaching, or at least to what they are assigned to accomplish in the classroom. And rare indeed is the elementary school teacher who has ongoing relationships with students and their families outside of the classroom, which is why, when it occurs, it is so celebrated.

When, instead of the traditional school, one utilizes the community as a flexible learning environment, the whole point is to find individuals prepared and willing to share their deepest passions and most highly developed expertise with our children. Ali and Meera learned early through personal experience that people make different and varied contributions to the community and that excellence outside of the teaching realm has merit. They don't have to wait for the occasional career day or be blessed with a rare glimpse of a schoolteacher's outside interests. Our children have become well-rounded individuals, not because they have learned to accept the fiction that all school subjects (and those subjects alone) should be accorded equal value in their eyes, since they take up the same amount of space on their report cards or count for the same in their grade point average. Rather they have been able to sample and experience over time and throughout their own development the richness and diversity our community has to offer. Instead of encountering teachers teaching, Ali and Meera have had serious and sometimes lasting encounters and relationships with scientists and wildlife biologists undertaking research, musicians composing and performing, theater directors directing, poets writing, and astronomers observing, and they have had continuing opportunities to learn from each of them.

This has been *hard work*. It has demanded consciously expanding our network of friends and acquaintances and carefully evaluating each new learning relationship into which our children enter. It has meant regularly perusing newspaper and community publications and calendars for potential opportunities, and a being willing to call strangers on the telephone and to ask questions which may reveal either our partial or total ignorance. It has dictated an enormous amount of schedule juggling and an ongoing day-to-day, month-to-month, year-to-year re-evaluation of the optimal relationship between our children's organized and unorganized activities. It has required learning when not to accept "no" for an answer and when to express just the right amount of impatience or indignation to overcome obstacles and cross over boundaries standing in the way of our family's unconventional educational choices. And we've had to figure this all out as we went along and as our children grew and changed. As we did so, we had to admit humbly to ourselves that each new solution we found was only tentative, not necessarily applicable to both of our children, or to anyone else's for that matter. We try to keep ourselves open, as we watch and listen.

We made career and income choices that facilitated our homeschooling efforts. Ellen's new career as a part-time massage therapist, with an office attached to our home, was a major factor in making our approach to homeschooling possible. She supplements our family income with two early morning newspaper routes. My mid-life career change from 80-hour-a-week publishing entrepreneur to mid-level public health professional working in state government freed up new energy for attention to our home and community life. We traded off career advancement, some job satisfaction, and income potential for the freedom to be with our kids, and it is a trade we'd make again.

We gratefully avail ourselves of the school district's resources. Meera regularly visits a well-utilized homeschool computer center created by the school district on our initiative. Despite warnings from other homeschoolers that we would find the school district unreceptive, we found the center easier to create than might be imagined. Two of the five school board members are personal friends and were thus easy to approach, and the school district receives extra revenue from the state based on the number of hours homeschoolers use the center. As it was in the district's best interests to maximize this revenue, they learned not to place any encumbrances upon its use, other than that homeschooling families complete the already-required home-schooling intent form. Ali is enrolled two half days a week in the district's "Program for Academically Talented Students" (PATS), which has been a good place for her to make friends. We were later to discover that the PATS teacher's own children were also homeschoolers. We don't resent what the school district is not doing for our kids; we are simply thankful for the opportunities they do offer, as we would be for those offered by any other community institution.

In making their way through this book, readers are likely to be confronted with the names of many people and things and terms and concepts they have never encountered before. I want to assure you that prior to our homeschooling adventures, we hadn't either. As an exercise, I went through the book and quickly counted more than one hundred. Here's a random sampling: Richard Dawkins; Bernd Heinrich; the birthplace of gray whales; Richard Feynman; amelanistic and anerythristic; John Dobson; where to find a moose in the woods; Maria Mitchell; Benjamin Banneker; perihelion and ephemeris; the difference between tortoises and turtles; rotating star wheels; ostrich polygyny; the life of Marian Anderson; fractals; E.O. Wilson and sociobiology; the Mozart *Requiem* (I'd heard it once 25 years earlier); monkey puzzle, sweet gum, thundercloud plum, and deodar cedar trees; Howard Gardner; trumpeter swans; how to figure a telescope mirror (I didn't know they *had* mirrors!); organelles; the imprinting of mallards; fuzzy logic; shape note singing; Newtonian reflector; *Simon Boccanegra*; Arctic Tern migration; Duruflé and Poulenc; xanthophyll/anthocyanin and how leaves change color; Cassini rings; doubling thirds and parallel fifths; birder lifelists; *Bison bison* and *Iguana iguana*; Trapezium; leptons; altricial and precocial; what Subaru means; the breeding of cornsnakes; E.D. Hirsch; monomorphic; ADHD; purchasing violins; punctuated equilibrium; mountain goats and bighorn sheep; Hilary Hahn; whole language approaches to reading; Mandelbrot sets; the difference between horns and antlers; *Lohengrin*; and the egg-laying habits of Eurasian cuckoos. Someone undertaking homeschooling their children in the same way will obviously not end up with the same list, as all children are different, as are the adults who help them learn. But I have absolutely no doubt that anyone who employs a similar method is likely to end up eventually with a list just as long or longer than ours.

As part of our commitment, but in the final analysis as one of our greatest joys, we've ended up educating ourselves — all of us together — as a family. A critical element of Ali's and Meera's education has been observing us as role models in the learning process. This is something children infrequently experience in their own parents, and never experience in their schoolteachers, who are viewed as virtually omniscient and never perceived as learning animals. Ellen was in massage school early in their lives. I went off to public health seminars. Ellen learned to weave and build telescopes with Ali. I took beginning piano lessons not long after Meera started (though she quickly lapped my efforts) and found a veena teacher only two hours away! Ellen took up the oboe again after a 28-year hiatus. Ali and I studied astronomy together, and Meera and I mastered the positions of the visible stars, neither of which had been part of my own childhood experience. We all learned about and experimented with breeding snakes and exotic birds, and explored wildlife ecology and ornithology. We continue to find educational opportunities as members of our local Friends (Quaker) Meeting. And in coming to know our community as our learning environment, we have taught our children the necessity of giving back so that the community can grow and change along with them. It has truly been, and continues to be, an adventure of which we are both honored and blessed to be a part, and we honor our community for making it possible.

Acknowledgments

We can't even begin to acknowledge all the people who have contributed to our family's learning adventures. I can only trust that they know who they are and that we as a family continue to strive to graciously give back in some small measure what we have received. Thank you!

"Dog Kitties"

I am set to light the ground
While the beetle goes his round.
Follow now the beetle's hum;
Little wanderer, hie thee home.

William Blake, "A Dream"
from *Songs of Innocence*

Ellen took nine-month-old Ali over to see the group of newborn puppies. "Kitties," said Ali in her newly comprehensible but still infantile voice. "Kitties." Ali's first word was "kitty," having been spoken or at least understood by us for the first time two months earlier when she attempted to crawl toward a small feline sunning itself on the sidewalk. "No," insisted Ellen. "Puppies. Dog. Baby dogs. Puppies." This dialog repeated itself several times. Ali sat pensively. Then, at last, with an exasperated look, she quietly but firmly announced, "Dog Kitties!"

I am persuaded on the basis of experience that young children from the very earliest age are far more adept at reasoning than most adults and many educators are willing to give them credit for. They lack experience, true, and the names of things, but young children spend most of their waking hours working to make sense of their world, contemplating similarities and differences, and categorizing their experiences through endless binary oppositions: movable/immovable; responsive: living/unresponsive: non-living;

49

touchable: not hot/untouchable: too hot; larger/smaller (than themselves); accessible, via crawling or climbing/inaccessible, out of reach; mothering: feeding possibilities/unmothering: no food; squishy/hard; light/dark; salty/sweet; wet/dry; dangerous/comforting. The list multiplies rapidly, as it is not tied to the narrow confines of language, and feeds on the acuity of all five senses (and maybe more), newly unwrapped and sparkling, neurons crackling with information in expanding convolutions of the developing brain. The associative rivers divide and redivide into eddies of knowledge, many of which turn into puddles and eventually dry up unless fed by new streamlets of information and experience. I am convinced that for many children past their earliest years, age brings with it a forgetting, as their stream of experience is so limited by societal, school, and home requirements for "efficiency" in childrearing, as in virtually everything else.

Ali's verbal precocity was well rewarded and reinforced by us with attentive listening and responsiveness, but it should not be assumed that young children who take more time to speak in words comprehensible to adults are in any sense intellectually slower. Most of the work going on for the young child is interior work. In some cases, the fact that individual children learn to speak "late" (if there is such a thing) may simply reflect the richness of their interior life and the difficulty of fitting that richness to words. Additionally, much of the effort involved in speaking reflects the development of auditory skills and the ability to manipulate facial muscles. And perhaps most critically, young children must figure out a way to ensure adults will listen to them!

When we moved to the West Coast from Philadelphia, I decided it was time for me to learn something about trees, or at least to be able to identify them by name. Whether it is my New York upbringing or some other factor I am not certain, but I have never felt wholly comfortable in a natural environment unmediated by human effort. I have tried to mitigate this discomfort — with only partial success — by the process of naming. Ali first taught me by her example that this is *not* the way to do it. Now she is able to be more explicit. "The name of a living thing doesn't tell you anything about what it really *is*," noted Ali as she read the beginning of this paragraph, and she's right of course. Plant or animal names are superficial, human-devised labels and tell us nothing about what the plants or animals and their interrelationships in the web of life really are, the stuff of which genuine nature education is made. Still, armed with a tree identification guide, I would push Ali down the street in her stroller, explaining, as if she fully understood, the names and characteristics of various species we encountered. I took especial delight in sharing the name of the tall monkey puzzle tree (*Araucaria araucana*) in the neighborhood, brought to Santa Cruz from Chile almost a hundred years earlier. Of course, for a long time, maybe to this day, I have been better at identifying trees on the printed page than when faced with the real deal. Looking back at it, I would have been better off taking a tree identification walk with a resident naturalist. It is a scary thought to consider that this is what the kids thought I was!

Nonetheless, walking down one particular street with 18-month-old Ali in front of me, I came upon a young tree with leaves similar to a type of maple or sycamore but with very different bark. I mused on this aloud, and scrambled through the guide to determine it was a sweet gum tree (*Liquidamba styraciflua*). Ali looked up at me from the stroller and uttered one word in her tiny, squeaky voice: "Library." "What's that, Ali?" "Library." "Library?" "Library." The next day I walked with her downtown to the library. There, lined up by the entrance, were no fewer than eight sweet gum trees.

When she was two or thereabouts, Ali befriended a Deodar tree (*Cedrus deodara*) on the corner. She would hold imaginary tea parties under it, sharing tea and conversation with her confidant. (I, unfortunately, will never know whether the conversation was two-way, although I have my suspicions.) For several years, Ali held birthday parties for Cedar. We would be invited down to visit and sing "Happy Birthday" while Ali tied a ribbon around a low-hanging branch. Cedar lived 30 feet from Fred, an extremely rare prehistoric species, I learned, not to be found in any popular tree identification book, which regularly dropped its leaves at the height of spring. To this day, Ali occasionally engages in conversation with plants.

The trees in our Olympia neighborhood, where we moved after leaving Santa Cruz, seemed to foster questions. Ali once asked me why all the trees in the area had green leaves except for the thundercloud plum (*Prunus cerasifera 'Nigra'*). She seemed to enjoy accompanying me to the garden stores around town to ask her question, and was amused by the inability of adults to provide an explanation. Finding an answer became a family project. A dozen library books and half a dozen phone calls later, a Washington State University agricultural extension agent was finally able to inform us that the thundercloud was unusual (but not unique) in that in addition to the usual green chlorophyll, the leaves contained two other kinds — xanthophyll and anthocyanin — which do not fade during the course of summer. Similar pigmentation can be found in unusually colored seaweed. This explanation, which Ali remembered for far longer than I would have imagined, is to me relatively trivial. What was important was allowing her to observe how we, as adults, went about ferreting out information.

A more momentous question was posed several months later. We were driving to a rural market to buy fruit for autumn canning. Ali was staring pensively out the car window as she was wont to do, when she inquired suddenly, "How does the tree know when to drop its leaves in the fall?" I paused for a bit longer than a moment, trying to judge the level at which to address the question and recognizing my own ignorance of the actual biological mechanism for tree thought. "Every living cell has a map and a clock inside," I said, "and knows exactly what is supposed to happen next. The cells communicate with each other so each knows what to do and when to do it, just like the cells in your body. The map and alarm clock are called DNA — deoxyribonucleic acid."

Ali provided the necessary corrective to my earlier miseducation efforts oriented around the naming process and, to be fair to myself, I did call attention to the characteristics of trees as well as naming them. And the labeling process is in fact important to the young child. As Joseph Chilton Pearce notes in his classic work *Magical Child*, naming provides the child with a common experiential ground which she shares with her parents and allows them both to refer to objects and experiences not manifest in the present moment. Through the naming process, parents grant sanction to a child's experience, and the shared process reinforces the parent/child bond, the secure underpinnings for future exploration. At any rate, Ali did learn tree names, but she didn't allow the name game to get in the way of her growing powers of observation, her knowledge quest, or her empathic understanding. After Ali turned six and a half, we contemplated an 80-foot-tall evergreen a block away from our Olympia home. We tried the tree identification book, but all we came up with was a giant sequoia (*Sequoiadendron giganteum*). But we had never heard of a giant sequoia outside of southern California where we had just stopped on a recent car trip to Mexico to see the General Sherman tree at Sequoia National Park. I told her I thought a sequoia unlikely. Undaunted, Ali carefully gathered up a cone, a small branch, some needles, and a piece of bark, placed them in a plastic bag, and took them on a trip to Washington, DC, to visit her grandmother, who volunteers as a Smithsonian Institution docent. The two of them took the bag to the National Arboretum where they left it overnight. In the morning they received a phone call informing them that it was indeed a giant sequoia and that cones had been brought to western Washington by settlers from California in the 1880s. Tree identification opened up into a series of lessons on plant geography and nineteenth-century history.

I am aware of the emphasis public school systems purport to place on computer skills and technology as the basis of their "education for tomorrow." Anyone familiar with the failures of the school system to teach basic math to large numbers of children using pencil and paper will remain justly skeptical. Regardless, to my way of thinking, this emphasis is misplaced. In an increasingly crowded world characterized by an escalating competition for finite resources and the degradation of the environment, I believe all education should be grounded in an understanding of and respect for the natural world.

Fortunately, my experience of children is that they unconsciously, and for different reasons, see it the same way. So much of early childhood is made up of coming to an understanding of natural processes and becoming competent in dealing with the physical world that I am convinced such learning becomes the template for later knowledge quests in a broad array of areas.

I envision the cornerstone of a sound environmental education to be based on five principles and processes:

- Preserve the child's sense of wonder and enchantment (this is by far the most critical);

- Allow the child's anthropomorphic tendencies to atrophy while at the same time reinforcing the child's sense of kinship with the natural world;
- Emphasize the environmental requirements for nature to thrive, and the fact that humans have these same requirements;
- Create understanding of the partnerships, the symbiotic relationships, which occur within the environment, and the cycles of birth and death; and
- Nurture the child's sense of belonging, ownership, and responsibility.

With our gentle assistance, all five of these processes have developed as part of our children's ongoing interactive dialog with the natural world. My caution is that this dialog, like natural processes themselves, takes time and should be respected. We have found that, rather than an elaborate curriculum, a few well-thought-out and well-placed questions at the appropriate moment to tune young children to be receptive may be all that is necessary to further their own explorations.

Our success in fostering this inner dialog was demonstrated to us by one of Ali's first forays into poetry:

THE TREES OF PEACE

The trees of peace,
The trees of the beasts,
They are so tall and green,
That nothing behind them can be seen!
What is behind them is as dark as night,
But in the trees it is very bright!
The trees of peace,
The trees of the beasts,
Of the promises they make,
They promise to save us,
From storms and floods,
Rains and winds,
And bring us good forever.

Through our learning adventures, we watched Ali, and later Meera, incorporate science and the natural world into their psyches through poetry, rhythm, and image. Indeed, these may provide the vital matrices necessary for having a young child take delight in her growing sensitivity and understanding of the natural world. The key word here is "delight," for it is that same delight which will be felt later by the lover reading a poem while lying under a tree in the hush of falling leaves, the scientist finding romance in the newly discovered DNA pattern of a segmented worm, or the amateur musician softly singing to herself while alone in the garden as the late afternoon sun fades away.

Much has been written regarding children's relationships with animals. I suspect young children initially experience animals as little different from themselves. Like children, animals eat, drink, breathe, explore, run, crawl, sit, climb, fear, defecate. In fact, very young children may find more in common with a family dog of similar size, sharing their four leggedness (though not their locomotive skill), than they do with two-legged, six-foot-tall bearded creatures, claiming to be relatives, who make a fuss over them and might even feel compelled to toss them in the air. This provides a tremendous advantage in the learning process if exploited thoughtfully. As the development of all animals is telescoped into a much shorter time period than that of humans, it provides a welcome analogy for children working hard to understand their own biological development. Children are also quick to draw analogies from the variations which occur as a result of animal evolution.

We saw an interesting expression of this readiness to draw analogies before Ali turned three. Ali developed a keen interest in whales and dolphins, I guess from an early bathtub companion, as she was yet to be exposed to "Flipper." As a gift from an uncle, she received a set of 18 anatomically correct plastic whales, nine adults of different species and nine babies. As one might expect, in her play she would often arrange these in their respective pairs or divide the adults and babies into two groups. What we didn't expect was that after a brief explanation that there were two major whale varieties — baleen and toothed — Ali started separating them according to their culinary habits as well as their biological development: the toothed eating fish and the baleen dining on "little shrimpies and krill." Culinary discrimination is an important unfolding in the lives of young children, as is the capacity for chewing, so there is really little wonder that Ali would latch onto an analogy for them in the natural order. We were later able to encourage this fascination with whales by visiting, on a rare car-camping vacation, the gray whale breeding grounds at Guerro del Negro in Baja California, Mexico (you can actually touch the whales!) and by going on a whale-watching trip out of Boston Harbor when on the East Coast for the gift-giving uncle's wedding. Ali's first serious subject of study was cetacean biology and prompted another early poem:

The Humpback Whale

Peaceful whale,
Graceful whale,
How I love the humpback whale.
She swims with her fins,
And dives with her tail,
How I love the humpback whale.

Twice a month for almost a year while Ellen was in massage school at night, five-year-old Ali, two-year-old Meera, and I paid a visit to Northwest Trek, a wildlife park run by the City of Tacoma Parks Department. Both Ellen and I have ambivalent feelings about zoos in general, but much less so about Northwest Trek. Within clear view of Mount Rainier, Northwest Trek is set up in such a way that most of the animals — bison, mountain goats, elk, bighorn sheep, pronghorn antelope, white and blacktail deer, caribou, trumpeter swans, and moose, among others — can roam freely over more than 500 acres, with re-created microhabitats ranging from marsh and meadow to woodland forest and steep hillside. Humans are confined to trams traveling set routes, which the animals can avoid if they so choose. Trained docents furnish information about the flora and fauna encountered. A nature center provides hands-on activities for children and displays several native snake species, freshwater fish, butterfly habitats, and living beehives. Small numbers of once-injured but now partially rehabilitated birds of prey — bald and golden eagles, barn, snowy and great-horned owls — are kept in open air enclosures, as are several small mammal species, from skunks to wolverines. All animals at Northwest Trek, except a few wild turkeys, are native to the Pacific Northwest. We have since visited a similar center, Homosassa Springs State Wildlife Park, north of Tampa, Florida, a rehabilitation home for injured manatees as well as a refuge for alligators, flamingos, foxes, and the endangered Florida panther.

The three of us would usually take the 45-minute journey out to Northwest Trek in the early evening, often taking a picnic dinner with us. The educational advantages of frequent visits became apparent very quickly and contrasted sharply with one-time visits we have paid to much larger zoos or nature theme parks over the years. During these visits, children (and grown-up children!) are for the most part attracted and wowed by what they consider (or are *taught* to consider) to be the most unique and unusual creatures: the largest (elephants and giraffes), funniest (monkeys and hippos), most ferocious (lions and tigers), cuddliest (pandas), and most entertaining (dolphins and seals). The areas where these are located receive, pardon the metaphor, the lion's share of the traffic. Information about habitat, geographical range, food gathering, reproduction, raising of young, or group behavior might at best be displayed on signs written in print too small for a child to read. Details regarding the interrelationships among animal communities and between animals and plants in the natural environment — predator/prey, symbiosis, parasitism — are rarely offered. Parents would have to work very hard indeed to remedy this deficiency for a child who is receptive while at the zoo, assuming they had such information at hand. A naturalist ready and able to answer questions from both children and adults is seldom available. But the biggest shortcoming of all is the failure of zoos and theme parks to convey to the one-time visitor any sense that animals, like humans, experience full life cycles — they are born, raised, learn, grow, mate, and die. Instead, the animals are static: the zoo lion sleeping under his tree is but a "life-like" virtual-reality representation of the animated cartoon version. Even if one undertakes a return visit, the animals are more likely than not to appear exactly the same, as if stuck in a time-warp. They might just as well be well-programmed robots.

This sensationalist but non-dynamic presentation of the animal world seriously shortchanges the intelligence and intellectual curiosity of even young children. In my experience, children as young as two and a half are prepared, even eager, to take in information on animal behavior and development, much as they do information about the human world around them, provided they are appropriately exposed to it over time.

During the course of the year, Meera and Ali made Northwest Trek a second home. They befriended all the docents, nature center volunteers, and tram drivers who looked forward to seeing them, and were often invited up into the spotter's seat beside the driver to look for animals and to help answer the questions of other visitors. Within six months, Meera could confidently identify the animals to be found in each of the microhabitats: swans, Canada geese, and beavers by the pond and in the marshes; bison and pronghorn in the fields and meadows; elk, caribou, and deer in the woodlands; mountain goats and bighorn sheep on the slopes. Ali discovered that baby bison and elk were born in the spring, that older males did not travel with the herd, and that they marked the mating season with ritual displays. She learned that caribou antlers, made of living tissue, grow into velvet and fall off, but that animals with horns, which are made of non-living material as are fingernails, never lose them.

For both Meera and Ali, the most exciting part of each trip was the search for the moose, only rarely successful. They learned that the moose bedded down around the swamp cabbage or hung out deep in the woods in summer, and trained their eyes to peer more carefully as nightfall approached and the weather cooled. A sighting would be great cause for celebration. They observed bison put on their winter coats and mountain kids grow from nurslings to adulthood. They both relished sharing the bison's Latin name, *Bison bison*, earnestly informing new visitors that these are *not* buffaloes, which are a completely separate Asian species. Both Ali and Meera attended short summer camp sessions at Northwest Trek, and Ali was invited on a special trip into the free-roaming area with one of the caregivers to feed the animals. By the time each of them turned six, Ali and Meera had more direct experience and understanding of the animal world than I had in a lifetime before they were born.

All Ali wanted for her fifth birthday was a snake. I presume she got the idea from Northwest Trek. She certainly didn't get it from me. As already noted, I'm originally from New York City, and the only pet I was allowed to keep as a child was a parakeet, and only after my mother had flushed several dead goldfish down the toilet. I'd never lived in a house with a reptile before, and rarely saw one. I think this was probably an advantage, as at least I had learned no fear.

A week after Ali insistently informed us of her desires, a young western garter snake serendipitously appeared outside our back door. The snake cooperated uneasily when I picked her up and placed her in the five-dollar terrarium we'd purchased at a neighborhood yard sale the day before. Ali was pleased, in her own quiet way. She spent hours watching the black rope of an animal with narrow green and gray ribbons running down her back and sides. We called her Olympia. Meera squealed with joy when Ellen allowed Olympia to curl around her wrist or slither up her arm.

One evening I returned home late from work, tired, but still wanting to take the family to a community event. Ellen suffered from a bad cold, and both kids were out of sorts, but I still had hopes, when we discovered Olympia had escaped! After 40 minutes of hunting with flashlights, the children in tears the entire time, we located Olympia hidden in the refrigerator coils. Many wrenches and screwdrivers and much pushing and shoving later, Olympia was back in her terrarium, both kids in bed, and Ellen and I sitting in the family room, drinking tea. A psychologist friend later informed me that Olympia, as a family member, was correcting an imbalance that night in the functioning of our family system.

Olympia did not eat well in captivity despite our best efforts, and we all agreed to let her go. For several years, whenever Ali and Meera saw a garter snake in the backyard, they would greet it as Olympia, their long-lost friend.

Olympia was soon replaced by a one-year-old cornsnake named Pop. Pop enjoyed slithering up inside people's shirts and blouses and had a very placid disposition. One of Ali's favorite activities was to allow Pop to wind himself through her long, dark hair and then to walk around as the family Medusa, to the consternation of visitors to our home. Alas, Pop didn't stay with us long. He escaped one evening from his terrarium and hasn't been seen since. For a while, we found diversion in warning squeamish house guests to tell us immediately if, in the middle of the night, they discovered a snake in their bed, so we could celebrate his return.

Ali's next two reptiles were also cornsnakes: Tassel and Silk. "They're both mutations," Ali would lecture any adult visitors prepared to listen. "Tassel, the male, is amelanistic ('without black', meaning a red and white mutation for a corn snake), while Silk, the female, is amelanistic, anerythristic ('without black or red', meaning white)." Then she'd launch into a learned dissertation of the potential genetic makeup of their future offspring, an understanding of which had been sparked by conversations with Sam, our local pet store snake breeder. Most of those on the receiving end of the lectures appeared genuinely mystified and noticeably ill at ease, as adults are not in the habit of taking in and evaluating scientific information offered by six-year-olds, and were rarely prepared to admit ignorance and ask her to explain things in terms they could understand. Ali learned how to do Punnett squares, simple charts displaying future genetic possibilities, prior to two-place addition and at about the same time she learned to read. Discussions of reptilian DNA were had by all, as well as interesting conversations about nature versus nurture. Ellen's massage school biology and knowledge gained from my professional work in public health stood us in good enough stead. After attending a reptile fair in Seattle, Ali joined the Pacific Northwest Herpetological Society as their youngest member and helped with reptile shows at the local library. Both kids took to giving away snake sheds as gifts to delighted friends.

Ali developed a somewhat annoying practice of correcting scientific or other misinformation offered by others within her earshot, whether these corrections were solicited or no, and it took some doing on our part to at least tone down if not cure her of the habit. It was especially difficult as she, in contrast with Meera, never did so in order to show off. She simply assumed everyone would want to have access to correct intelligence about just about anything, just as she would herself. Ellen explained to her that this practice might make some people feel uncomfortable and that she should curb the urge, at least around her friends. Ali still struggles with this. She has managed to learn to control herself, but maintains that hearing wrong information stand uncorrected continues to "drive me crazy."

When Tassel and Silk arrived, they were only three months old and eight inches long. Watching them grow to their current four-and-a-half-foot lengths turned out to be a great learning tool, and an introduction to the science of measurement. Each month after they shed, Ali or Meera measured the skin length and weighed the snakes on a balance scale. Then we plotted the weight and length on graphs hung above the enclosures.

Not long after we acquired the two snakes, my daughters were given two rats — one male, one female — by one of their friends. Nightingale Ocean and Snowflake came with a solemn pledge: their offspring could not become snake food. That day should go down in rat history like the Emancipation Proclamation. Close to a hundred rat babies were raised and sold to the local pet store, which paid us enough to feed the next litter. Meera took on the role of official baby rat handler, so that when the six-week-old rodents made it to the pet store, they fetched a premium as hand-tamed. Meanwhile, we warn house guests that if they go looking in the freezer for a late night snack, they shouldn't take *all* the frozen microwavable mice. Tassel and Silk would not be pleased. We've now taken to raising fresh white mice for the snakes' dining pleasure. In our house, mice are totem, but rats are taboo.

After being introduced to them at a Herpetological Society meeting, Ali told us she wanted to spend her savings on an eastern box turtle. "Really a tortoise," she insists authoritatively, and who am I to argue? Terra Rosa, a five-year-old female, arrived just in time for one of our town's biggest annual events, the Olympia Pet Parade. Almost a thousand people gather with their pets in our downtown area and compete for prizes offered by local merchants. Then they march up our main street to the cheers of the multitude, led by a troop of bagpipers, horses thoughtfully assigned to bring up the rear.

We taped a fan of white feathers topped by a single peacock feather in the center to Terra Rosa's back, and a few stray feathers to the sides like a fringe. Then I helped the kids rig a sign for the back of their wagon, reading "Rare Olympia Peacock Turtle — *T. Olympianus Ridiculi.*" When Ali and Meera, dressed in their Halloween wolf costumes, pulled the wagon up to the judge's area, we knew we had a hit. Children and parents gathered round, and among the ferrets, snakes, guinea pigs, bunnies, goats, geese, ducks, dogs, cats, and tarantulas, the judges awarded Terra Rosa a cash award for best animal costume. It was just enough to purchase a second box turtle for Meera, a male incongruously named Fluffy. Terra and Fluffy both enjoy eating bananas and flopping around in the bathtub.

For my birthday, the children informed me that the family room was being converted into a nature center. A sign written in a six-year-old's scrawl appeared, tied to the tree outside the house, proclaiming "This Way to Fun," with an arrow pointing toward the door. Ellen built a floor-standing terrarium made of 2 X 4s and an old sliding glass window, which now housed Terra Rosa, Fluffy, and a male green iguana named Mendel after the founder of modern genetics. (The Latin is *Iguana iguana*, Ali reminds me, paralleling *Bison bison*.) In and around the nature center are or have been two turtles, two iguanas, 40 white mice, 22 rats, two black-masked lovebirds — so similar ("'Monomorphic' is the word," says Ali) we named them Victor and Victoria, to Ali's great amusement (she loved the Julie Andrews' movie, after having had it thoroughly explained by us) — and a host of offspring, a green-cheeked conure (a little parrot) who likes to help us wash dishes, a Holland Lop rabbit, a Catalan sheepdog, and a group of inscrutable Asian stick insects. Caring for them all became part of the family regimen. Meera and the reptiles became regulars at various show-and-tells about town. I am still allergic to cats.

Even before Ali could read by herself, the thread of earlier exchanges about DNA and mutations led us into fresh discussions about biological adaptation. "Would Silk — the amelanistic, anerythristic (that is, white) cornsnake — survive in the wild?" "Yes, and more likely if she could find white sand to hide in." "What about Tassel, the amelanistic red one?" "His chances would increase if he could live around red clay soil." "What about white tigers?" "Where it snows a lot." "And pink ones?" "Are there pink tiger mutations?" "No. But if there were, they'd be valued for television commercials." For months and even years, our dialogs about biological adaptive and survival values have deepened, even to include instinctive and behavioral characteristics of animals, and those of humans as well. Enrolled, as already noted, two half-days a week in the school district's Program for Academically

In full wolf regalia, with canid relative

Talented Students, Ali chose to write a long essay on Darwin's theory of natural selection. At our suggestion, she learned "An idea is a greater monument than a cathedral," the climactic oration delivered by the character portraying Clarence Darrow from Jerome Lawrence and Robert E. Lee's *Inherit the Wind*, a dramatic rendering of the 1925 Scopes "Monkey Trial." By the time Ali reached nine, I was struggling to keep up with her in this area and could only do so by delving into the works of contemporary Darwinists such as Oxford University's Richard Dawkins (which I thoroughly recommend). But Ali's powers of observation kept her one step ahead. I learned the theory, but when I tried to illustrate the complexity involved in the evolution of spider webs, I found out that she'd not only read about it, but had conducted simple experiments by throwing heather flowers onto different parts of various webs to see how the different spider species would move around the diverse web strands.

As a birthday present, my coworkers bought me a membership in Wolf Haven International, a sanctuary for captive wolves that had been used in scientific experiments or that people had tried unsuccessfully to keep as

pets. This internationally recognized facility, which also sponsors educational programs and is involved in a national Mexican wolf breeding and reintroduction program, is located in Tenino, Washington, only 16 miles from
our home. Yet it took about six months after receiving the gift for me to take
the family there to visit, which is a fair indication of my own initial lack of
interest. Five-year-old Ali was immediately and absolutely captivated,
whether by the alertness of the wolves' eyes, the eeriness of their howls, or
the information or enthusiasm offered by the tour guide. Ali was pleased to
offer hypotheses to several adults on the potential adaptive value of mutations in wolf eye color as the tour guide listened open-mouthed. On weekend evenings in summer, Wolf Haven International plays host to "Howl-
Ins." Storytellers and musicians entertain children and adults alike. There are
arts and crafts and education exhibits, and visitors and staff try to provoke
the 40 or so resident gray wolves and two coyotes into howling. We began
to attend regularly. For one of these Howl-Ins, Ali wrote a lullaby which she
sang, and later adapted for her violin. The chorus went:

> When the night comes,
> When the moon rises,
> Then the wolves come
> To sing us to sleep.

Upon returning home that evening, Ali began to badger us: she wanted to be a Wolf Haven volunteer. Three separate inquiries over a period of
months netted little response. Finally, I wrote to Wolf Haven International's
founder and president, noting they would be gaining the services of our
entire family, and Wolf Haven would profit greatly by having a child work
with other young visitors. The president got back to us and said if Ali would
take the same required 16-hour course in wildlife ecology and wolf biology
and pass the same written examination, Wolf Haven would accept her volunteer services.

Ali, now turned six, was game. She sat through the two-day course
with two dozen other potential volunteers, all adults up to age 70, but without taking any notes — she couldn't write yet. A week later she took the

exam, which was made up of 20 long-answer questions, dictating her responses to us to be written down. "She passed," said Beth, the volunteer coordinator, "and actually did better than some of the adults."

Safety issues precluded Ali from becoming a tour guide, and she was not mathematically equipped (or tall enough!) to help out in the gift shop. Beth found the perfect position for Ali. She would assist the education director in setting up and running the education table and educational displays at Howl-Ins. Ali had to learn to furnish information and explanations fluently to both children and adults about all of the following: the diverse North American wolf species and their geographical ranges; pack behavior; hunting and feeding habits; territorial marking and migration; predator/prey relationships; sensory acuity; breeding, biological development, and population variation and control; wolf/human relationships and myths about wolves; wolf reintroduction efforts; and the role and contribution of Wolf Haven International. Ali mastered all this information through classes, films, and books, and learned to present it by apprenticing to the education director.

Within a year, Ali ran the education table herself. She'd set up skulls of bears, wolves, coyotes, and mountain lions to explain the dissimilarities in their dental and jaw structures and to elucidate differences in their respective faculties of smell and sight. "If you were a wolf, you could smell your mother's spaghetti sauce cooking six miles away, if the wind was right and your mother cooked spaghetti," was one of her favorite illustrations. Small canisters with cottonballs soaked in scent-producing materials of various concentrations demonstrated the acuity of the wolf's olfactory sense. Plaster casts of bear, bobcat, wolf, and coyote footprints showed how animals could be identified from the tracks they left. Sample radio collars, old and cruel leg-hold traps, antlers and horns of wolf prey, and pictures of animals in their natural habitat were set up and displayed on all sides of the large table. A choice hands-on activity led by Ali consisted of a plastic hotdog and pieces of carpet pads that could be affixed with velcro over elbows so they couldn't be bent. After the pads were attached, Ali would request participants to keep their hands in fists and then to try to figure out how they might manage to get the hotdog to their mouths while on all fours. Participants realized quickly that by necessity wolves are very messy eaters!

Ali's most significant innovation was her use of a set of small plastic wolves and a larger plastic caribou to spin an elaborate yarn about pack hunting behavior. Included were scientific explications of the roles played by various pack members, eating habits, hunting techniques, and the basics of wolf-related population biology, all woven into a child's "toy story," which could be quite gripping. Ali learned to direct questions she couldn't answer herself to the facility's research director or one of the more experienced tour guides.

Since Ali began her work at Wolf Haven International three years ago, several other children have become volunteers. Ali has taken her display into school classrooms and helped promote Wolf Haven International at county fairs in the area. Wolf Haven started an "Ask Ali" column in its children's newsletter.

The educational value of Ali's involvement in Wolf Haven is incalculable, and the benefits of her finding ways to make use of her newly acquired knowledge cannot be overestimated. The learning process put her in direct contact with research scientists, wildlife experts, and a devoted cadre of adult volunteers who shared her preoccupation and provided camaraderie. The repetition of activity at the education table, at least twice a month, allowed her to master both the information and the entire situation as teacher, and gave her room to express her own creativity and the opportunity to share her enthusiasm with young and old alike. The subject matter itself led to broader and deeper reading and study, progressing rapidly over the years.

I need to emphasize that while we provided the initial opportunities for this interest in wolves and wildlife ecology to develop, it is Ali's, not ours. She has been the leader. Ellen's and my main contribution has been to listen and to open doors. Again and again, I think back on what might have happened or, more to the point, what might *not* have happened if I had not followed up after our third rebuff from Wolf Haven with a letter. Similar instances of Ali and Meera sensing and then communicating their particular learning needs, and of us then strategizing ways to meet them regardless of barriers based on their chronological ages, have been a continuing feature of their education.

Victor and Victoria, the black-masked lovebirds, happily turned out to be male and female and have produced many offspring, most of which we

Ali, age seven, working the Wolf Haven Education Table

sold. Meera looked into their nest daily to check on the eggs and was entertained by watching the development of the young from scrawny hatchlings
to fully fledged adults in six weeks. "They're altricial," explained Ali, utilizing a word I'd never heard before to apprise me of baby lovebirds' complete
dependence upon their parents, in contrast to other birds who are precocial
and can fend for themselves almost immediately after birth, such as ostriches, chickens, or ducks.

Ali got her new words from a book I bought for her when she accompanied me to a large bookstore in Portland, Oregon. Unlike me or her sister,
Ali hates to browse in either bookstores or libraries. She will withhold judgment on a book until she has read at least two chapters. But the cover of *The
Lives of Birds: Birds of the World and Their Behavior* by Lester Short, Curator
of Birds at the American Museum of Natural History, caught her attention,
and by the time we left the store, she had read just under half of it. For days,
Ellen and I received impromptu lectures about the imprinting of newly
hatched mallards; the egg-laying of Eurasian cuckoos, whose eggs, laid in the
nests of other birds, mimic the host species' eggs in color and markings; the

abstract reasoning of blue jays; the polygyny of lark buntings; and the flight navigation of lesser black-backed gulls.

Needless to say, questions arose: if the Arctic tern spends most of the year migrating, when and where do they lay and incubate their eggs? The book didn't say. With my assistance, Ali came up with several hypotheses: the mating terns stay behind one year; or stop in the tropics in the middle of migration; or the eggs have an extremely short incubation period and the chicks mature very quickly (this is the correct explanation). No amount of library research or queries of birdwatching friends netted an answer, so, with our encouragement, Ali struck up a correspondence with Dr. Short, who provided one. This process of reading and observing, questioning, theorizing, and then researching, utilizing not only books but finding knowledgeable individuals who will take the time to respond, has become a continuing feature of Ali's education.

Ali retained her capacity to draw out distinctions from earliest childhood. "Ostriches and wolves are completely different in breeding habits," she announced to us out of the blue one day. "How so," I asked, knowing I was in for something special. "Well, the main female ostrich scoops out a hole in the ground for her eggs, but several other females lay their eggs in the same hole. The male (ostriches are polygynous, she noted) will sit on the eggs at night, and the main female does so in the daytime. And when the eggs hatch, the babies are precocial and can pretty much fend for themselves. But with wolves, the pack prepares the den, only the alpha female gives birth, and many different wolves care for the helpless pups until they are ready to join the hunt."

Ali pointed out to me that there are few animals which seem to recognize their parents throughout their entire life cycle. "Just some primates, orcas, and sperm whales, although we don't really know for sure. A dead 13-year-old-sperm whale was found to have milk in its stomach. Orcas live in the same pod as their mothers their entire lives, but they always breed with one from another pod. That's how they prevent inbreeding." To ask a question about parent recognition in the animal kingdom had never occurred to me, but it is easy to appreciate why this would interest a nine-year-old growing into independence.

As she raised one of the hatchling lovebirds as a pet, Ali became interested in the degree to which animals can reason and express emotions in the human sense of the terms. She was particularly amused with my retelling of the proof offered by nineteenth-century American philosopher Charles Sanders Peirce. Peirce noted that when his father came home from work, closing the door and throwing his umbrella in the hallway rack, the family dog would come running down the stairs to greet him excitedly. A pet parrot learned to imitate the sound of the door slamming and the umbrella dropping and would cackle with malicious amusement after causing the dog to fall all over itself scrambling down the stairs to greet its non-present master.

Meera enjoyed the menagerie, her experiences at Wolf Haven and Northwest Trek, and the flurry of activity surrounding her sister's interest in botany and animal behavior. But her early biological science interests were oriented toward people. She wanted all the details of how my brother lost both legs in an automobile accident, the details of his care, of how his prosthetics were made and how they worked. At age six, Meera went to the doctor for vaccinations. This trip prompted a round of questions: what diseases did each of them prevent and what are their symptoms, how do immunizations work and can they make you sick, do these diseases exist in other countries, and what really causes them? As I work in public health, these were questions I was better prepared to answer, together with providing an explanation of what I did in my job. She asked about the major causes of death among dogs. She inquired after one of our friends, a recovering alcoholic. "Will she die if she has one drink? Two? Well, how many would it take?" "Why do people smoke if it makes them sick?" Meera enjoyed brief periods looking at blood cells through the microscope, but she really wanted to know how diseases were transmitted from person to person and how they could be prevented.

We sought outside avenues to help structure Ali's natural science studies as they were growing beyond our capacity to organize them well. Ellen made several failed overtures to the local school district to see whether Ali, now nine, could sit in on a high school biology course. So we enrolled her in a high school life sciences course offered by the University of Missouri's Center for Distance and Independent Study. Several times a week, Ali reads her textbook, and Ellen and she review the discussion and workbook materials. Ali completes a review quiz which she sends to the University. An evaluation is returned, with detailed explanations of any questions she answers incorrectly. Ali has developed her own mnemonics for nucleotides, and she has taught me about how mitochondria are used to study genetic history.

When Ali commenced the course, we were not concerned about whether she would succeed. I did have some small initial anxiety, however, that her independent inquiring frame of mind, which we had so carefully nurtured, might be stifled and she'd become slave to the text. I needn't have worried. From her room as she studied the very first chapter, we heard Ali splutter aloud, "That's not right." "What's the problem, Ali?" I asked. "My textbook has a big mistake. It says, 'In 1975 the United States sent the Viking space mission to our nearest planet, Mars, to see if life existed there.' But the closest planet is Venus!" I couldn't have devised a better object lesson myself if I'd tried, and we reinforced the lesson by having Ali write both the textbook publisher and the instructor at the University of Missouri. Just prior to her mid-term, I took her out for a snack at a local café. She looked at me, blueberry muffin only half-chewed in her mouth, and mumbled, "You know, dad, I wish my biology textbook was more up-to-date." "Oh, how so?" "Well, it includes statements about organelles as only hypotheses which we now know to be true." I shrugged, muttered something about the progress of science, and looked up "organelle" in my out-of-date dictionary as soon as I got home.

A final concern we had with Ali undertaking more formalized studies was that the pursuit of evaluation (i.e., grades) might replace her love of the knowledge quest. Fiercely competitive, I can remember that happening to me, and it took years (decades, actually) for the damage to be undone. We hoped success would come to be defined by the self-fulfillment she would experience in new learning, rather than by the number of questions she might not answer correctly on an exam. Again, we needn't have worried. On the day Ali chose to take her final exam, she went into her room to spend half an hour on last minute review. She emerged an hour and a half later. "What have you been up to?" asked Ellen. "Well," she said, "I quickly finished studying for the test, but the material in my textbook for next semester's course (on organic chemistry and genetics) was so interesting, I could not stop." She completed the 90-minute multiple choice final in 20 minutes, and went back to her reading.

———◦•◦•———

One of the most obvious realities about school-based education, and also one of the most overlooked, is that it takes place almost entirely indoors. Pets are excluded. Plants are prohibited for fear of potential allergic reactions. Classrooms and hallways are repeatedly treated with toxic chemicals to eliminate pests. Windows, when they exist, are kept tightly closed and secured, and are not meant to be peered through. It is as if for education to happen, nature must be shut out at all costs, for it cannot be controlled and does not conform to the school's architecture, administrative structure, or timeframes.

The result, not surprisingly, is an overwhelming natural illiteracy among children and, later, among adults. Intimacy with nature is denied. The natural world is to be dissected, analyzed, experimented upon, but there is no room for cultivating the art of long-term and continuous observation, something for which children are well or, I should emphasize, *naturally*, even uniquely, equipped. The fundamental lesson inculcated in children in this restrictive environment, regardless of curriculum, is that nature is, above all, foreign. At best, the natural world is to be viewed as a giant amusement park; at worst, as an overgrown golf course waiting to be tamed.

It is also seen as disposable. Many schoolteachers recognize the need to bring some representative of nature back into the classroom and may be praised for doing so. The baby chicks pecking through their shells and chirping in a box under a light bulb in the corner, the hamster exercising on the flywheel, the Chia Pets growing on the windowsill, all introduce their small elements of welcome chaos into the classroom environment. Some schoolteachers can regale one with stories of just how much chaos is involved in figuring out how to dispose of the chicks once they have outgrown the box (and the classroom) or who will care for the hamster during spring break. But nature illiteracy shows even through these well-meaning efforts. There are now programs that encourage schoolteachers to hatch monarch butterflies in classroom terrariums and to release them to the wild. They come in kits. No thought is given by these teachers to the fact that the monarchs released in Washington State are grown from larvae bred in New York and Pennsylvania with different genetic migratory programming. There are potentially devastating ecological consequences to the monarch species and predators and plants along their migratory paths if and when interbreeding with local stocks occurs. Regardless, students are not permitted as part of their education to take the time to observe caterpillars or butterflies in the wild, or anything else for that matter. Children, too, are part of nature, and the fear is that they too cannot be controlled.

Nature illiteracy and lack of intimacy with nature have enormous social and environmental consequences. The effects of toxic waste, pesticides, automobile exhausts, and polluting, energy-inefficient production practices upon our air and water and, ultimately, upon our health and that of all living things are at least partially a result of habits of mind grounded in school-based education. Despite our own natures, we learn from an early age to ignore our intimate connection in the web, and as a society we are paying an immense price for it.

The answer to this natural illiteracy, however, does not lie in attempting to inculcate a love of nature in our children, at least not directly. This is despite the fact that the best aspects of adult initiatives for environmental conservation and rehabilitation are driven by such a deeply realized attachment. For a young child, love of nature is a pretty abstract idea. I doubt that children are born with an instinctive nature affection, but freed of indoor tyranny and gently nurtured, they are more likely to find an affinity with nature deeper than their elders can ever hope to reclaim for themselves. In our experience, time in nature provides the grounding, but nature education best proceeds from the specific to the general. Kids may not make sense out of the idea of loving nature, but they may become very attached to their own, sometimes secret, places. They might not feel a generalized sentimental affection for all of creation, but they may become obsessed with ants, spiders, mushrooms, horses, or, yes, even dung beetles. Feed the child's chosen nature quest, and she will find herself intimately entwined. Still, and this is an open question: can people, and especially children, who are now living more and more isolated lives indoors and who are losing their stories, tales, myths, and experience of the wisdom and power of the natural world, nevertheless learn to honor and protect it?

———————◆◆◆———————

Even as Ali was completing her life sciences course, she spent increasing amounts of time on daily jaunts to the 25-acre woods in our neighborhood. Equipped with magnifying glass, binoculars, plastic bags, nature guides, occasionally a journal, or, more commonly, just waterproof boots, she quickly became the resident naturalist. She also joined the local chapter of the Audubon Society so she could go birdwatching. I got to tag along on trips which we now schedule weeks in advance. With chapter members averaging more than 45 years of age, and some with decades of experience, each excursion provided Ali with 12 to 15 knowledgeable teachers ready and eager to explain bird behavior, to identify wildflowers and mushrooms, to discuss butterflies. Critically, and unlike in many similar adult-oriented settings in which she has found herself, birdwatchers understand and appreciate the value of silence and contemplation. Nature itself is the best teacher. We purchased a "birder's lifelist," a journal and checklist including the 720-plus bird species native to North America as well as space for observation notes. In an expression of humor absolutely typical of her, Ali used one of the blank spaces on the list to report sighting an astronomical object, the Wild Duck Cluster. The lifelist is an important educational tool. It provides Ali with a working reminder of how much more there will be to observe and learn throughout her lifetime. Audubon outings and meetings have become elements of Ali's life sciences learning lab, but have not displaced her tireless efforts to catch the gilded leaves from the alder tree outside our home as they cascade in the autumn wind.

There is a recurrent theme running through our natural science adventures, but one which rarely becomes apparent in the school process of stuffing children's heads with disconnected facts, whether the kids express interest in them or not. Namely, the first duty of the naturalist, as of all scientists, is to describe accurately what one has perceived, and to communicate it within the context of a growing understanding of the larger natural order, both for oneself and for others. This can be taught formally, but our experience suggests it doesn't have to be. What is required is for the child to acquire the tools and opportunity to make explicit what is already going on in the evolving journey of self-awareness, of which nature awareness is an integral part. Long after the great natural historian's and scientist's discoveries have been superseded, their writings, like the knowledge quests of children, continue to engage and inspire because, ultimately, they awaken us to something enduring about ourselves.

What I hope my children have gained through our learning adventures is a deepening recognition that the process of science itself is a conversation, with the world of natural phenomena of course, but also with scientific understandings of the past, with our perceptions and those of others around us, and with the future. It is this dynamic of conversation, its inherent reciprocity, which coaxes nature to yield up her secrets, as to an intimate friend. To quote from "The Dispersion of Seeds," the last work of Henry David Thoreau, America's greatest naturalist , which I gave to Ali when she embarked on her high school life sciences course:

> Though I do not believe that a plant will spring up where no seed has been, I have great faith in a seed. Convince me that you have a seed there, and I am prepared to expect wonders.

Brown, Tom and William Jon Watkins, *The Tracker: The Story of Tom Brown, Jr. as Told to William Jon Watkins*. Englewood Cliffs, NJ: Prentice-Hall, Inc., 1978. The first of many books by and about Tom Brown, revealing a timeless wisdom about the natural world and our place within it. I think Ali has read just about all of them! This book cannot fail to fire the imagination of young and old alike. In Washington State, we are privileged to be home to the Wilderness Awareness School, founded by a student and close apprentice of Tom Brown. The School is a community-based institution dedicated to engaging humans' natural intelligence and awakening our innate abilities to perceive and connect with the world around us. The Wilderness Awareness School offers programs lasting from several hours to a period of years. Its Kamana Naturalist Training is a comprehensive program, offering a sophisticated inquiry into ecology, biology, botany, natural history, ethnobotany, and cultural anthropology. It involves hands-on field work, observation, and extensive journaling, and develops life-long research skills. The correspondence program is meant for adults or teenagers and takes between 18 months and five years to complete. Extensive mentoring and support is provided. Ali is likely to undertake the Kamana program shortly. For a list of offerings and more information, contact the Wilderness Awareness School, 26333 NE Valley Street #5-137, Duvall, WA 98019; Tel: 1-800-340-6068; 425-788-1301; Website: www.NatureOutlet.com; E-mail: wasnet@natureoutlet.com

Connor, Richard C. and Dawn Micklethwaite Peterson, *The Lives of Whales and Dolphins.* New York, NY: Henry Holt and Co., 1994. One of the two volumes in the American Museum of Natural History's animal behavior series ever published, and "almost as good as Lester Short's book on birds," says Ali. The series editor, Theresa Burns, upon my calling her to tell her how much Ali enjoyed Dr. Short's book and to see if there were others in the series, went out of her way to send Ali a free copy, now out of print.

Cornell, Joseph Bharat, *Sharing Nature with Children.* Nevada City, CA: Ananda Publications, 1979. Now considered a classic, and justifiably so. Cornell's maxim "Share more, teach less" should be at the heart of any sound nature or science education.

Dawkins, Richard, *River Out of Eden: A Darwinian View of Life.* New York, NY: Basic Books, 1995. See also *Climbing Mount Improbable.* New York, NY: W.W. Norton, 1996.

Northwest Trek, Eatonville, WA 98328; Tel: 1-800-433-TREK; 360-832-6117; Website: www.nwtrek.org

Penn, William, *Some Fruits of Solitude*. Richmond, IN: Friends United Press, 1985. For more than 300 years, Quakers have held a testimony regarding the importance of education, and of nature education in particular. Perhaps the earliest and most poetic statement of this testimony comes from William Penn, the founder of the "Holy Experiment," which became the Commonwealth of Pennsylvania first published in 1693:

> The first Thing obvious to Children is what is sensible; and that we make no Part of their Rudiments. We press their Memory too soon, and puzzle, strain, and load them with Words and Rules; to know Grammer and Rhetorick; and a strange Tongue or two, that ten to one may never be useful to them; Leaving their natural Genius to Mechanical and Physical, or natural Knowledge uncultivated and neglected; which would be of exceeding Use and Pleasure to them through the whole Course of their Life ...

> It were Happy if we studied Nature more in natural Things; and acted according to Nature; whose rules are few, plain and most reasonable. Let us begin where she begins, go her Pace, and close always where she ends, and we cannot miss of being good Naturalists. The Creation would no longer be a Riddle to us: The Heavens, Earth, and Waters, with their respective, various and numerous Inhabitants: Their Productions, Natures, Seasons, Sympathies and Antipathies; their Use, Benefit and Pleasure, would be better understood by us: And an eternal Wisdom, Power, Majesty, and Goodness, very conspicuous to us, thro' those sensible and passing Forms: The World wearing the Mark of its Maker, whose Stamp is everywhere visible, and the Characters very legible to the Children of Wisdom.

> And it would go a great way to caution and direct People in their Use of the World, that they were better studied and

known in the Creation of it. For how could Man find the Confidence to abuse it, while they should see the Great Creator stare them in the Face, in all and every part thereof?

Short, Lester L., *The Lives of Birds: Birds of the World and Their Behaviors*. New York, NY: Henry Holt and Co., 1993.

Thoreau, Henry David, *Faith in a Seed: The Dispersion of Seeds and Other Late Natural History Writings*, edited by Bradley Dean. Washington, DC, and Covelo, CA: Island Press, 1993.

University of Missouri Center for Distance and Independent Study, 106 Clark Hall, Columbia, MO 65211-4200; Tel: 1-800-609-3727; Fax: 573-882-6808; Website: indepstudy.ext.missouri.edu

Wolf Haven International, 3111 Offut Lake Road, Tenino, WA 98587; Tel: 1-800-448-9653; Website: www.wolfhaven.org; E-mail: WolfHvn@aol.com

Mr. Newton's Rules

Look on the rising sun: there God does live
And gives his light and gives his heat away;
And flowers and trees and beasts and men receive
Comfort in morning, joy in the noonday.

William Blake, "The Little Black Boy"
from *Songs of Experience*

Ali's first science lesson was earth-shattering. Literally. We lived just three blocks from the center of downtown Santa Cruz, when a week before Ali's second birthday, the 1989 Loma Prieta earthquake hit. Five people dead, hundreds made homeless, the downtown heavily damaged, with entire buildings reduced to rubble. People lined up outside stores waiting for water. Highways were buried under debris. Visible damage existed for months and even years after.

For several days after the quake, we camped in the backyard. On the ground, we could feel every aftershock course through our bodies. When we turned on the television, we could not avoid witnessing more of the same, a wave of destruction having swept across the San Jose Valley and the San Francisco area.

We knew Ali was upset, or at least we assumed so. We certainly were. All of our daily patterns and routines, from picking up the mail to savoring coffee and sweets at our favorite café, were disrupted. How does one explain this to a two-year-old?

We could have tried to make light of it, pretending it didn't happen. Instead, we taught Ali what amounts to a mantra. "What happens in an earthquake?" we'd ask. She would reply at each prompting: "First the tectonic plates go ..." "POP!" "Everything ..." "*SHAKES!*" "And then, ..." "KABOOMEE!" Together, we repeated the ritualized formula, bouncing Ali on our knees, playing with blocks or with constructions in the sandbox. Ali seemed genuinely pleased, especially since whenever the conversation turned to the earthquake, which was all too often, she had something to contribute.

Was this "science"? Or mere parroting? Surely Ali had no idea what tectonic plates were, nor what it meant for them to go "pop." But I'm not sure that mattered. What did matter was that Ali had a shared explanation for her world, a comforting, if embryonic and imprecise, understanding of natural phenomena which made her the master of, or at least commentator upon, rather than a helpless bystander to, her experience.

Ali retained much of her seismic education. Four years later, she spent a day involved with the Junior Ranger program at Mount Rainier National Park. We highly recommend these programs, not so much for their content (which varies widely in quality) as for the opportunity for children to interact with park rangers. While Ali's program in mountain geology was designed for children ages 8-12, the park ranger reported back to us that six-year-old Ali was already familiar with most of the material and concepts and readily referred back to her earthquake experience.

After Ali turned four, we began to have fun with "Newton's Rules." We constructed an elaborate evolving tale of a "Mr. Newton," based loosely on the historical Isaac who, sometimes with his imaginary wife's assistance, made rules for how things in the world work. We conceived of him ordering individual apples to fall from trees and imagined what happened on the day he overslept (no apples were allowed to fall). We blamed Mr. Newton for unfortunate occurrences at the dinner table, and thanked him for ensuring that water remained at the bottom of the bathtub and for making the droplets fall from the showerhead. Mr. Newton was responsible for my difficulty in getting out of bed in the morning, for marbles rolling around the linoleum, or for balls bouncing on the pavement. Ali would laugh with delight when Ellen and I, both a bit overweight, would try to occupy the same chair at the same time.

Following several months of this activity, Ali and I began to speculate on how flying insects managed to rest on the ceiling. We came up with several "hypotheses." Perhaps there was a special sticky glue on bug bellies. Or maybe there were suction cups on their feet. Or conceivably there were little hooks on insect legs. Or just possibly the bugs bribed Mrs. Newton and she wheedled special permission from the Mr. for them to be allowed to ignore the rules. (This, by the way, is metaphorically closest to the true explanation, as the mass of insects is so small that the force of gravity has little effect.)

Of course, we did this all in a spirit of play. However, behind it was a serious educational issue. In school, both Ellen and I were taught, beginning at a fairly early age, that the scientific method involved drawing up hypotheses, conducting experiments, observing what happens (or collecting data), and coming to conclusions. Public schoolteachers have told me they still use this formula to teach how scientists supposedly think and, by implication, how children should learn to think as well. The only problem is that this is *not* the way scientists think, or at least not the way scientific inference works. Well before settling on any particular hypothesis to test, scientists examine already available data and experience to develop contrasting hypotheses which might lead to a 'best possible explanation'. Only after this initial process of inference is undertaken and a potential best explanation chosen would the formula kick in. The crucial difference is that scientific inference is open-ended, with the questions to be examined or the directions to be taken chosen by the scientist.

The gifted writer and field biologist Bernd Heinrich, in his superb work on avian sociobiology *Ravens in Winter*, explains how this process works for him. He writes:

> Right now I have nine hypotheses. Not theories, just hypotheses. It could take a lifetime to go through this list of hypotheses exhaustively testing each one, one at a time. And I might *still* not have the answer at the end. I have to go on hunches.

But I have to work to get the right ones.

> Every (field) trip is exciting because I try to set up an experiment to "test" one of the different ideas. But they are not rigorous tests — just probes to get at the general features, to allow me to have good hunches so I can later bear down on the *relevant* ideas ... Gradually the focus will get sharper as I pare away the chaff.

Heinrich notes that to sharpen up his hunches further, he seeks out other documents and draws on his experience about how other related birds species behave. He makes inferences drawn upon analogies and comparisons, all based upon his past experience, whether from books or direct observation. Anyone who has observed a young child try to figure out whether water is too hot before touching it or food too spicy before tasting it, based solely on limited data garnered from past experience, is watching true scientific inference at work.

The physicist Richard Feynman has emphasized that while the test of all scientific knowledge is experiment, its foundation lies in the imagination. Albert Einstein wrote, "When I examine myself and my method of thought, I come to the conclusion that the gift of fantasy has meant more to me than my talent for absorbing knowledge." More than a few other scientists have written that what has made their new discoveries possible is the ability to think like children, that is, to make imaginative leaps by considering a wider range of hypotheses than might more normally be entertained. Discoveries are made by those who are able to see things with new eyes.

In contrast, the esteemed Harvard educator Howard Gardner, writing on the abject state of scientific knowledge even among graduates of prestigious universities, has stated that formal education must contend with children's deeply entrenched understandings if disciplinary understandings are ever to supplant intuitive ones. He suggests that for education to succeed, there is a need to create a radical disjuncture with what children think they already know. In other words, *get them to stop thinking like children*. With all due respect, I am convinced Professor Gardner is wrong. Expecting human beings — children or otherwise — to reject the data and insights they have gained through experience in favor of the pronouncements of authority figures, texts, or prepackaged demonstrations is not only bad science, it is educationally destructive. This is especially true for those usually considered to be good students, whose ability to retain and regurgitate responses for which they are rewarded is predicated upon their becoming dependent on others for their learning, a condition from which they may never recover. Perhaps the failure of Professor Gardner's university graduates to remember and articulate scientific facts may not be so closely tied to the schools' failure to teach them, (after all, these students all aced their exams and got into Harvard) but rather on the schools' inability to teach in a manner which overcomes students' inner reluctance to believe these facts once their usefulness as correct test answers is exhausted.

The textbook error Ali discovered in the preceding chapter (Mars having been designated as the planet nearest to the Earth) may merely have reflected poor copyediting, which could easily be corrected. However, surrounding it, I believe, is a deficiency of understanding which is a powerful example of how public education's methods of imparting information may actually inhibit the development of basic scientific reasoning skills. I would challenge you to ask yourself, any high school or college graduate you know, or any non-science public school teacher (you can try science teachers too if you like) the following question: "What planet is most likely to be closest to the Earth at any particular point in time?" To answer, people will likely rely on the few factoids they gleaned in school, if they remember them at all, beginning with the order of the planets ("Mercury, Venus, Earth, Mars, Jupiter ..."). They will also probably have been taught that planetary orbits are elliptical (some, relying on their second-grade education, might say "circular"), and the better educated will remember being told that the further the planet is from the sun, the longer it takes to make a full revolution. About 60% of respondents will answer Venus, the bulk of the rest Mars. Venus does indeed occupy the orbit closest to Earth's. But the correct answer? Mercury! It's simple to derive from the three factoids that were taught, too. Venus and Mars spend a large portion of the time in their orbits on the opposite side of the sun from the Earth. Because it revolves so quickly, Mercury spends more time than either of the other two on the same side as the Earth. And when all three planets — Mercury, Venus, and Mars —

are on the other side, Mercury is closest to the sun and hence to the Earth as well! My strong suspicion is that schools expend so much energy getting kids to parrot back facts of which they have neither tangible nor indirect experience, and then testing for them, that they actually inhibit the capacity of children (or adults!) to make any sensible use of these facts once their utility as test answers has faded away. Millions of kids graduate from high school having been taught the basics of planetary astronomy, just as an example, while believing they've never actually seen a planet. They're wrong of course, but no one has even thought of the necessity to assist them at an early age in picking out the planets from among the thousands of seemingly indistinguishable points of light in the sky, or helped them come to an imaginative realization of what it might mean to be standing on one!

Ellen's and my experience with our children suggests the need to stress continuity, to respect, validate, and build on the store of information and insight already gained, to nourish sensory awareness and to act as gentle guides, and to nurture imagination and self-awareness of the thought process. Of course, the real problem with applying this latter approach in the school setting is that teachers rarely if ever have the time to find out what insight and self-awareness each of the kids already possesses, no less to systematically build upon them. Darwin's friend and advocate Thomas Huxley once wrote that the scientific method is nothing but the normal working of the human mind, to which, I would add, the machinery of public education, in my judgment, stands in radical and profound opposition. Administrative necessity drives educational approach. Be that as it may, children need to have affirmed the idea that they already know how to think, to learn that what they already have *are* understandings (which initially may have been based on intuition but have grown beyond it) and that these understandings can and do change and are refined, given new information, experience, and imagination. Perhaps above all, a child needs to know that what distinguishes a genuine scientist is not her capacity to memorize facts, but her ability to synthesize the raw materials of observation to tell a good story.

We have repeated the pattern of working with our kids to develop contrasting hypotheses about natural phenomena that interest them. Sometimes this results in a round of supervised or unsupervised observation or experimentation, other times in exercises in deductive reasoning. Often it leads to a trip to the library, which is then encountered not so much as a repository of books but as a storehouse of explanations — scientific stories — awaiting discovery.

Much later, we introduced Ali to the terms 'gravity' and 'inertia' and the classical formulations of Newton's laws. But Ali began to actively use them well before then. Once, at age five, having fallen off her bicycle and scraped up her knees and elbows, she came running into the house beaming, eager to explain to me that "two of Newton's Rules (the first being the one that pulls her bike to the ground, the second being the one that keeps her going even after she stops pedaling) fight!" Quite simply, in this case as in her seismic adventures, the intellectual understanding took hold because it was rooted in her making sense of her own sensory, and more particularly, her own bodily experience, the stuff of which early childhood is made.

Ali went through a period when she became infatuated with painting and painters. She looked through book after book and became quite adept at identifying various French Impressionists, and even tried, with very limited success, to copy them. Cézanne could be identified by the use of brown tints, the dark outlines of objects, and the still-life subject matter; Degas by the depiction of anorexic female dancers; Gauguin by scenes of Tahiti; Renoir by the use of orange and yellow and of diffuse and fuzzy outlines; Monet by the interplay of light and shadow upon water, vegetation, or buildings; Manet (Ali reminds me, while reading through the draft of this chapter, that she doesn't like Manet) by the re-creation of crowd and café scenes; Sisely for depictions of countryside and winter; and Seurat by the tiny paint dots used to build up the images. She became interested in perspective and color, which provided the impetus for a series of science experiments. We played with shadows and light. We measured the fields of view of first one eye and then the other, and drew diagrams of optical triangulation (simply put, what we see with each eye, and what happens when we see with both eyes at the same time). We bent light through a prism and through a glass of water. We combined pigments. We looked for vanishing points on the highway and watched objects shrink in the distance.

Like with many of our "lessons" — occasions when inklings of my kids' interests have sent me scrambling to provide solid, organized explanations — the total time expended was short, probably not exceeding two hours in all (plus some time for me to think up and in some cases do some library research about how to present material). But Ali's retention rate was very high. What was critical, what is critical, is finding that magic moment when the gates are open and the river of knowledge can flow in. Evaluating the level of material to be taught is much less important: if too low, a round of questions will be forthcoming; if too high, some of the material will be retained as 'bric-a-brac' for exploration at some future time, provided the child isn't put off by the mode of presentation. But lessons taught at a time a child is not prepared to receive them are always a tremendous waste of energy for both child and parent/teacher.

——◆◆◆——

When Ali told us she wanted to use some of her violin earnings to purchase a telescope, we weren't all that surprised. More than a year earlier, before her eighth birthday, she had asked for and received a subscription to *Astronomy* magazine. The glossy monthly, with stunning color photographs of astronomical phenomena on the cover, would appear in the mailbox, and quickly disappear onto the elevated platform of Ali's bed. During the first year of the subscription, neither Ellen nor I read a single article, and I cannot remember any articles from it prompting dinner table conversation. I think I thumbed through an issue once, filled as it was with references to terms I had never encountered and pages of ads for large and complex telescopes and astral photography equipment with prices running into the thousands of dollars. I now have a much healthier respect for this well-written and beautifully illustrated publication, but it took me a long time and a reawakening of my own long-dormant curiosity to appreciate it. A negative side effect of the subscription was that Ali began to receive multiple credit card offers and applications through the mail.

I discovered the depth of both Ali's preoccupation and the fruits of her information-gathering quite unexpectedly. Ali and I drove up to Seattle to attend a South Indian music concert. Prior to the event, we went to a local music store. I offered to buy her a volume out of an excellent pictorial book series on the lives of the great composers, and after much consideration, she settled on Wagner. Just as I was about to pay the cashier, Ali came up to me and said that rather than a book, she'd prefer to have a recording of Gustav Holst's *The Planets*, which she had recently heard on the radio. We paid for the recording, which she clutched closely in a plastic bag, and left for the concert.

South Indian music concerts can take upwards of four hours, during much of which Ali was allowed and even encouraged to dance around in the back of the hall, but after an hour she was clearly unsettled. I asked her quietly whether she wanted to leave, and she nodded. I assumed she wanted to hear her new recording, but I was not prepared for what followed. For the next 50 minutes or so while we drove home, I received a non-stop astronomy lecture about each of the planets as the relevant musical section came on the compact disc player. I learned of the carbon dioxide atmosphere on Venus, the lack of atmosphere on Mercury, and Kepler's discovery of Mars' elliptical orbit. I learned of the four largest moons of Jupiter discovered by Galileo with the aid of one of the first telescopes, the possibility of life on one of them, Europa, based on the thick layer of water ice on its surface, and the crash of Comet Shoemaker-Levy into Jupiter's atmosphere. She lectured me on Saturn's Cassini Rings, its more than 21 moons, the discovery of Uranus by Sir William Herschel (who was also a musician), the Hubble Space Telescope photos of Neptune, and the fact that right now, Neptune is the planet in our solar system farthest from the sun. "Why isn't Pluto in the music?" I asked. "That's silly, dad," she impatiently admonished me, as if I should have known better, "Holst wrote *The Planets* in 1913; Pluto wasn't discovered until 1930. And actually there are ten planets because Pluto has a twin named Charon."

I gleaned from Ellen that, besides reading and rereading all of her issues of *Astronomy*, at the homeschool computer center Ali had been downloading from the Internet everything she could find on the planets, comets, meteors, the Hubble, and the newly discovered Comet Hyakutake. Together, they found a number of good Internet sites set up by the National Aeronautics and Space Administration, Hubble Space Telescope Laboratory, and the University of Colorado, but the best were set up by amateur astronomers on their own. From these, Ali prepared her own textbook containing the most up-to-date information. Soon, pieces of a planet mobile appeared in her room, not built on any prodding or even suggestion from us. An earlier version, Ellen reminds me, was constructed about three years earlier, again without our urging. Ali also invented a "Nine Planets Board Game." Participant/space travelers have to answer questions in order to return to earth. Sample questions include: "How many spacecraft have visited Neptune?" "What is the most prevalent gas in Uranus' atmosphere?" "What is the best-known feature on Jupiter?" "Who first observed Saturn through a telescope?"

We took advantage of an infrequent visit to grandparents in South Florida to take the kids to the Kennedy Space Center. I'm not at all sure how much of a lasting impression it made, as so many of the exhibits dealt with the technology, or even the business, of space travel, and much less with what is to be found once one gets there, wherever "there" might be. There was a film about the first "Martian" to visit earth, a boy born in a Mars-mission space colony traveling back to the home planet for the first time. It was a fine film and a cute idea, but there was no information about living on Mars! Ali and Meera tried on spacesuits and walked through space capsules, and we took a bus to the launch pad. Meera was impressed by the armadillos and feral pigs inhabiting the surrounding nature preserve. The highlight of our trip came as a result of our having scheduled our visit to coincide with an evening launch of a communications satellite.

Our trip to Kennedy Space Center was more valuable than many of our excursions to local or regional "science" centers have been. These are not to be confused with the superlative exhibitions and well-supervised hands-on science activities we once found at the Smithsonian Institution in Washington, DC. We have visited a variety of these science centers from Florida to California, the best we found being the Museum of Science and Discovery in Fort Lauderdale. We were members of the Pacific Science Center in Seattle for several years. But we and, more to the point, the kids usually came away disappointed. The problems with each of them, with rare exceptions for special exhibits, were always the same. The displays were placed in a manner which seemed close to random, except as they were designed to overwhelm those entering with sights and sounds. Science is usually treated like a magic show. A gaze into curved mirrors would reflect distorted faces, but there would be no explanation of the optical principles behind the distortion. An anatomically correct Tyrannosaurus Rex would roar, perhaps no more than 20 feet away froman apparently unperturbed plant-munching Brachiosaurus standing across the aisle from a tail-swishing Stegosaurus baby (gosh, the dinosaur world must have been awfully crowded!), but there would be no explanation of robotics, or of how paleontologists work or how you might become one. There might be bubbles and whirligigs and slide and light shows and computer screens and buttons to push, which were often frustrating, with information on nutrition located near a tank of new-born sea turtles followed by a display case of moonrocks, with nary a scientist or a serious amateur who could answer a child's question. As these science centers are sometimes built like airplane hangars, the reverberating roar of children can be deafening. There would occasionally be an exhibit that would command the attention of one child or the other, but finding it could be considered an accident. Indeed, I think that is the point, as the science center by itself neither creates nor fulfills an intellectual need. It is rather like walking through a disorganized three-dimensional multimedia maze hoping that something, *anything*, will capture a child's imagination. Ali suggests she would prefer a living library where she could specifically choose the information she wants to explore, to be displayed in multimedia fashion or in a working laboratory, with adults who are themselves engaged in the subject matter. I often came out of one of these general science centers with a headache. Ali and Meera, being good little troopers, might express appreciation (they knew we went ostensibly for their benefit), but neither has ever displayed any enthusiasm about going back.

More successful from Ali's perspective was a trip with Ellen to the University of Washington observatory to behold Comet Hyakutake. The glimpse through the telescope was arresting enough, but what was most memorable for Ali was standing in line with other amateur astronomers, even a few kids, who shared her enthusiasm. Ali was hooked!

I began reading through the back issues of *Astronomy*, trying to figure out what kind of telescope to buy, how much to spend, and how to buy it.

Despite the fact that, for better or worse, I am an inveterate shopper, this seemed to me like a daunting task, given that I had not even looked through a telescope in almost four decades! I told Ali we would proceed slowly.

Ali and I spent time educating ourselves on the differences between refracting and reflecting telescopes. Refracting telescopes are what we non-astronomers usually think of and have encountered in department stores, a long tube with a large lens at one end through which light is bent toward a small eyepiece at the other end. Galileo used one of this kind to make his famous drawings of the lunar surface and to discover that the Milky Way is awash with stars. The Newtonian reflector (named after its inventor, that real-life brother of the apocryphal Fig) dispenses with lenses, which are apparently very difficult and expensive to manufacture without chromatic aberration, especially in large sizes. Instead, in a Newtonian reflector, light bounces off two mirrors (one large, one small,) into an eyepiece. Mirrors, as I learned later, are easier to make than lenses, although they require a bit more maintenance, as they are wont to tarnish. The majority of the great observatories of the world, as well as the Hubble, utilize giant reflectors.

Ali and I undertook a cursory study of optics, using some old lenses and magnifying glasses, with which we had equipped both kids, and hallway mirrors. Soon, with the aid of some books (which I describe in the next chapter) and a few lessons from us on how to use her new compass, Ali was off teaching herself the basics of trigonometry and two-dimensional map-and-compass reading. I assumed — correctly, it turns out — that this would stand her in good stead when we got to star charts, which I'd never to this point ever looked at. I now marvel that schools do not teach trigonometry (the science of measurement dealing with sides and angles of triangles, which can be used in computing distances), optics, and astronomy all of a piece, so naturally do they flow together and so clearly would there be motivation to learn the dry mathematics. But thinking back on my own education, I can't remember any such connections being made, and Ellen can't either.

Early on, Ali picked up an important piece of information that had frankly never crossed my mind before. The main purpose of a telescope is not magnification (except for peering at surface features of the moon or the nearer planets); neither is the utility of a telescope best expressed by its power. This came as a revelation to me, having observed "565X" plastered all over telescope boxes at our local department store. (You'll see the same advertising hype on the Home Shopping Network.) The great telescope at Mount Palomar usually employs a magnification of 300X or less, and fine telescopes have their best performance in the 40-50X range. If the magnification is higher than 200X, even small atmospheric disturbances will blur vision. After all, from earth, what we are doing is the equivalent of looking up at a beacon on top of a skyscraper from the bottom of a swimming pool filled with water. Magnification is for the most part determined by the eyepiece, not by the telescope itself. The essential purpose of a telescope, directed as it is toward a dark void sprinkled with celestial bodies tens of thousands of millions of miles away is to gather and focus light. Being so far away, even under intense magnification, stars remain points of light. Eyepieces can be rated at "565X," but if no light gets to the eyepiece, or the mount is even a little bit unstable or the air is unsettled, the high power is useless. What really matters is *aperture*, the diameter of the lens in front, or the mirror in the case of a reflector. The greater the aperture, the more light gets in. A telescope with an eight-inch aperture gathers 1,150 times more light than the eye can normally see. It is this light-gathering capacity of either telescopes or binoculars that multiplies our ability to behold the heavens' illumination.

Meanwhile, we were still no closer to owning a usable telescope, though our next-door neighbor Evelyn found a small toy-store refractor at a yard sale which we were never able to make work effectively. And we still hadn't looked through any, at least of the amateur sort.

This was soon remedied by a member of our Quaker meeting, a retired professional astronomer married to a friend with whom Ali played violin duets. Alfred and Marjorie invited us out to examine their telescopes. Alfred spent about a half hour setting up his excellent 90mm refracting instrument. The spectacle of Saturn and its rings was breathtaking. Ellen commented on beholding the planet for the very first time, "It looks just like one of Meera's stickers," and indeed it did.

We were impressed, but while the rest of us were having such a good time, I observed, from the look on her face and what was even for her an unnatural reticence, that Ali was troubled. The tripod was bulky and awkward, and difficult to set up. The manipulation of the weights and counterweights necessary for the functioning of the mount looked daunting. Using such an instrument would require many different operations: setting up the scope; locating the object in the sky via charts, and then through the viewfinder; setting the weights and counterweights utilizing both gross and fine adjustments; choosing and then focusing with the eyepieces; and then mechanically adjusting the weights to track the object across the sky. These are too many steps for a nine-year-old; they likely would try the patience of most adults. A telescope is only worth its investment to the degree it is actually used. Knowing Ali, I realized that after the necessary training, she would want a telescope she could manipulate herself.

From Alfred I found out that the president of the local astronomical society was a singer and had performed with Ali in the Mozart and Fauré *Requiems*. I called him, and he remembered Ali. "Is there a solution to this problem?" "Sure is," Bob replied. "A Dobsonian reflector. Most of our members have them." He proceeded to explain that the Dobsonian is not really a type of telescope, but describes a unique mounting system. Instead of having positioned a six-, eight-, or ten-inch or larger reflector on a complicated high-tech mount, a Dobsonian rests on the ground, in a plywood rocker box. It, in turn, is mounted on a wheel which can rotate one way or another on Teflon pads. Besides ease of use (it can be repositioned with a gentle touch of the hand) and greater stability, the lack of sophisticated and costly mounting hardware means a Dobsonian reflector of similar aperture and quality can cost less than half of one with a high-tech mount.

In my book (this is, after all, my book), John Dobson should be considered a hero of contemporary amateur scientists and of homeschoolers. As science has become more technologically complex, opportunities for amateurs to participate meaningfully have become increasingly limited. John Dobson is one of those rare individuals who has opened up scientific vistas for people, promoting serious participation through hands-on exploration.

Born in Beijing, and a 1943 University of California-Berkeley graduate with a degree in chemistry and mathematics as well as a former dancer, Dobson quit his job on the Manhattan Project where he helped develop the atomic bomb, and entered a Vedanta monastery to devote himself to Hindu religious philosophy and practice. After borrowing a book on telescope making from the library, he built one with a two-inch lens found at a local thrift shop and an eyepiece scavenged from an old pair of binoculars. Over the next 20 years, besides serving in his role as monastery gardener, he turned to building reflectors, grinding mirrors using carefully sifted sand as an abrasive and polishing material made from gardening supplies. He perfected the Dobsonian mount, which bears his name, and loaned the finished telescopes to local children.

In 1967, Dobson left the monastery to devote himself to sharing his new-found skill with the world. His hope was and remains that a glimpse of the heavens will spur people into more serious speculation and study of the origin and meaning of creation. He has built literally thousands of telescopes and has helped as many other people build their own, all by hand. On clear nights, he and his students — the San Francisco Sidewalk Astronomers — set up telescopes on the streets for passersby to peer out at the stars. Devoted to a very simple lifestyle, Dobson in 1969 bought four tons of ships' glass portholes at auction for $1,000 and has since partially made his living from selling them to students to grind and polish. Now in his eighties, Dobson has been known to take his larger telescopes out to the Grand Canyon and other national parks in an old school bus, offering tourists and especially children a grand look at the universe.

On Halloween, there was a small newspaper announcement that a telescope viewing would be held in a local supermarket parking lot. Ali and I arrived on an extremely cold and clear evening (very rare in Olympia in mid-autumn) and saw two men standing behind what looked for all the world like a pair of black medieval cannons, an eight-inch and a ten-inch Dobsonian. There were no weights or counterweights or high-tech metal alloy mounts here, just spectacular sights of Saturn and several of its moons. Ali spent almost a half hour in the cold going back and forth between the two telescopes, climbing a small stepladder each time to peer through the eyepieces. We were sold! I was struck by the fact that for every person willing to stop and peek, ten walked right by. Some hurried past, apparently fearing they were about to be panhandled.

I learned the names of various brands of commercially available

Dobsonian telescopes and put out word to the local astronomical society, of which Ali was now a member, and to a new friend at Tacoma's Pettengill-Guiley Observatory that we were in the market for a good used model. Meanwhile we began to learn the positions of the stars, making use of our old binoculars which had spent years gathering dust in the closet. Ali enjoyed this activity, but it was six-year-old Meera who became the star of our little stargazing group. Extremely farsighted, she easily located the Pleiades without the binoculars, which to me in our semi-urban neighborhood was only a murky blur. "There's Subaru," she'd exclaim, amused by the fact that we drove an automobile carrying the Japanese moniker for the constellation. "There's only six stars there," Meera observed, having hit on one of astronomy's great mysteries, namely that diverse cultures call these six stars visible to the naked eye the "Seven Sisters."

Meera learned to manipulate the rotating star wheel, lining up date and time and turning it upside down over her head to orient it with the sky, the only problem being that she didn't realize the guide had to face north toward Polaris (the "North Star") for it to work. "How do you find Polaris?" she asked. "Measure three fists on a line from the two stars at the end of the Big Dipper," I replied, relying on my 40-year-old summer camp lore. "Oh," she said, and broke out in the chorus of "Follow the Drinking Gourd," which Ellen had taught her years earlier. A gaze at the firmament was quickly transformed into an extended American history lesson and conversation about race.

Every evening, Meera would peer out the back door at the dark sky, hoping to catch a glimpse of her new-found friends. In the Pacific Northwest winter, it didn't happen often. When it did, we bundled up and outside we went. Within a month, Meera could easily identify the belt and dagger of Orion —home of the "baby stars" in the Trapezium — and Orion's orange beauty with the entertaining name Betelgeuse and his fiery blue-white giant Rigel; Orion's dog featuring the dog star Sirius, the brightest star in the northern hemisphere; the great square of Pegasus; Castor and Pollux, the Gemini Twins; Capella, the resplendent star in the constellation Auriga directly overhead; the big "W" of Cassiopeia; and Cygnus the Swan. We have yet to clearly locate her namesake in the constellation Cetus the Whale, the earliest-discovered variable star Mira (in Arabic "the wonderful one"). Meera has since become interested in meteorology and cloud formations, looking out toward the southwest to predict our next short-term weather change. She has choice words of healthy skepticism for the television weatherman's predictions: "Just because he says it doesn't mean he's right!"

Meera was also quite intrigued with the idea that it takes time for light to travel, that the stars we see are not the stars as they are now. We joked about the fact that she never sees me as I am, only as I was, a reflection. "What I see is kind of like an echo of you," she concluded, with an image full of philosophical and poetic possibilities. But does the principle hold when looking at oneself? And what are we, really? Atoms? Cells? Thoughts? "Do we only 'see' our thoughts after we have thought them?" she wondered. I tried hard not to give Meera a straight answer to these queries (I couldn't have anyway) and restrained myself from furnishing what would have likely turned out to be an overly pedantic lecture on notions of reality.

As each of us took up this new preoccupation with the heavens, I took note of our individualized attitudes toward what we were learning. For Meera, becoming familiar with the positions of the stars is another step toward making the world around her feel more like home. For me, increased awareness of living upon a tiny, floating fragile sphere within an expanding and immeasurable void is unsettling and makes me a bit queasy. My nighttime driving has definitely suffered. For Ali, the astronomical universe represents nothing so much as the largest possible intellectual playspace. Ellen simply enjoys the celestial light show.

Ali and I began to attend local astronomical society lectures. Some of them went well over Ali's head and mine, which does not mean we didn't enjoy them, even if they weren't "age-appropriate" for either of us. A healthy sharing of ignorance can help turn education into a learning partnership, and openly educating oneself provides the best possible role model. We attended a lecture on the "Physics of the Big Bang." Ali understood about a quarter of it, I maybe a third. We learned that bosons, mesons, leptons, gluons, quarks and antiquarks, and Z particles, none of which I had ever encountered before, are now regular features of physical cosmology discourse. We were both amused for days by a description of the electrical force: when one punches a wall, one never really touches it, but only meets its electrical resistance. We both asked lots of questions, and came home ready to learn some more.

We were close to purchasing a telescope when I thought to call the organizer of the Halloween telescope viewing. Recognizing that Ali enjoyed knowing how things are constructed, I asked Carl if there were opportunities for her to watch a Dobsonian get put together. Carl instantly remembered Ali from their encounter six weeks earlier, though he was clueless about who I was. "Do you know what I do?" he asked. "Not exactly," I replied. "Well, once a year I run a workshop to assist ten individuals or families in building their own telescopes. The course takes about three months, one evening and one weekend day a week. And in four years I have never lost a student. My next workshop starts this coming Saturday, and it's full. For Ali, I'll make room." Ellen said she could fit it into her already complicated schedule, and so the two of them joined the Nisqually Valley Telescope Maker's Workshop to build an eight-inch reflector.

Much of the grinding and polishing work required strong hand pressure and body weight, so Ali could only watch, though she did learn how to measure a mirror's wave pattern and calculate the focal length of its curve. She took an occasional turn around the grinding barrel. Carl, himself a student of John Dobson, engaged the class in cosmological discussions. Is the universe truly expanding, or is this an artifact of our perceptions? Did the Big Bang really happen? What lies beyond the edge of the universe? To this last query, several of the participants immediately replied that there was nothing. After sitting quietly for quite some time, Ali looked up. "Nothing does not exist," she said, "The moment you think of nothing, your brain is involved in an energy exchange, changing matter to energy." To this day, we are awestruck by this neurobiological variant of the Heisenberg uncertainty principle (that there is uncertainty associated with every measurement; when one attempts to measure something, one must disturb that which is to be measured).

We have had lengthy conversations about the possibilities of intelligent extraterrestrial life. Ali is one of the few willing to put up with my facetious question regarding whether it can be shown conclusively that there is intelligent life on earth. She thinks there may well be life within other planetary systems, though the organisms probably breathe methane. Have we been visited by life from other planets? Perhaps, she says, but we've been looking for them on the wrong scale. The organisms are probably much, much smaller than humans. Following the discovery of possible traces of life in meteorites of Mars origination, we are both amused that we all just might be descended from Martian pond scum.

During the long periods of mirror grinding and polishing, we fed Ali a steady stream of books on skywatching and mapping techniques, and biographies of famous astronomers. Two historical figures in particular stood out. Maria Mitchell was the first well-known woman astronomer, the discoverer of Mitchell's Comet in 1847. A Nantucket Quaker, Mitchell became the first woman professor of astronomy in the U.S., the first faculty member appointed at Vassar College, and the first woman elected to the American Academy of Arts and Sciences. Ali was intrigued by how she got started. At age 12, Mitchell filled in for her father in setting chronometers by the stars for ship captains who came into port. Mitchell provided Ali with the reminder that "Entrance to astronomy is through mathematics," and that one should not be overly wowed by large accumulations of scientific equipment. "A small apparatus well used will do wonders ... Newton rolled up a cover of a book; he put a small glass at one end, and a large brain at the other — it was enough." We are all especially appreciative of her motto, "Every formula which expresses a law of nature is a hymn of praise to God."

The second historical figure to stand out was Benjamin Banneker (1731-1806). Banneker was the free-born grandson of an enslaved African prince and a transported English milkmaid who carved a homestead out of the Maryland wilderness near the shore of Chesapeake Bay. Befriended and educated by Quakers, he became in his adult years a farmer, mathematician, and astronomer, and helped survey the site for the nation's future capital in Washington, DC. He was best known as the fabricator of the first completely American-made clock and author of an almanac which outsold *Poor Richard's* and for which he calculated his own ephemeris, a collection of charts and tables of the ebb and flow of tides, the rising and setting of the sun, and future positions and motions of the moon, planets, and stars.

At long last, the telescope was completed. We all went out to the workshop to celebrate and take photographs with Carl. Several days earlier, Ali had gone to the library to look up the Latin for "sky eye," which she wanted to name the telescope. Ellen and Ali painted "Oculus Caelestis" a beautiful shade of blue, with bright yellow carrying handles, giving a child's feel to a sophisticated astronomical instrument.

Oculus Caelestis was completed during Comet Hale-Bopp's perihelion (its closest approach to the sun). For weeks we observed the comet brighten and helped out at various events sponsored by the local astronomical society. To mark the completion of the telescope, I presented Ali and Ellen with the following certificate signed by Carl and myself:

NON FRUSTRA SIGNORUM ORBITUS SPECULAMUR ET ORTUS
("Not in Vain Do We Watch the Setting and Rising of the Stars.")
This certificate is hereby presented to
Aliyah Meena Shanti and **Ellen J. Sawislak**
to commemorate completion of an 8-inch Dobsonian Reflector Telescope
"Oculus Caelestis" ("Sky Eye")
Awarded during the Perihelion of Comet Hale-Bopp, April 5, 1997

We are now beginning to become more adept at using the telescope, although Ali was extremely pleased that the first time we took it out we caught a glimpse of the Trapezium in Orion's dagger. Ali has started to keep a journal of her observations. Oculus Caelestis has become a very popular attraction at local homeschool fairs. Ali helped teach a summer school class on astronomy at a local college, explaining with the help of her own diagrams how the various types of telescopes work.

We had the opportunity to put Oculus Caelestis through its paces at what might have been the finest educational event I've ever attended. The Table Mountain Star Party, sponsored by the Northwest Astronomical League, brought together more than 1,000 astronomers (and over a hundred kids), from rank amateurs to university professors, for three days and nights of sky viewing, lectures, and fellowship on a 6,500-foot-high mountain

Creosoting the telescope tube

plateau. Classes were held on subjects ranging from mirror grinding to constellation archeology. Three hundred telescopes of all sizes and description dotted the landscape, with people invited to go from scope to scope to peer out at every conceivable observable astronomical phenomenon.

For me, the most remarkable aspect of the Star Party was how it functioned as a paradigm of educational democracy. Age or occupation could not be assumed to be accurate determinants or even indicators of knowledge. Information about the universe beyond our earth has changed our understandings so rapidly that an intelligent and well-read, Internet-surfing teenager at the event was likely to be better informed than a college science instructor outside of her own field. We met auto mechanics, preschool teachers, nurses, astrophysics professors, and short-order cooks all united in their knowledge quest. Several families camped near us did not own telescopes and knew less about astronomy than I (or even Meera, Ali already being an expert), with our kids quickly becoming docents of the night sky. Of the eight families and individuals, ranging in age from nine to 70-plus, who had brought telescopes crafted in Carl's workshop to the Star Party, seven had had no significant interest in astronomy even five years earlier, and none had previously owned a telescope. Fifty-year old men squealed like children at their first glimpse of Jupiter's four Galilean moons. Meera played "planetary bingo" and fell asleep on a lounge chair covered by a sleeping bag while looking for meteors. Ali found the Ring Nebula in the constellation Lyra (looks like a smoke ring or a donut or, if you're a New Yorker like me, a heavenly bagel) and explained the difference between supernovae remnants and planetary nebulae to captivated novices. John Dobson was there, sporting, to Ali's surprised amusement and approval, a button proclaiming "Nothing does not exist!" and lecturing children, amateurs, and professors alike on competing theories of the universe's creation, comparing it to a raisin pudding expanding in the oven (the raisins being galaxies). Dobson tells *great* stories. "Your own existence is what you're surest of," he concluded to Ali's delight as she sat on the edge of her chair, "Everything else is problematical." He signed Ali's telescope at her request and left her with a message: "All kids think that grownups are nuts. They're right. But watch out — it could happen to you!" Later in the summer, Ali was able to join Dobson with Oculus Caelestis for an evening session of sidewalk astronomy outside the very supermarket where she had met Carl and tried out a Dobsonian for the first time.

Ali and two other friends from our homeschooling group have participated in the Boston Museum of Sciences "Science-By-Mail" program, which is supported by the National Science Foundation and links small groups of students to a working scientist. Children are encouraged to correspond, to write "scientist's journals," to work up simple inventions, and to explore scientific ideas with the assistance of an adult group leader. The 1996-1997 topic was simple machines and flight. The kids had a good time with the hands-on activities related to gears and pulleys, aerodynamics and hot-air balloons. Ali has written to her scientist friend, a Cornell University reptilian biologist, on several occasions and had a serious exchange theorizing on why the outer needles of a Norwegian blue spruce tree are blue, but the inner ones green. She can now explain the third-class leverage principles behind the use of chopsticks when we go out to our favorite Korean restaurant.

At Table Mountain Star Party with John Dobson

I sense that as Ali and Meera grow, their education in the physical sciences will prove a challenge to us. Neither Ellen nor I feel we come well-equipped in this area, and it will take a special effort to continue to find the mentors and opportunities necessary to meet our children's learning needs and interests. I find this ironic. I grew up as somewhat of a "science nerd" (even before such a term existed) and attended a highly competitive and prestigious high school in New York City that specialized in science, where I always earned straight A's. Yet, to this day I feel inadequate and often fumble with explanations of the simplest machine. Don't dare ask me to explain the internal combustion engine or the inner workings of my computer. I've never successfully changed a tire or the oil in my automobile, though Ellen is a pro and is prepared to teach the rest of us shortly. The test of the effectiveness of our approach to homeschooling will be whether their parents' well-schooled ignorance becomes our children's destiny.

In a lecture on cosmology and human evolution, Dobson ruminates on the evolutionary significance of the genetic mechanism called 'neoteny,' the retention of juvenile characteristics into later life. Unlike in a cat, asserts Dobson, the human brain continues to grow, and, if allowed, our insatiable curiosity carries over into adulthood:

> We are the children of children who never grow up. And it is the lingering wonder of childhood which gave rise to Newton's *Principia*, to relativity, to quantum mechanics, and to all the religions of the world. And the beauty and freedom of childhood follow us still.

Astronomy. Kalmbach Publishing Co., 21027 Crossroads Circle, PO Box 1512, Waukesha, WI 53187; Tel: 1-800-533-6644. Subscriptions: $34.95/year. The magazine publishes an updated list of star parties occurring throughout the U.S., with contact names and addresses.

Berman, Bob, *Secrets of the Night Sky: The Most Amazing Things in the Universe You Can See with the Naked Eye.* New York, NY: William Morrow & Co., 1995. Ali and I agree this is the best single introduction to modern stargazing we've come across, and we've read a lot of them!

Gormley, Beatrice, *Maria Mitchell: The Soul of an Astronomer.* Grand Rapids, MI: William B. Erdmans Publishing Company, 1975. A 'young adult' biography.

Heinrich, Bernd, *Ravens in Winter.* New York, NY: Summit Books, 1989. A well-told detective story of how a field biologist spent years trying to find an explanation for seemingly altruistic behavior among ravens. You get right inside his mind, feeling for yourself the tedium of fieldwork, and the satisfaction which comes with discovery.

Krupp, E.C., *Beyond the Blue Horizon: Myths and Legends of the Sun, Moon, Stars, and Planets.* New York, NY: HarperCollins Publishers, 1991. Dr. Krupp, Director of the Griffith Observatory in Los Angeles, takes us on a wonderful illustrated tour of the heavens as presented in celestial stories from six continents. Enough introductory astronomy is offered for even a rank amateur to make sense of the tales, which will excite the imagination of young and old alike. I gave this book to Ali (with the certificate) to mark completion of Oculus Caelestis.

Patterson, Lilli, *Benjamin Banneker: Genius of Early America.* Abingdon, PA: Parthenon Press, 1978. A fine, inspiring account for young people (and adults, too!).

Science-By-Mail, Museum of Science, Science Park, Boston, MA 02114; Tel: 1-800-729-3300; E-mail: information@mos.org Check out their fine website at www.mos.org

Scientific American. Scientific American, Inc., 415 Madison Avenue, New York, NY 10017-1111. Subscriptions: $34.97. If you haven't seen *Scientific American* in the past five years, you're in for a treat. Gone are the footnotes, abstracts, and articles too abstruse for all but the most committed devotee; in are photographs, excellent diagrams, and, yes, even real editing. The mission of keeping the public abreast of the latest in scientific thinking remains the same. Highly recommended for all homeschooling parents, and for children when they decide they're ready, too.

The Sidewalk Astronomers have contacts across the U.S. and maintain an excellent Internet website, with information on cosmology, John Dobson, etc.: www.magicpubs.com/dobson

Fearful Symmetry

Tyger! Tyger! burning bright
In the forests of the night,
What Immortal hand or eye
Could frame thy fearful symmetry?

William Blake, "The Tyger"
from *Songs of Experience*

Symmetry really is the point of a child's earliest arithmetic, isn't it? Mother and me are two, and Daddy (or sister) makes three; one mouth, one nose, two arms, two hands, two ears, two eyes; five fingers, five toes; two grandmas; three aunts?; one dog, one cat, two animals, each with four legs; fork and spoon; light and dark; up and down; in and out.

Symmetry is comforting. Finding it is one of the main strategies very young children use as a coping mechanism to deal with a new existence characterized by seeming disorder and chaos and to provide themselves a feeling of security. Discovering symmetry leads to some of the earliest realizations of self-mastery. Long before a child is able to use her hands or feet effectively, she realizes she has two of them, one conveniently located on each side. The rhythms of speech, of motion, and of music provide yet another kind of symmetry, a balance and a grid upon which to plot new realms of experience.

Soon, the young child learns to gauge distances and to estimate time-distance continuums ("once I cry, how long will it take for Dad to bring me my bottle, given he is already in the kitchen fixing it?") Later, she masters simple spatial relations, comes up with her own measurement tools, compares weights, heights, volume, force. She learns to divide — objects, groups of objects, and time — as part of her social learning about sharing. She engages in abstract logic, formulating syllogisms to come to new understandings of the relationships between parts and the whole, individual and class, and constructs discrete sets from the plenitude and variety of her experience so that things 'fit together.'

Abstract and mathematical reasoning is a natural part of a child's development. One can help to nurture this reasoning, but it will develop of its own accord and on its own timetable, provided the child's environment is reasonably secure and stable and there are new opportunities for its application.

What became by far the most popular 'toy' in our home for both Ali and Meera, once they could be trusted not to put the pieces in their mouths, was a set of pattern blocks. They remain so even to this day. These are small blocks of wood, with facets one inch long, and color coded according to shape: orange squares, green equilateral triangles, yellow octagons, red trapezoids, beige and blue rhombuses. Both Ali and Meera's pattern block play has changed over time, though several different kinds of play could co-exist. They would segregate the blocks according to color/shape or lay them out in long strings, one abutting the next. They might copy patterns from a book to make small animals, cars, kites, or can openers, or perhaps attempt their own. The shapes might be used with other block sets to build forts and castles. At a later stage, Ali and Meera began to construct intricate wheels — flowers or suns like Buddhist mandalas — with angles conjoined in such a way as to create circles out of straight edges.

Ali's second favorite toy is a box of half-inch round solid glass beads. They come in various colors, and Ali can spend hours sorting and resorting them by color or according to the irregularities in their shapes, or counting in groups of five or eight or ten, or aligning the red ones in long rows with a green for every sixth or ninth or whatever other number strikes her fancy. Meera is more taken with actual beads which she can string into necklaces using whatever arithmetic pattern appeals.

I am old enough to have witnessed through the media the seemingly endless debates about mathematics education, and have noted with secret delight that the industrialized countries where students perform best on standardized mathematics tests are not those with the longest school year (Japan), but those with some of the shortest (Hong Kong, Taiwan, Flemish Belgium). I would like to believe that the shorter school year allows children greater opportunity to actually use what they have learned, which accounts for their greater success, but I'm sure it would take another 30 years of educational research before I could fairly make such a statement. I'll be patient, and frankly, I don't care that much — I'm not father to a nation, just to my own two kids, and that's hard enough! Why a country's ability to perform well on standardized tests should matter is also not self-evident. As Neil Postman points out in *The End of Education*, there is no evidence that the productivity of a nation's economy (or, I would add, the self-fulfillment of its people) is related in any way to the supposed quality of its schooling as measured through standardized testing.

I have seen school districts and leading educators by turns embrace and discard old math and new math, extol and condemn rote drilling and contextual math, praise and denounce applied math and abstract math, call for more/less use of manipulatives and more/less memorization of the times tables. It's all fearfully symmetrical and, at least as portrayed in the popular media, indicates the most 'childish' understandings masquerading as educational theory being churned out from our graduate schools of education. One doesn't have to be Einstein (indeed, being Einstein wouldn't help!) to see that any and all methods might have their place at different times in the development of each individual child and mifht be suited for complementing the particular learning styles of specific children.

It is equally obvious that success or failure might have nothing to do with the teaching method at all. I was an honors mathematics student throughout my own public school career, scoring in the 98th percentile on all standardized tests and gaining college advanced placement status in calculus. Yet, and this was in the days before electronic calculators were virtually standard issue, I never learned the manual method for calculating square roots. Was it the teaching method? No. During the two weeks square roots were taught in my accelerated seventh grade class, I was hospitalized with an intestinal disorder. When I returned to class, the unit was completed, and no one bothered to ascertain whether I'd mastered the material. Since I could estimate square roots quickly and accurately enough and was pretty adept with a sliderule, I was never found out. When I got to 12th grade calculus, my ignorance was glaring to me, but I would have been ashamed to ask my high-school teacher to take the time to instruct me in seventh grade material.

I still can't manually calculate a square root, but I was creative enough to work my way around the deficiency. Nowadays, most schools no longer teach this skill, as it is thought to be too difficult and students have calculators. So much for educational progress. My Achilles' heel did not hinder my 'educational performance,' and hence the nation can express its gratitude for my past contribution to the national test score average, thank you. But the negative is that the school system never learned how it had failed me. Thousands of children with self-esteem or egos not as substantial as mine may not be so resilient. If and when the unit train passes them by, they may find themselves relegated and resigned to the caboose, and, much too often, they do.

What underlies the dichotomies in approaches to mathematics education is a deeper reality which my children have shown me. Namely, mathematics requires two distinct learning modalities for mastery to be achieved. On the one hand, mathematics is a language, with its own symbols, grammar, and syntax. Like a foreign language, much of it can be learned unconsciously as it were through whole language or total immersion approaches. Here we locate progressive school-based and homeschooling strategies to allow children to come to an understanding of mathematics as part of everyday life — baking cookies, opening up a lemonade stand, charting their own height and weight, figuring out gas mileage, reading maps, dividing pies, weaving rugs, computing baseball players' batting averages, measuring rainfall, playing music, pouring liquids from one container to another. Conscientious parents could easily expand this list and would note that it happens as part of their children's expanding experience. And just as language has nouns, verbs, and vocabulary to be committed to memory, so mathematics has its parts and terms of speech: the names and written forms of the numbers, cardinals and ordinals, the appellations for basic operations (addition, subtraction, multiplication, squaring, etc.), the written forms of problems, measurement terms and relationships (centimeters/meters, inches/feet, ounces/pounds, degrees, etc.), shapes and angles, both in their simple forms (squares, circles, triangles) and their complex forms (obtuse, acute, equilateral, hypotenuse, perimeter, radius, etc.), and the list could go on. The language of mathematics is rich and the vocabulary large, but for the most part it can be learned contextually, provided the experiences are equally rich and furnish a continuous flow of meaning and utility to the child in meeting her own learning needs.

On the other hand, there are mathematical operations that simply must be learned as building blocks in order for further development to take place. I think of these as rather like learning scales in playing a musical instrument. Without mastering them, preferably in some kind of rational sequence, a child is likely to experience significant frustration. Carrying subtraction, long division, adding or multiplying fractions, finding the perimeter or area of a circle, or computing the hypotenuse of a triangle might all fall in this category. Of course, most of these operations could be performed on a calculator, but if we don't make sure that children understand the basic principles behind these mathematical operations, use of the calculator condemns them to mathematical illiteracy. This becomes especially apparent when a child undertakes algebra. Try as she might, S can never be divided by P on a calculator.

Ali and Meera taught us a series of five lessons about helping them learn mathematics:

- Never expect that what worked for one child at a particular chronological age will work at that same age for another.
- Never assume anything has been learned until you see your child try it out in the real world. And make sure she has opportunities to do so!
- Never underestimate the capacity of your child to go forging ahead at the precise moment she is ready, and don't worry too much when she seems stuck in a rut. I have watched both Ali and Meera seemingly make no progress at all for months, only to churn through huge amounts of new mathematical material in a matter

of days and weeks. Think of yourself as a *learning accelerator* — sometimes it makes sense to step on the gas, but sometimes it's okay to allow your child to coast, too.

- Watch for the moment, and be aware of the fact that the learning style that worked before may no longer be effective, and vice versa! Don't let that frustrate you or your child. Be experimental rather than prescriptive.

- While the timing will take care of itself, don't assume learning the building blocks will. I imagine it is possible for a motivated child to teach herself everything she needs to know about mathematics, but assuring solid conceptual foundations can make a world of difference in the effort required and can in the long run, enhance a sense of fulfillment in the learning process.

Meera is a whiz at basic addition, subtraction, and multiplication operations, which she treats like a game. She competes with herself to find out how quickly and accurately she can complete a set of problems. And she is very quick and very accurate. She loves computer-based mathematics drills and quizzes. She often carries around a bag of coins which she will count again and again and is delighted to help us make change at the supermarket. It has been fascinating to watch how Meera handles the introduction of new concepts or operations, which closely parallels her response to taking on a new piece of piano music. The almost automatic response is a ritualized complaint — "It's too hard!" — followed by half an hour of playing with and mastering the concept, after which it becomes almost second nature. We believe she picked up the complaint language from a gymnastics class she takes with predominantly school-enrolled children, as it is not a phrase she would likely have ever encountered in our household.

Ali's mathematics learning turned out to be a challenge to manage, and it is only in retrospect that we can see the wisdom of our having taken an experimental and experiential approach to its development. At age nine, she had a grasp of mathematical concepts that was far ahead of her skill at arithmetic operations. The standardized tests she took as part of her state-required homeschooling evaluation suggested her conceptual skills were some seven years ahead of her putative third-grade level, whatever that is supposed to mean. We knew of the leapfrogging of her conceptual skills over her operational ones early. Grocery stores or coin bags did not initially interest her. We would occasionally sit her down to a page of math problems. This practice was conceivably useful in increasing her comfort with rote skills, but was a vestige of our earliest wrong-headed thinking that we had to "do school at home" and perhaps reflected a failure of our own imagination. Ali would take a stab at long division or two- or three-place multiplication, taking ages and often forgetting where she was in the middle of a problem. She couldn't care less if she got the wrong answer, as she saw the assignment as a somewhat noxious chore or irritation rather than as an absorbing game. "Besides," Ali said, to our combined amusement and exasperation, "I know *how* to get the right answer [and by implication, we knew she did, too], so what difference does it make if I get it wrong?" The standard rejoinder, "You wouldn't want to drive over a bridge constructed that way," had little impact, probably because, Ali would choose to worry about that when she was actually building bridges. She'd be right, of course, and we all might have done better with a sophisticated model bridge-building set or a couple of meetings with an architect or engineer. Purely arithmetic problems posed orally could be troublesome, as she'd often forget the problem in the middle of performing mental operations.

However, the very same questions posed as word problems, requiring her to provide the framework for a solution as well as to perform the required operations, never gave her any trouble, and rarely would there be a wrong answer. She mastered fractions early as part of her prodigious musical note-reading skills. Probability was encountered as part of genetics; percentages in figuring out how close she was to paying off her violin.

For a while, we imprudently fought her inclinations, and to no particularly useful end. Ali made her way, albeit reluctantly, through the progressively more difficult exercise books, though slowly but surely she weaned us off those and toward workbooks composed exclusively of word problems. We found a book of "mental math," problems she could read aloud and compute while in the car. Not having to worry about forgetting the terms, she became adept at solving them very quickly.

But what we intuited was Ali's hunger for more mathematical theory and conceptual stimulation, and she still loved her pattern blocks. After much searching, we found a series of manuals focused on geometric concepts that could be used in self-teaching. The University of Illinois at Chicago "Maneuvers with Mathematics Project" produces a series of student lab books dealing with angles, rectangles, circles, and triangles, which impart a broad range of skills. Carefully designed so that each new skill builds on mastery of the previous one, the series also provides an immediate sense of how each of the skills might be used outside of the mathematics lesson context. Within seven months of beginning work with the series, Ali mastered map and compass reading; the use of ruler, protractor, and compass; English and metric system conversions; the beginnings of trigonometry; and the formulas for the perimeter and area of various geometric forms. Along the way, she learned to operate her calculator, to find squares and square roots, to multiply and divide fractions; to understand the function and value of $pi=\pi$ and comprehend basic algebra. Ali's arithmetic operations improved rapidly when employed to calculate distances, areas, angles, heights, and weights. Pattern blocks took on entirely new meaning, and figuring out the height of neighborhood trees was a new source of stimulation.

The knowledge gained was immediately put to good use. Degrees, arc minutes, and arc seconds became routine elements in understanding astronomical positions, as were calculations of object distances. The mathematics necessary for optical computations utilized in building her telescope became a place where she could exercise her new-found capabilities.

We began taking long trips to the supermarket. But before we began, we had lengthy discussions regarding our own nutritional and shopping principles. Ali already knew quite a bit about animal nutrition from her work at Wolf Haven International and her biological studies, enough at least to perceive the fallacies behind the U.S. Department of Agriculture's food pyramid and other dietetic marketing schemes. "Just because you eat protein doesn't mean your body automatically makes protein," she noted. "The body knows what it needs to make." We both agreed there is important value in a balanced diet, but balanced over a period of weeks, months, and years, not daily. Our nomadic foraging prehistoric ancestors would move from area to area, eating only one or two kinds of food at a time for as long as six weeks before moving to new pastures, forests, or seashores. We also recognized that they got a lot more exercise and that it would be a good idea if we did too. Unlike her sister, Ali abhors junk food.

We read and analyzed food labels on the backs of cans and bottles, noting calorie counts and percentages of FDA requirements contained in each. After some discussion, we agreed that our family seemed to have three principles behind what we purchased: food should have sound nutritional value; it should taste good; and we shouldn't spend money unnecessarily, as we liked to use it on other things.

Then it was off to the supermarket. The first time it took us slightly over two hours to purchase ten items. Ali came equipped with her calculator. She would estimate produce weights before weighing and convert scale fractions to ounces and pounds, and then to decimals to calculate actual prices. We discussed the geography of where various kinds of produce were grown, speculated on how it was shipped to our town, and recognized that the wide variety of produce available to us came at some environmental cost. We talked about what farm laborers were paid to pick our fruits and vegetables, and the fact that in some cases they could barely afford to provide these same items for their own families.

We spent the bulk of our time in the breakfast cereal aisle, for it was here that we could most readily discuss the economics of marketing. Why are there five brands of cornflakes, two of which (one the house brand) being produced in the same factory but priced substantially differently? Why are the per ounce prices lower on the larger packages? How much of the cereal price represents the cost of raw materials and production? What kind of art work is used on the packaging to attract customers? What about shelf placement? Are the cereals marketed as healthful really better for you? Why are the bagged cereals less expensive per-ounce than the boxes? And why the strange packaging sizes (25.5 ounces, 32.2 ounces, 1 pound 3 1/2 ounces)? Are consumers really well served by having such an array of choices? Ali will never walk down the cereal aisle the same again. Finally, when we got to the checkout stand, we discussed payment options: cash, check, credit and debit cards, and how each works. Now, each time we go to the market, it is like having a refresher course.

I am aware that Ali would have been equipped to take on some of this mathematics learning at an earlier age, and she did catch bits and pieces of it over time. But there was method in our waiting. While it is true that the context provided Ali the opportunity to use her mathematical skills (which is why 'innovative' school teachers may take their classes *once* to the supermarket and be featured in the local newspaper), I view this contextual deployment as entirely secondary and perhaps even backwards. After all, our schools, and our society as a whole, have amply demonstrated their effectiveness in turning our children into a nation of shoppers. What is primary was learning that mathematics helps make sense of the larger world and that personal decisions take place within a larger socioeconomic framework. Sure, mathematics will help one determine what two pounds of broccoli cost, and 'gifted' students could figure out what percentage of a parent's hourly wage goes toward purchasing it. But by itself, mathematics provides no information about how wages are set or why they differ from job to job or from country to country; about what pesticides are used in broccoli cultivation; about what the nutritional value of spinach is; about how a supermarket works and who owns it; about what marketing strategies are employed to get people to buy produce; and about why some people end up going hungry when so much good food is thrown away and what can be done about it. One could expose a child to any or all of these matters as separate 'units,' and in schools some few are, *once*. The essence, however, is that the use of mathematics in shopping, and not just in the initial learning experience, can be the starting point to ponder all of these issues, if and when the kids themselves express an interest.

This would seem on its face to pose an impossible educational standard. And it would be, except that our 'shopping math' lesson does not happen only once, but occurs over a period of years. This approach is not just applied math or contextual math, but lays a foundation for a 'values-based' mathematics. After the initial delight in figuring out how numbers work wears off, a few children will retain a love of mathematics for itself. But the central point is that if kids learn early, repeatedly, that mathematics is a tool that helps them understand their world and answer *their own* questions, they will have greater reason and incentive to learn the tricks and techniques.

"U.S. Twelfth Graders Receive Failing Grade in Math and Science," screamed the February 24, 1998 local newspaper headline. In the Third International Mathematics and Science Study (TIMSS), U.S. students about to graduate from high school scored among the lowest among youth from 21 countries tested in mathematics, just ahead of those from Cyprus and South Africa. President Clinton used the results as an opportunity to hold several media events in schools to promote increased federal funding and, some believe, control of public education. U.S. Education Secretary Richard Riley referred to it in speeches to spur the nation's teachers to action. Radio talk show hosts bemoaned the decline of schools, the abject state of American families, and the dismal future of the nation.

"With data on half a million students from 41 countries, the TIMSS is the largest, most comprehensive, and most rigorous international study of schools and students ever," trumpeted Dr. Pascal D. Forgione, Jr., Ph.D., U.S. Commissioner of Education Statistics, U.S. Department of Education. "The questions were developed by international committees ... International monitors carefully checked the translations and visited many classrooms while the assessments were being administered to make sure instructions were properly followed ... The quality standards for the sampling process for TIMSS were higher than in any previous comparison of education systems." Dr. Albert Beaton of the TIMSS International Study Center at Boston College coordinated and managed the study; the U.S. National Research Coordinator (much quoted in the newspaper) was Dr. William Schmidt, Professor of Education, Michigan State University. High-powered advisors for the study included professors from Harvard, Stanford, and Northwestern Universities, the Universities of Chicago, Michigan, Wisconsin, Colorado, Georgia, and California at Berkeley, and representatives of the Council of Chief State School Officers and the National Council for Accreditation of Teacher Education. Millions of dollars in funding came from the National Center for Education Statistics (NCES) of the U.S. Department of Education and from the National Science Foundation. (Further information on TIMSS can be found on the NCES website: nces.ed.gov.timss)

The test's mathematics portion consisted of 80 questions, three of which were chosen for inclusion in the NCES-TIMSS report appendix.

Apparently only one was circulated to the media, for all newspapers ran the same sample question:

Experts say that 25% of all serious bicycle accidents involve head injuries and that, of all head injuries, 80% are fatal.

What percent of all serious bicycle accidents involve fatal head injuries?
A.   16%
B.   20%
C.   55%
D.   105%

Correct Answer: B   U.S. Average: 57%   International Average: 64%

"This is strange," said ten-year-old Ali after studying the problem for a few minutes. "The answer they want is B [20%], I guess. The real answer is probably closer to 16% [A]. But actually you can't tell. And they don't give you 'Not enough information' as a choice."

"What makes you say that?" I asked, and we teased it out together. If 25% of all serious bicycle accidents involve head injuries, and 80% of all head injuries are fatal, then 80% of 25% is 20%. That's simple enough, or at least it was for ten-year-old Ali. But it doesn't say 80% of serious head injuries incurred *on a bicycle* are fatal. Probably 95% of serious motorcycle accidents involving head injuries are fatal. And probably less than 80% of those which occur on bicycles are fatal. So the real answer to the question might be closer to 16%. But one can't know from the information provided.

And why, I asked myself, did 57% of U.S. students answer 20%, but 64% of international students answered 20%? After all, much was made over this failure in relative performance by the would-be test analysts. Possibly, more of the American students were trained well enough to realize the question didn't make any sense. Perhaps some figured out that the answer was likely to be less than 20%, so they chose A. Maybe the international students just thought the question was translated incorrectly, so they gave 20% as the answer for which the testmakers were fishing. But who knows? Now, mind you, this sample question was chosen by the TIMSS experts as the representative example of their work for all the world to see. One can only imagine what the other questions looked like. Certainly neither parents nor teachers will ever find out.

With Ali now thoroughly amused, we decided to conduct a scientific experiment. I wrote to Professors Schmidt and Beaton, Richard Riley, Dr. Forgione, NCES, the Department of Education, and the President, enclosing copies of the question, and noting the danger with coming to conclusions and making policy decisions based on suspect data derived from questions poorly formulated to begin with. The hypothesis was that we would never receive a response from any of them. We didn't.

———•◆•———

In our experience, the timing of contextual math lessons is often unplanned, but one must be prepared to take advantage of the openings when they occur. Ali had already set up a credit union account for her violin earnings, had read about trade expansion during the Renaissance, and had learned about the basic differences between capitalism and communism in discussions about Russia. We talked about personal banking options during our shopping expeditions. Yet it was a much more unusual context that sparked a discussion of interest and credit. We were watching a video performance of Ali's favorite opera *Simon Boccanegra* (opera is discussed in the following chapter). After Act II, she asked me what a moneylender was. It seems a rival to the title character for election as Doge of Venice was a moneylender who, by the way, never actually appears in the opera. That evening we never got to Act III.

For parents who experienced some degree of math trauma when in school themselves, being ready to take on the contextual math challenge will require some extra courage, advance planning, and commitment, either to relearn alongside their children — the most optimal scenario — or to find mentors, be they family friends or neighborhood teenagers, ready and willing to make themselves available. For no doubt there is danger in parents passing their own math phobias on to their children. If parents are unwilling to deal with their own math anxieties, at least to the extent of recognizing them and finding other resources for their children, the kids are likely to grow up with similar fears.

Actually, parents who have experienced math phobia are in an especially good position to prevent such fears from developing in their children, if they just take the time to re-create what it was that resulted in their own phobias in the first place and to re-envision how it could have been different. There is now a widely shared "Math Anxiety Bill of Rights" writtten by Sandra L. Davis for adult college students. By relating it to their own experience and taking it to heart, parents will stand a better chance to instill a sense of self-confidence, free of anxiety, in their children:

Math Anxiety Bill of Rights

- I have the right to learn at my own pace and not feel put down or stupid if I'm slower than someone else.
- I have the right to ask whatever questions I have.
- I have the right to need extra help.
- I have the right to ask a teacher or tutor for help.
- I have the right to say I don't understand.
- I have the right to not understand.
- I have the right to feel good about myself regardless of my abilities in math.
- I have the right not to base my self-worth on my math skills.
- I have the right to view myself as capable of learning math.
- I have the right to evaluate my math instructors and how they teach.
- I have the right to relax.
- I have the right to be treated as a competent person.
- I have the right to dislike math.
- I have the right to define success in my own terms.

Ali and I attended several lectures related to mathematics presented by the local astronomical society. One of our favorites was about "fuzzy set theory," offered by a professor of mathematical engineering. Humans use "fuzzy" logic all the time, especially when we make use of adjectives or adverbs. For example, when we use the word "tall" or say a number is "large," it is our own personal and social context that determines whether it is accurate in the first case in relationship to a child or to a Boston Celtics basketball player, and in the second, to our expectation of a number's size. But getting computers to 'think' this way is a 'tall order.' The use of fuzzy logic allows one to program voice recognition tools or video cameras and, in the case of astronomy, enables scientists to adjust the mirrors on the Hubble Space Telescope when images relayed down to earth seem beyond the relative parameters of what might be expected. Both Ali and I were somewhat overwhelmed by the formal mathematics, but each of us came up with other scenarios where one could use fuzzy logic, such as programming a robot working in a doughnut shop to help with marketing efforts by giving out free samples of a new variety to only those customers who are most likely to be induced to purchase them later.

I discovered Ali had mastered the concept quite unexpectedly. Sitting in the back of the car one day, Meera informed Ellen that she wanted a voice-controlled miniature truck. Ellen replied she might get her one for her birthday. "That's three months off!" complained Meera. "But you've been telling everyone how soon your birthday is," Ellen reminded her. "Fuzzy set theory," harrumphed Ali under her breath.

Abbott, Edwin A., *Flatland: A Romance of Many Directions*. Mineola, NY: Dover Publications, Inc., 1992. This 1884 novella describes the journeys of one A. Square, a resident of two-dimensional Flatland, and his discovery that there are worlds beyond. Part mathematics and part social satire, this is the perfect book for the child who has just encountered formal geometry for the first time.

Burns, Marilyn, *Math: Facing an American Phobia*. Sausalito, CA: Marilyn Burns Education Associates, 1998. My painstaking and long-suffering editor at Holt Associates, Pat Farenga, has asked me to tutor him in math. He says that he still gets spooked by it and that it was all a confused jumble that he muddled through in school. And Pat has three wonderful homeschooled daughters! Well, I don't have time, and I live more than 3,000 miles away, but this book will definitely help. Burns, a gifted classroom teacher herself (yes, there are some!), offers a gentle and humorous account of the way math is often taught: "Yours is not to question why, just invert and multiply." She uncovers the reasons behind adult phobias (math ranks up there with snakes, public speaking, and heights) and outlines excellent ways to ensure we don't re-create such phobias in the young. She places heavy emphasis on thinking and reasoning skills and making sense of the world, rather than on a limited focus on computation, memorization, and speed.

Page, David A., Wagreich, Philip, and Kathryn Chuval, *Maneuvers with Angles*. University of Illinois at Chicago Maneuvers with Mathematics Project. Palo Alto, CA: Dale Seymour Publications, 1993. We liked these so much that we ended up purchasing the entire series!

Scieszka, Jon and Lane Smith, *Math Curse*. New York, NY: Viking/Penguin Books, 1995. A children's book for young and old alike. Mrs. Fibonacci has put a curse on one of her students so that everything the child looks at or thinks about turns into a math problem! "Estimate how many M&Ms it would take to measure the length of the Mississippi River." She breaks free, and life is great until science class, when Mr. Newton says, "you can think of almost everything as a science experiment ..." Highly recommended.

Exits and Entrances

Bring me my Bow of burning gold:
Bring me my Arrows of desire:
Bring me my Spear: O clouds unfold!
Bring me my Chariot of fire.

William Blake, "Milton"

Consider the toddler in the sandbox. Hour after hour she spends her day shaping and reshaping hills, carving valleys, building walls, sprinkling grains of sand upon the ground. Toy cars and trucks surround her; dolls and plastic animals, spoons and shovels, twigs and tree branches, and whatever flotsam and jetsam she has managed to pick up may have found their way onto the scene. Occasionally, with the sweep of the hand, a stomp of the foot, or an outpouring from a bucket, contours are obliterated and, if there is enough time, the process begins again.

No parent would be deceived into believing that what keeps the child occupied is fascination with sand, although trying to fathom the actions of gravity, inertia, and friction certainly makes up part of the preoccupation. No, the sandbox is a theater. Within its boundaries, the child works out her understanding of who she is and her relationships to the natural world, to her family, and to the more expansive, though still limited, social order into which she has been newly introduced. She conveys meaning and order and rhythm to her experience. At a later stage, she takes stories and tales told by others, internalizes them, and represents them as her own through a complex process of reinterpretation. If there are two children in the sandbox, plots may be combined, exist simultaneously, or be brought into open conflict. Story and song, symbol and myth, dream and magic are linked together in a re-creation of the world as vision and reality.

If by now the toddler's sandbox sounds like the setting for a late Wagnerian opera, it is because it should. The child is at once playwright, architect, costume designer, and theater director, and the fabric of her vision is little less than the nature of reality itself.

Don't be put off by appearances into thinking that the representation is 'childish.' On the contrary, the hallmark of this childishness is its complexity. The child's understanding of symbolic representation is so keen that she is able in the course of her play to distinguish between the real, the representative, the non-present, and the fictional. What is poorly developed, and only comes with experience, is a discernment of what part of the real is truly representative of the wider human or natural frame. This is why the sandbox creation rarely ranks as great art.

I have never met a healthy child, or a healthy adult for that matter, without a fantasy life. It is no more necessary to extol the existence of a child's fantasy life than to glorify her breathing. But the important thing is to respect it. Not to do so can be as crippling as suppressing breath itself.

The child's fantasies grow and develop, making use of new materials and skills and new understandings of the world as well as of a larger circle of experience as she grows older. They punctuate the round of her development and her evolving sense of self.

And then, like a bomb detonated in an already crowded theater, school hits. Without any regard or even the slightest acknowledgment or attempt to understand what is going on for that individual child, school constrains her to abruptly exit the absorbing autonomous construction of her experience for a whole new and initially barren set of symbols which are foisted upon her. No recognition is given to the fact that the child already knows the stuff of which symbols are made and ways to manipulate them. Worse still, the symbols — letters and numbers — are presented as devoid of feeling, of song, of color, or, at best, as being 'happy.' They are, to the world of the child, flat.

Don't misunderstand me: both reading and arithmetic have very secure places in childhood. Used to advantage, they can enhance the unfolding drama of self, exposing the child to alternative stories and different ways of seeing, providing an opening to wider experience and more elegant modes of symbolic manipulation and understanding. They can widen the entrance to rather than signal the exit from the dramatic construct.

But the problem is that the child is not immediately aware of this potentiality, and little that happens in the classroom even suggests it. Worse still, mastery of the techniques — constantly measured in grades, checkmarks, and report cards — is given priority over the end toward which they can be used. Even from the point of view of imparting competencies, the narrow focus on technique subverts its own end, as it is meaning and utility to the child's own story that can, if allowed, readily provide the prime impetus for skill-building.

Amidst the rubble, in this vacuum, in those little chairs and desks never encountered anywhere else in the real world, with an adult at the front of the room determined or desperate to remain in control as she is surrounded by two dozen children hungry for attention, hungry for praise, hungry for escape, or just plain hungry, 'education' is suppose to happen.

And it does. Nature abhors a vacuum. If children are compelled to abandon their own stories, they will learn to make use of the available ones. Barbie and G.I. Joe manufacturers are more than prepared to step into the breach.

Some years ago I edited a well-received book by childhood educators Nancy Carlsson-Paige and Diane Levin titled *Who's Calling the Shots? How to Respond Effectively to Children's Fascination with War Play and War Toys.* The book's central thesis is that given the reality that children, particularly those in the four-eight-year age range, are being captured by the war toy manufacturers and their violent television cartoon tie-ins (as well as by sexist representations aimed at girls), parents must strive to humanize the play stories that accompany the toys or at least facilitate the children's crafting of their own scripts. But I would take the analysis a bit further. The G.I. Joe and Barbie scripts may have their own appeal, yes, but the reason many school-age children are drawn to them is that these are the only scripts consistently being offered when their own stories are in the process of being wrenched away. The toy manufacturers know how to fill a vacuum, and they understand far better than school administrators how to 'educate' their potential customers. And should Barbie and G.I. Joe begin to wear thin, the successors to Joe Camel are waiting in the wings. Carlsson-Paige and Levin argue convincingly that children need to be in control of their own play. Where the authors fall short is in a failure to recognize, firstly, that schools themselves are the agency singularly responsible for children's loss of control and autonomy and, secondly, that without the institutionalization of children in schools where they are held captive, there is no compulsion for arbitrary distinctions to be drawn between a child's play and her learning. Child's play is child's work.

Our homeschooling experience taught us that it is neither necessary nor desirable to oblige children to exit their rich dramatic constructions in order to master academic skills. On the contrary, we learned that allowing for and enriching the former, over time, stimulates mastery in a whole range of areas far beyond what might have been expected or possible otherwise. We also learned to acknowledge that what from our perspective might have seemed incidental or tangential to any particular lesson often turned out to be integral to our kids' learning development.

Between the ages of two and a half and three, Ali decided to try out a new persona as Dorothy from *The Wizard of Oz*. We humored her somewhat; I wasn't allowed to be the Wicked Witch of the West, so I settled for Toto (known better in those days as "Toe-Doggie"). She divided up her zones of self-presentation so that within the family she would only answer to "Dorothy," but "Ali" worked just fine to outsiders. We provided a large dress-up box so both children could costume themselves as required. We had the privilege of watching sequels to the movie being developed as part of ongoing play activity.

With the family taking an airplane trip to Washington, DC, Ellen informed Ali that she could only take one of the multitudinous bears that inhabited her room and that it couldn't be a large one. Ali insisted it had to be Pooh Bear, one of the larger members of the collection. After determining Ellen's resistance could not be overcome, Ali came up with a solution: she deputized a small green bear as "honorary Pooh Bear" for the period of the trip.

One evening when Ali had just turned four, I was sitting in my recliner and channel surfing between two basketball games. Ali came out of her room and after several changes asked me to stop on a channel between the two games. I did so, and what we saw was a stage with a relatively rough-hewn set depicting a country village, two very fat men sitting on a bench, drinking from large wineskins, acting tipsy, and singing at the top of their lungs. The more massive of the two turned out to be Luciano Pavarotti in a broadcast performance of the nineteenth century Donizetti opera *L'Elisir d'Amore*. The singing may have been wonderful, but I was not allowed to find out. For the next hour, I was required to read aloud each and every subtitle translation as it flashed across the bottom of the television screen.

As if that wasn't enough (sometimes we are a little slow on the uptake), one afternoon about a month later, Ellen lay down to take a nap. Ali was playing outside, leaving 18-month-old Meera by herself in the living room. When she awoke, Ellen was astonished to find Meera perched on the living room couch, thoroughly engrossed in watching a video of the ballet *Swan Lake*, which we had received as a present. Meera had found the tape (which she had seen once before), plopped it into the machine (we certainly hadn't taught her how to do so), and turned it on, and was now mesmerized by the music and by the controlled physical expressiveness of classical dance.

We got the hint. In the months and years that followed, our house was filled with video performances of famous operas, mostly for Ali, and ballets for both kids. I needed an entire re-education to feed the kids' burgeoning interests. I made sure they didn't watch any of these performances until I had at least explained the story, and perhaps alerted them to some musical or dance highlights to watch for. I have met so many adults who have gone to the opera or ballet once, never to go again. The reason they don't return is not because they don't like music or dance, but because they cannot overcome their insecurity at being confronted with a whole new set of stylized storytelling conventions to which they have never been properly introduced — whether it be menprancing around the stage in tights representing kings and princes or a generously full-figured soprano singing at the top of her lungs as she dies of consumption. My efforts were aimed specifically at helping my kids feel secure in encountering these conventions so that they could unlock for themselves the imaginative power inherent in performance.

For a while, both Ali and Meera took ballet classes. Neither chose to continue with them for very long, but the classes revealed to each what their real interests were: for Meera, it was gymnastics, at which she quickly became extraordinarily accomplished; for Ali, it was the stories themselves. Ali turned an old dress into a peasant dancing smock so she could play Giselle. Building-block structures became the castle of the Black Prince from Tchaikovsky's *Swan Lake*, the tree outside our house the setting for the garden scene from Mozart's *The Marriage of Figaro*. For the next two years, I may have run up a record number of library overdue notices for *The Metropolitan Opera Stories of the Great Operas* and George Balanchine's *101 Stories of the Great Ballets*, until grandparents eventually remedied the situation by providing these two books as birthday presents.

In very short order, Ali was constructing her own ballet scripts, which we had the foresight to write down. A favorite was an amalgam of themes and ideas from *Giselle, Swan Lake, Sleeping Beauty,* and *Firebird* titled "The Duck Goes Off in the Puddle":

THE DUCK GOES OFF IN THE PUDDLE

Once upon a time there was a duck who lived by the side of a magic puddle. Her friend the Fruit Lady lives next door. One day, the Fruit Lady jumps into the puddle and pulls the duck in after her. They both swim across the puddle and the duck turns into a beautiful ballerina and the Fruit Lady into a flower maiden. The Fruit Lady dropped her scarf into the puddle when she goes in and it floats across. The transformed Fruit Lady (now a flower maiden) takes the scarf out of the puddle because she knows it now contains magic. The duck ballerina realizes that the flower maiden is her mother.

A prince goes down to the puddle and falls in love with the duck ballerina. The ballerinas come to tell the duck ballerina and the flower maiden that the prince is in love with the duck and wants to marry her. The flower maiden realizes that if the duck gets married, the magic scarf will turn them both into real princesses. She tells the duck to agree to the marriage. The ballerinas go off to tell the prince the good news.

The wedding takes place in a park surrounded by a deep forest. The guests include a dancing bush, dancing broom, dancing water, and dancing stairs, all dancing with the ballerinas and flower maiden. There is a big party. The magic scarf turns the flower maiden and duck ballerina into real princesses, and all the guests do special dances for the newly married couple.

———— ⋅•⋅•⋅ ————

Olympia is blessed with a large, private nonprofit out-of-school theater for children. Capital Playhouse — A Northwest Theater for Youth — attracts more than 600 children ages 6-18 annually to participate in workshops, performances, and summer camps led by theater professionals. Shortly after her first exposure to opera, I took Ali to see a youth performance of Gilbert and Sullivan's *The Pirates of Penzance* put on by the Playhouse. Before going, we discussed some basic theater etiquette and how long the performance would actually take. I also made it clear, as I always did when taking the kids to cultural events at an early age, that she could ask to leave at any time. Parents are often reluctant to make such an offer, feeling that the child's urge to leave somehow represents a failure on their part to adequately prepare her or to choose an event that would capture the child's imagination. The result is often seen in fuming parents feeling a mixture of anger, guilt, and above all, a need to control, sitting next to bored or squirming children, with neither enjoying the event very much. It's even worse when the activity is chosen ostensibly for the child's benefit and provides little diversion or amusement to the now-resentful accompanying adults. And, unfortunately, parents or children may become extremely leery of repeating such an encounter: the parent may remember the previous 'failure' more vividly than the changes which have occurred in the child since, and the child picks up on the parent's cues. Failures to prepare the kids adequately or in making mistaken choices do occur, so one learns to choose wisely, without, however, limiting possibilities to what is already known to please. When Meera was five, I would never have taken her to a play of any kind, but she sat perfectly entranced for two and a half hours of the Peking Acrobats. However, our experience suggests it is just as likely that a child may wish to leave because she has taken in enough to process valuably well before the show is over.

Ali and I sat through the entire production. Some of it was cute, and some well sung. Occasionally kids mumbled their words, or forgot their lines. Overall, it was a spirited effort. On returning home around 10:00 p.m., Ali didn't want to talk about the performance, and we all went to bed. Except Ali. What had apparently caught her imagination had occurred during the overture. The stage was bare except for a two-dimensional wood cutout of the pirate ship. While the music played, a cardboard cat mounted on a dowel chased similarly mounted mice across the bow and stern of the ship, and dowel-mounted seagulls landed and flew off from the first deck. Ali must have stayed up all night, for in the morning there were almost two dozen paper cutouts of animals and fish, sun, moon, and stars, all outlined in crayon and marker and crudely mounted on chopsticks with cellophane tape. And along with them came an elaborate story.

The following week Ellen and the kids constructed a very simple stage of cardboard and scrap wood. Hooks were attached to the back where chopstick characters could rest so others could be brought into the scene. Ali and Meera painted the stage and decorated it with cutout stars.

One of its major uses became a family tradition. As Quakers, we do not as a matter of religion celebrate any holidays (more correctly, *all* days are to be considered holidays because they have equal potential for revealing the Divine to us), but as a cultural matter we celebrate all kinds: Hindu, Christian, Jewish, ethnic, birthdays of famous composers, artists, writers, and scientists, π Day (March 14th — we bake several pies and divide them into fractions before eating), even some we just make up ourselves. As an amateur storyteller, I sometimes try to imbue old traditions with new stories. One favorite is titled "Another Chanukah Story," in which I removed what we perceive as the Jewish holiday's glorification of militarism, and placed family togetherness in hard times at the center. Each year in December, the kids get out the stage and make new chopstick characters for the story as needed for an animated retelling, following the traditional lighting of candles. We now have a collection of the same characters redrawn by the children as they have grown, and the story takes on new richness each year. Meera and Ali and I have appeared on our local television cable access channel to present our Chanukah tale. More consequential in terms of learning, they witnessed an adult compose a story, write it down, and tell it for pleasure, which has prompted them to engage in similar activities.

The cardboard stage became the setting of other dramatic presentations, most notably scenes from the great Indian epic *The Ramayana*, re-enacted as part of our celebration of the Hindu holiday Diwali. (*The Ramayana* played an important role in Ali's reading development — see the "Letters!" chapter.) Diwali, the Hindu festival of lights ("kind of like Hindu Chanukah," says Ali), commemorates the return of the Indian hero Rama and the monkey warrior Hanuman after having defeated the forces of Ravana, the ten-headed King of Lanka, who had abducted Rama's wife Sita. What I thought worthy of pointing out to the kids was that the moral implications of the story are different, depending upon one's point of view, and hence ambiguous. In Sri Lanka, King Ravana, portrayed as the villain in the Indian versions, is considered the hero. Ravana's ten heads and 20 shoulders, according to this retelling, are symbolic of what is necessary for a king to govern wisely.

In fact, my object lesson was superfluous to Ali's and Meera's learning needs. I had been taught to believe by a host of experts on early childhood development that all children express their understanding of and their need to manipulate power relations through the creation of good and evil characters (or monsters) who they can then orchestrate as part of their play. And, we are told, the children's toy manufacturers and television and movie producers play on this universal need. Well, despite the claims of ubiquity, the universalizing angel must have passed over our house. Without any intervention on Ellen's or my part, the to-be-expected battles between good and evil never took place, and so there was no need for me to gratuitously add ambiguity, human or divine, to the calculus. Rarely did monsters visit our home, and when they did, they were just as likely to be benign as sinister. Other children (even boys!) playing at our house quickly abandoned their "Mortal Kombat," "Ninja Turtle," or "He-Man" scenarios for substantially different fare.

I only have hypotheses as to why this is so. My main one is that Ali found so many ways to express her own power and self-mastery at a very early age and so many outlets for her creativity encouraged by us, that the 'universal need,' and any potential interest in the television-scripted stories that prey upon it were radically reduced. Following in her sister's footsteps in these ways, Meera was more likely to participate in and then emulate her sister's creative directions. Neither of the girls ever spent very much time in daycare, where they might have been regularly exposed to what have come to be considered the more normal childhood fantasy preoccupations or might have felt the need to express anger or a sense of betrayal at being left by their parents.

Power dynamics were overtly expressed in Ali's and Meera's play, though most often in relation to natural phenomena: volcanoes, thunderstorms, blizzards, and the like. The one script they (and we) enjoyed best was called "Mile High Flood." Ali, now five and a half, and Meera, two and a half, would affix simple pulleys and baskets to the upper bunk of their double-decker bed, and the object would be to pull up all their stuffed animals, dolls, and related belongings to safety before they could be swept away by the raging torrent.

Given our kids' natural history interests and understandings even at this young age, *Little Red Riding Hood* and *The Three Little Pigs* were not likely to be popular in our household. Both girls would have rooted for the wolf. At age six and a half, Ali helped Wolf Haven International's education director lead a workshop for children ages 8-12 on making and using Inuit finger puppets. On the spot, Ali composed a story to be told along with using the puppets:

Four Friends

There were four friends in the wilderness — a wolf, a crow, a snake, and a whale. One day a hunter came upon the wolf. He had the wolf in the sight of his gun and was about to shoot, when from behind the hunter the crow let out a loud "caw, caw" and the wolf ran off.

The hunter was angry and decided to shoot the crow. The crow flew up high into the treetops. The hunter started to climb a nearby tree in order to get a better shot. Just as he was getting into position, he saw a snake at the base of the tree open its mouth wide and swallow a whole mouse. Amazed by the snake, the hunter fell out of the tree. The fall startled the crow who flew off.

The forest was on the edge of an ocean beach. The hunter sat down on a log to decide what to do next. It was evening. The snake slithered out of the forest and up to the log. The hunter jumped up, grabbed his gun, and was about to shoot the snake when, to his astonishment, a whale breached close to the shore, almost completely out of the water. The hunter ran to the water's edge to see if he could get a good shot. But all he could see was the bare edge of the whale's flukes and the gleam of the moon on the water.

And while gazing into the water, he heard the distant howl of the wolf. The hunter put down his gun and went home. And he hasn't gone hunting since.

"Four Friends" has since been performed dozens of times for both children and adult audiences and has been published in several magazines and nature education manuals. It should be noted that Ali does not oppose hunting per se, only those who do so for sport and waste what they have killed. "Other hunting species never waste food," Ali reminds me.

Ellen and I have always felt strongly that children must be empowered with complete control over their own play scripts as well as their own magic, rituals, and fantasies. Specifically, Ellen objects strenuously to adults creating fantasies for children whereby the adults conspire to withhold information from them for purposes of mystification. This has sometimes put us in conflict with the culture at large, and even with some of our friends. We have no truck with Santa Claus or the Easter Bunny and believe they devalue those things which are truly 'magical,' such as the writing of the Mozart Requiem or the painting of the Sistine Chapel, or 'miraculous,' such as the original creation of life from inorganic matter. In our experience, when many children grow old enough to have the Santa Claus myth debunked, they feel betrayed and may even wonder what else their parents have deceived them about. To avoid being deceptive without seeming like total spoilsports, Ellen and I have invited the kids to join us in poking fun at the lack of creativity in these adult fantasy rituals foisted upon children. When Meera placed one of her newly lost baby teeth under her pillow (Ali simply chose to save hers), she awoke to find an envelope containing a dog bone, a cowrie shell, two postage stamps and a note from the Tooth Fairy, apologizing that she'd run out of money and informing Meera that she could redeem the stamps for cash from her mother. Meera cashed in her stamps, and then promptly demanded and received her tooth back.

------◦◆◦------

Ali's interest in opera burgeoned rapidly. Well before her seventh birthday, she knew the plots of the major Mozart and Puccini operas, a smattering of Verdi and Rossini, and various more modern works. Her earliest favorites were *The Marriage of Figaro* and *Madama Butterfly*. Later, she would tell people who inquired that Verdi's *Simon Boccanegra* was her choice and Sherill Milnes, singing the part of Boccanegra, her favorite male singer. I thought this work a very strange preference and not one I would have shared, given its dark, brooding character. Her answer often met with blank, wide-eyed stares. It is noteworthy that what the three — one being a comedy, and the other two being tragedies — have in common is that none has a

Performing "Four Friends" on behalf of Wolf Haven International, age eight

villain or presents a struggle of good versus evil as so many operas do, but rather focus on complex, shifting human interactions. Ali and I sat through video performances of Richard Wagner's *Tannhauser* and *Lohengrin* twice each, neither of which I had ever seen before. Much to my surprise, I enjoyed them almost as much as she. It was a distinct advantage to experience them first on video rather than on the stage, as we didn't have to watch them all in one sitting. Wagner's *Lohengrin*, in particular, seems made to delight a child, being the story of a prince transformed into a white swan pulling a boat and then transformed back again, and a hero who champions a maiden but who can only remain so long as the maiden does not ask his real name or where he is from.

On a visit to Washington, DC, her grandmother took Ali to see *Hansel and Gretel* and *Madam Butterfly*, the first live operas she ever saw. Given she already knew the stories and some of the music from each, how long the performances would last and, just as significantly, when to anticipate the intermissions, she had no difficulty sitting through them in their entirety. This last point deserves more attention when one thinks of taking a younger child to a live performance and is another reason sound preparation will increase everyone's enjoyment. Many children's and some adults' sense of time is not all that keen; if you tell a child that the first half of a show will take 45 minutes, you are simply encouraging her to look at your watch. Tying the intermissions to expected points in the action keeps the child (or adult for that matter) more fully engaged with what is happening on stage. *Madam Butterfly* made a very distinct impression. On her return home, Ali asked to write out a version of "Un bel di" ("One Fine Day," Butterfly's most famous aria), so she could play it on her violin. This was not an easy task for me, non-Western musician that I am, given that it was originally written in a key with six flats.

Ali loved operatic performances, but what particularly captivated her was trying to figure out how they are put together. After all, opera is just the most expansive adult version of the sandbox, from which she was never banished. Once it became clear she could read a vocal score with some facility, I wrote a letter to the directors of both the Seattle and Tacoma opera companies, inquiring whether Ali could be allowed to attend staging rehearsals. We received positive responses and cordial invitations from both of them.

Ali's first time attending a staging rehearsal of *Rigoletto* (lots of villains and characters taking revenge in this one) may have been one of those defining sentinel moments of her development, if there is such a thing. Of course, only time will tell. We reviewed the opera with care before she went, learning the characters and noting the names of the various arias and ensembles. As she clutched her used libretto, vocal score, and pencil tightly, Ali and I made our way through the prop room where we saw walls of costumes, horses hanging from the ceiling for *Die Walküre*, a large statue of a man in armor standing on a pedestal (the Commendatore from *Don Giovanni*), a white swan (*Lohengrin*), and a huge dragon (*Siegfried*). In the staging room, a small table in the corner was set aside for Ali. She opened her libretto and score at 10:00 a.m., and I don't think she moved a muscle until 12:45 when she turned to me and said, "You know, Dad, I wish we could come back this afternoon." There wasn't a rehearsal that afternoon, but Ali and I or Ellen, or occasionally an adult friend who wanted to get in on the opportunity, returned dozens of times to observe working sessions at both opera companies over the next several years. Ali met and had discussions with many of the singers and stage directors, often getting them to sign her libretto, and was especially befriended by Tacoma Opera's director, who got a particular kick out of just watching her page through a score.

Ali soon decided to try her hand at writing her own operatic plot:

The Importance of Change

Act 1: In the Main Street of Portaga: In the Kingdom of Portaga, there was a King Robert and his twin children, Prince Charles and Princess Amelia. Prince Charles had been away for a very long time, and everyone thought he was dead because Moral, the princess' lover, told the King that he had seen Charles killed. The King suspects Moral had something to do with Charles' death and so banishes him from the Palace.

One day, Prince Charles returned to Portaga, but does not realize that it is Portaga. As he is standing in the main street, the royal procession of the King and his daughter pass by. Prince Charles does not recognize his father or sister, nor do they recognize him. The Princess waves at her lover Moral, who she spots in the crowd standing near Charles. Charles thinks that the Princess has waved at him and he falls in love with her. He turns to Moral and asks, "who is that?" Moral answers that it is his love, the Princess Charlene, her father the King. (Amelia has changed her name in memory of the brother she thinks is dead.) Charles then overhears Moral tell a friend that he is to meet the Princess in her garden after dark.

Act 2: In the Princess' Garden at Night: Charles arrives in the garden madly jealous of Moral. Moral arrives after him and Charles confronts him, fights with him and accidentally kills him. Fearing what he has done, he drags the body off and buries it in the woods. The Princess comes to the garden but finds no one there.

Act 3: In Charles' Room at the Inn: Charles attempts to disguise himself as Moral so he can win the Princess' love. He has created a mask of Moral's face but it will not fit over Charles' beard and moustaches, so he shaves them off. Now he looks much more like the Charles who left Portaga many years before. Charles dresses himself as Moral for the Ball at the Palace that evening, not knowing that Moral has been banished from the Palace.

Act 4: At the Palace Ballroom: Everyone is at the Ball, including the King, Queen, and Princess. Charles comes dressed as Moral. The King sees him and thinks he is Moral. He rushes towards him and attempts to kill him. The Princess tries to stop her father, but the King says that Moral is the one who killed her brother Charles and deserves to die. The King grabs Charles and strangles him. As Charles falls to the ground dying, the mask comes off in the King's hands. Charles says with his last breath that Moral is dead. Amelia rushes over and realizes who her father has killed and cries, "You have killed my brother!" The King recognizes his son and cries as well.

Lest you think this tale too melodramatically contrived or unlikely for opera, check out the plot of Verdi's *Il Trovatore*! Ali had not, to my knowledge, become familiar with it when she wrote *The Importance of Change*.

That fall, Ali enrolled in an eight-session introductory Italian class in the city's Adult Education Program. We had no difficulty in signing her up; the application didn't ask for age. We accompanied her to the first class session, introduced her to the teacher who was surprised but quite open, and left. In truth, she didn't learn very much Italian, though she followed along quite well and did her homework. But that wasn't the point. She could now pronounce all the words!

Ali continues to make use of her operatic knowledge in a broad and sometimes surprising array of contexts. Upon completing the last chapter of Richard Dawkins' *River Out of Eden* on the evolutionary replication of DNA mutations, she told me, while we were crossing a busy intersection in downtown Seattle on the way to a concert, that it reminded her of Don Basilio's famous aria from Rossini's opera *The Barber of Seville* ("La calunnia é un venticello" — "Let me teach you the art of slander"). "I'll bite," I said, surprised she would refer to a piece from an opera she had not seen or listened to in almost two years. "How?" "Well, the mutation begins almost imperceptibly and is scarcely noticed; it slowly sneaks up, and finally it has taken over the entire population!"

<hr />

Looking through the newspaper at summer camp opportunities, Ali told us she wanted to go to Shakespeare camp, run by the Olympia-based Washington Shakespeare Festival. "Shakespeare camp?" I probed with some surprise. "You don't know and haven't even seen any Shakespeare." "No, I haven't," replied Ali. "But I know Verdi's *Macbeth* and *Falstaff* and *Otello* and they're all based on Shakespeare, right?" I set her an assignment to learn Jacques' "All the world's a stage" soliloquy from *As You Like It* as a kind of readiness self-assessment, and she succeeded just fine.

When we went to New York City for Ali's Carnegie Hall performance, we were fortunate enough to wangle tickets for the opening night of Shakespeare's *The Tempest* in Central Park, featuring Patrick Stewart (of Star Trek fame) as Prospero. This was Ali's first live Shakespeare, and considered the finest Central Park Shakespeare performance in 20 years. Of all of Shakespeare's plays, with the possible exception of *A Midsummer Night's Dream*, *The Tempest* is the most tailor-made for children. It is filled with magic, budding love, sprites and spirits, mistaken identities, outrageous slapstick, song, and a happy ending. *The Tempest* has the most accessible language of all of Shakespeare's plays, and this particular performance added outlandishly costumed Brazilian stilt-walkers, all under an open sky.

Ali was enchanted, and so was I. Over the period of the next two years, she performed in three youth productions and saw live or movie performances of *The Tempest, A Midsummer Night's Dream, Twelfth Night, Macbeth, As You Like It, Taming of the Shrew, Much Ado About Nothing, A Comedy of Errors, Hamlet, Henry IV Part I, Richard III, Henry VIII, Romeo and Juliet, Love's Labour's Lost, Two Gentleman of Verona, Othello,* and *Julius Caesar,* all with deep and abiding pleasure, and able to discuss each intelligently.

I distinctly remember being taken on a school trip to my first Shakespeare play at age 12, and it was a disastrous experience. As a result, I chose not to endure any further Shakespeare until I went off to college. No explication of the plot was offered in advance. In fact, I'm not convinced my sixth-grade teacher could have explained the plot — the play being *A Comedy of Errors* — if he'd wanted to. The play was apparently considered too difficult to read, even for those of us labeled "academically gifted." Whether this was true, I'll never know, as no copies of the play were furnished to my class, no encouragement offered to find it in the school library (there may not have been any), and certainly no communication with parents urging them to read or review the play with their children. In fact, I don't even recall being told that this or any other play could be found in books at all. We were provided no sixteenth century English history, no theatrical context (many children had never seen a play of any kind), no plot summary, and no concept of why the school thought this would be important for us. We *were* told that Shakespeare was the greatest dramatist who ever lived, which, after attending, we knew for certain to be an out-and-out lie, just one of the many deceptions we were inured to receiving from our schoolteachers. I have no idea whatsoever whether the performance was any good. Even if some few of us tried to comprehend what was going on, the presence of hundreds of children who were forced to attend but couldn't care less, some of whom had become car sick from gasoline fumes during the one-hour trip on the school bus, and the constant shushing and admonitions of mostly bored and angry teachers made any concentration or enjoyment absolutely impossible. "It's good to expose our sixth graders to it," I'm sure some school administrator was thinking, rather like exposing young ones to the chicken pox in early childhood, so they'll never have to suffer from it as adults. Once we returned to school, the play was entirely forgotten, as if it had never happened.

Now I know there are both schools and inspired and well-meaning schoolteachers who have tried and sometimes succeeded in improving the experience for some few children. One of the unfortunate tendencies, though, is for schools to arrange for Shakespeare productions that radically simplify both the language and the plot, often leaving the play almost beyond recognition. I can appreciate the intent of this approach, as it may at least ensure a positive theater experience for children who might not otherwise have one at all. But what is gained this way has a price: children may achieve no recognition that Shakespeare has anything more to offer. If the play encounter is seen as the end rather than the beginning of exploration, and children do not pursue it themselves later, they may never find out.

Our approach has been quite different. Once we are convinced each child is ready and truly interested, our objective is to build children up for the most optimal theater encounter (as for any other experience) rather than seeking to play down to them. Our process of preparation for all live Shakespeare performances, which might take place over several weeks, would usually go like this: Ali would read the wonderful plot synopsis in the classic *Tales from Shakespeare* by Charles and Mary Lamb; after reading their summary of *The Tempest*, Ali decided to read this magnificent volume cover to cover. Ali then might read the play itself. Often we will agree on a short speech or soliloquy for her to learn by heart or to be at least discussed in detail. A short history lesson may be in order, as, for example, in preparing to see *Julius Caesar, Antony and Cleopatra,* or *Richard III.* If there is an opera based on the play or a well-known movie version on video, we will likely watch it together. If there is classical music based on the drama, I will try to find a tape or compact disk at the library. By the time of the performance, Ali is ready to appreciate the play on its artistic merits, rather than simply struggling, like most children and adults, to figure out what is going on. Afterwards we almost always have a spirited discussion. More significantly, she knows she can look forward to many more plays and performances in the future. She is, I assume, likely to forget the details, the characters, maybe even the names of many of the plays she has seen, and she will never have to take a test from us to prove to someone else's satisfaction that at one time she knew them. If we are successful, she will have learned that the theater can be a source of inspiration for her own introspection, imagination, and creativity.

Ali's theater experience has not been confined to Shakespeare. We make it a regular practice to attend 'pay what you can' previews at college and community theaters which, together with Ellen's and my volunteer ushering as already noted, helps keep the family budget under control. One of Ali's favorites was a performance of Christopher Marlowe's *Dr. Faustus*. At intermission, while sitting on the floor in the theater atrium munching on a cookie, she turned to me and commented, "You know, what's really interesting about this play is that it all takes place inside Faustus' mind."

———◆•◆•———

Ali had already been writing poetry for some time and had met and worked with a friend who was an excellent, well-published poet and member of our Quaker meeting. I had, however, deliberately avoided suggesting she learn 'about' poetry until she turned nine. Perhaps I haven't known where to look, but much poetry I have perused expressly written for kids is really meant to appeal to parents' wistfully rosy view of their children as uncomplicated beings who can be captured by humor but little else, despite their own experience to the contrary. Certainly this was not material upon which it was worth spending much time. We of course enjoyed reading A. A. Milne's "Pooh Poems" and the silly verses of Ogden Nash to our children. Meera was inspired by these and at six and a half composed her first verse for a home-school poetry contest, which she won:

RAINBOW FRUITS

I like fruits and you do too.
Bananas that are red and oranges that are blue.
Pumpkins are black and pineapples are brown,
Especially those pineapples that
live underground.
I like to eat grapes that are hot pink
And spit the seeds right out in the sink.

The seeds grow through the drain and into the ground,
And hot pink grapes are all over town.
I like to eat orange cherries and white apples too,
Especially white apples that
always say MOOO!
Purple tomatoes make a lot of noise,
But most of all I like them as toys.

Silver peaches are quite delicious,
But now it is time to wash the dishes.

But in my experience, most children grow up thinking of poetry as rhyming doggerel (if they think of it at all). The success of our schools at teaching an appreciation of poetry can best be ascertained by noting poetry's hopelessly shrunken share of the book market in this country. That this doesn't have to be the case, even in a nation with wide access to television, can be demonstrated by the tens of thousands of people in South America who regularly flock to amphitheaters and soccer stadiums to listen to their favorite poets read their work live.

Meera actually has a favorite poet, though she probably doesn't know it (please excuse the rhyme): Ira Gershwin. After a piano recital, I presented her with three compact discs of Gershwin songs, two with performances by Michael Feinstein, and one sung by Ella Fitzgerald. Later, I also found a printed piano collection of these for her. For six months or more, Meera listened to Gershwin songs incessantly and now not only knows and sings them all by heart, but will discuss the different treatments and various nuances given the songs by the two artists. She also sent us on an unsuccessful search for the piano music for one of the songs sung by Michael Feinstein which, we finally ascertained, is as yet unpublished.

Ali had been introduced to the language of poetry through Shakespeare, and it was in that context that I more formally initiated her into the larger poetic realms, beginning with the two Romantic poets Blake and Wordsworth. My lesson, really just a directed discussion with examples, was less than 30 minutes long, but I spent significantly longer than that preparing it. I suggested Ali think of the Romantic poets, and of most who came later, as operating within their own "theater of self." With Shakespeare, one might rather quickly discover his support of monarchy, his dislike of Puritans, and his distrust of the mob, but little about the Bard himself. With Blake and especially with Wordsworth, one learns little else. Ali appreciated Wordsworth's insight that "The Child is Father to the Man," immediately associating it with her own educational process. She was interested and amused by my account of how Wordsworth wrote "The Prelude" three times over a period of 50 years (and, in my judgment, making it worse each time), and we compared selected passages. I thought this an important lesson to provide early, for through the comparisons she could witness the editorial process of a poet's mind, rather than thinking of poetry as something that springs full-blown from the poet's brain onto the printed page. Ali was particularly attentive to the explanation of how, for Wordsworth, the crystallization of memory into words came first, with meter (and, rarely, rhyme) only coming as an afterthought. She thought long and hard about Wordsworth's theory of perception, of how we half-perceive and half-create the world around us. Finally, as she committed to memory the climactic verses of "Lines Written a Few Miles Above Tinturn Abbey," I challenged Ali to think of Wordsworth as a dramatist who wrote monologues for only one character: himself.

It was the poetry of William Blake, however, which truly caught Ali's fancy. There are periods in the development of youths when childish understandings and those of maturity coexist, and it is precisely the ability to reflect this characteristic which marks Blake's genius and which took immediate hold of Ali's imagination. Blake was the first poet in the English language to take as his subject the secret richness of childhood and its collision course with modern industrial civilization. And for that, Blake has been banished to the university classroom where, with students' childhood outlooks on the world appropriately withered, his work is to be appreciated at a secure and remote emotional distance.

Unbeknownst to me at the time, Ali spent much of the day following my introducing her to Blake reading the *Songs of Innocence and Songs of Experience* aloud to her pet lovebird Blossom, delighting in the fact that one of the poems had the same title. The next day I took her to a bookstore so she could see reproductions of Blake's original colored printings of the poems. (I later bought her a used copy, which is now well-thumbed.) I quickly discovered Ali had memorized approximately half of them and, moreover, had read all the editor's notes in the back of her book as she knew what changes Blake had made in the poems' order of presentation. Both Ali and Meera have rather prodigious memories, which I attribute at least in part to their early musical training. Within three months, Ali started to set the poems to music: first, "The Ecchoing Green" for youth choir and violin obligato, then "Ah! Sun-Flower" for soprano solo and piano.

I am acutely cognizant of Ali's precocity in both writing and literary understanding, but I am also aware of how assiduously we have labored to feed and foster such understanding in both of our children. I am persuaded from my own experience that we do our children a serious disservice by not immersing and actively engaging them, at whatever age they display readiness, in the best the world's cultures have to offer. We know total immersion works: by the time children grow up, most have successfully completed a total immersion course in violence, mindless competitiveness, unthinking consumerism, and passivity from the relentless curriculum of school and the surrounding society. The real reason a higher order engagement doesn't happen in schools, I'd suggest, is not due to a lack of intelligence, capacity, or interest on the part of children, but to the systemic inability of schools to optimize the potential of each individual child at the moment it manifests itself. When the child's potential is wasted at an early age, it is extremely difficult to re-energize later. Those who bemoan our contemporary cultural wasteland and decline should not have to look far for a culprit.

Perhaps the best theater experience Ali and I shared together was the night I took her, age eight and the only kid in attendance, to see Eugene Ionesco's comedy *The Bald Soprano* at an experimental theater. Yes, the play is full of both adult language and themes, though certainly much more tame than half the shows on weekday evening major network television. But now what seems obvious to me is that the "theater of the absurd," perhaps especially that based on adult themes, is absolutely splendid for kids, as it reflects rather precisely the way they are likely to see the adult world. In the play, adults repeat themselves ad nauseam and to no discernible purpose, characters show little self-awareness, and individuals may not even know who they are themselves unless something in the environment triggers their identity. Sex and gender simply complicate matters. I don't think I ever heard Ali laugh so hard as during this performance, and her joy was infectious. At the intermission, a middle-aged woman came over to her and asked whether she was having any trouble understanding the play, being so young (as if anyone at whatever age could truly be said to understand Ionesco). Having had to crane her neck for much of the evening, Ali's retort was blunt and decisive: "My problem is not that I'm young, but that I'm short!"

Balanchine, George and Francis Mason, *101 Stories of the Great Ballets*. Garden City, NY: Doubleday & Co, 1975.

Carlsson-Paige, Nancy and Diane Levin, *Who's Calling the Shots? How to Respond Effectively to Children's Fascination with War Play and War Toys*. Philadelphia, PA and Santa Cruz, CA: New Society Publishers, 1990.

Freeman, John W., *The Metropolitan Opera Stories of the Great Operas*. New York, NY: The Metropolitan Opera Guild and W. W. Norton

& Co., 1984. Ali perused several other books of this kind but always returned to this one. When grandparents offered to buy her a book about opera, she insisted only the Metropolitan book would do.

Lamb, Charles and Mary Lamb, *Tales from Shakespeare*. New York, NY: Puffin Books, 1995. The Lambs leave out most of the subplots, and not all the plays are covered, but this book is a literary masterpiece and has delighted both children and adults for almost two centuries. Unlike the practice in some of the other volumes of Shakespeare stories, the Lambs' versions make use of language from the plays themselves, so that when readers encounter it upon the stage, there is a favorable shock of recognition. Whether you're brushing up on your Shakespeare or learning to appreciate it for the first time, this is a great place to start.

"Letters"

No bird soars too high, if he soars with his own wings.

William Blake,
"The Marriage of Heaven and Hell"

Ellen and 20-month-old Ali were driving through a parking lot on a typical summer day, when Ali looked up from her car seat and, pointing out the window at a sign atop a passing building, exclaimed "Letters! There are letters!" For the next month and more, letters were discovered everywhere — on license plates, milk containers, crayon boxes, mattress tags, and record jacket sleeves.

Taking a walk along the Santa Cruz Municipal Pier that evening took an hour and a half longer than we had planned. Ali discovered that at her eye level there were signs — with letters! — attached to every parking meter, and she had to "read" each and every one of them.

By 14 months, Ali had divined the names of letters one of the usual ways, through the Alphabet Song. We also had an alphabet book based on items of Egyptian art from the Brooklyn Museum, given to us as a gift. I was a proud and captivated father when I awoke one morning with 14-month-old Ali lying next to me in our family bed, happily chirping "*H* is for Hieroglyphics ... *O* is for Obelisk ..." And of course both Ellen and I delighted, like most parents, in having Ali show off her precociousness in having acquired these greatly-to-be-admired new skills.

I am not convinced mastering either of these two proficiencies, or games, as they seemed to Ali, has much of anything to do with reading, or even, as the current jargon goes, "reading readiness." Of course, providing children with a sense of mastery is always important, as are general associations with books and letters and the startling fact that the latter do appear outside of books, as Ali and later Meera discovered. But the Alphabet Song does little except furnish a child with an arbitrary order of letters, one she will never encounter in making words, and an association between this order and a particular, to my ears not very pleasing, musical sequence. The commercial alphabet book is a little bit better, but not by much. It illustrates the physical shape of letters, and some kind of mysterious relationship between them and certain objects ("Question #1, for ten points: What do hieroglyphics, José, horse, and hour have in common?"). It may also teach an occasionally misleading association between the name of the letter and its phonemic content — the sound it makes when spoken — which is rarely and sometimes never encountered in the course of reading ("Question #2, for 20 points: What word begins with the sound made by the name of the letter W as it occurs in the Alphabet Song? For triple bonus points, try the same exercise with the letter H!" ["oh my *aching* back!"]). To date, Ali has rarely encountered an *ibis* and, as far as I know, nary a *scarab*. I suspect if a family wants to utilize an alphabet book with a child, the best choice would be one they make together, with the child choosing the objects to be signified.

For more than a decade, and for all of Ali's first four years, Ellen and I were book publishers working out of our home. I spent a good part of every working day trying to figure out how to convince people they should desire to read our books and hence buy them. I associate the buying of books with reading, though every major study of American book-buying behavior I have ever seen casts doubt on this association. But not to belabor the obvious, writers write and readers want to read because they are interested in *content*. Everything else from the paper to the printing ink, from the array of letters on the page to the illustrations (except when illustrations are the point), is no more than the United Parcel Service to the brain.

We read to our kids, like all good parents are supposed to. Our children associated us as particularly pleasant parts of the delivery mechanism they could get close to, even if the story lines were weak. I'm not sure that until they were close to age four or so they particularly cared what the words had to say, though they certainly delighted in the words themselves. Favorites in our family included: Joanna Cole's *This is the Place for Me* (Poor Morty's plight was a vivid reminder to us of the horrors of house-hunting); Maurice Sendak's *Chicken Soup with Rice* and *Where the Wild Things Are*; Mick Inkpen's *If I Had a Pig*; Vera Williams' incomparable trilogy *A Chair for My Mother, Something Special for Me,* and *Music, Music for Everyone*; Eric Carle's magnificently illustrated *A House for a Hermit Crab*. A particular favorite of Ali's was the misadventures of poor Murdley Gurdson in Helen Lester's hilarious *It Wasn't My Fault*. Great agitation was created one day when Ali began demanding the "aardvark" book; we didn't have any books about aardvarks and couldn't remember any. A trip to visit the local children's librarian and a literature search aided by Ali revealed an aardvark to be one of Murdley Gurdson's good friends.

We avoided, and still do avoid, stories (as well as videos, television shows, and movies) with commercial tie-ins, and Disney tie-ins in particular. It is not that such stories are necessarily badly written, or even that they teach the wrong message. Rather we didn't want our children to associate purchasing behavior with the pleasing aspects of the reading delivery mechanism. This has had interesting effects: if today you were to ask Ali three questions: "Who was Heinrich Schütz? What did Kepler discover about Mars and how did he make that discovery? Who was the Little Mermaid?", she would readily provide answers to the first two and draw a complete blank on the third.

We were struck by observing Ali manipulate a book at ages two to three. Ali would take a book, any book, and 'read' it to several of her stuffed animals. The content of the printed words was irrelevant as was the order of the pages; more often than not, she would turn the pages backward. I don't think she thought they were in Hebrew! The illustrations might have had some value, at least as the starting point for her verbal riff. From Ali's point of view, she was mastering the art of the book by figuring out how to hold the bound volume on her lap, turn the pages, and provide warm fuzzies for her stuffed friends, all in imitation of her parents, and inventing more imaginative and emotionally satisfying, if unprinted, content for herself.

As former publishers, and as parents, we understand that writing — or more precisely, the act of constructing content and representing that content, whether in dramatic, story, or song form, so that it can be symbolized on the page — comes *before* reading. We were assigned the task of committing the content to paper. The characters most often came from among the myriad of stuffed animals in her room or from artifacts of songs Ali had assimilated. We wrote Ali's stories down for her, and she illustrated them as she wished.

One of the interesting qualities of these early stories was the fluid nature of the characters. Once about to be converted to book, characters from the physical realm could be transmuted to new forms in the symbolic one. One of Ellen's favorite stories, which was popular for months, was called "Babe's Adventures." It begins:

> Know why they call him Babe? 'Cause he was a baby — a baby ox, a baby blue ox. His parents were named Dave and Sally. Dave is a stuffed bear who pretends he's a bull. Sally is a stuffed donkey who pretends she's a cow.
>
> This is how they got Babe. They found Babe in a mailbox! They knew they should take Babe because he was a baby ox and he wanted to be their baby.

Ellen and I enjoy this story, but frankly I don't think it is that unusual. It shows a normal child making sense out of her surroundings and her family and figuring out how the "Babe" fits in. More important, though, from the point of view of reading, the story reveals the twinkling of an understanding that once objects make it to the printed page through symbols, they can be transformed in all kinds of strange and wondrous ways.

Now, in contrast, consider for a moment the child who reaches kindergarten or first grade without having discovered how books are written or constructed. Schools may have long since graduated from the Dick and Jane series, but the point would be the same regardless. "Why am I learning about Sally and Spot, and why do I care? Will Dick and Jane help me make sense of my environment? Will I ever meet Spot and Sally and where do they live? Who put Dick and Jane in my book anyway and how did they get there? Why does the teacher want me to be interested in *them*?", a child might ask. I remember wondering about this more than 40 years ago, and I'd still like to know the real answers!

Ellen and I put little stress on early reading. We'd both lived around children for more than ten years before Ali was born and had learned that, barring organic problems like brain damage or extremely poor eyesight left uncorrected, or severe psychological or emotional trauma which carried over into a fear of symbols, *all* children learn to read. Our own experience demonstrated to us, and repeated studies have confirmed this, that there is no relationship between early reading and school grades, subject mastery, or personal success three, five, ten, or 15 years later. We also had the soothing advantage of knowing our kids could master complex symbol systems — both Meera and Ali read music well before they learned to read words fluently.

Most of the major discoveries young children make in their lives — the existence of a heaven populated by clouds, the luminosity of stars and moon, and the sun's rising and setting; the panoply of lifeforms and their motions, from the suddenness of cats to the deliberateness of turtles, the butterfly's flutter, and the seagull's gliding; the dangers of automobiles and fire; the mystery of snow, the melting of ice, and the delight of puddles; the pleasures of melody and rhythm and, for some, warm baths; culinary discrimination, partiality, and fancies; vague notions of birth, death, and even sex; the daily movement of adults to and fro from work to shopping and home again; the comfort and variety of families; and the clockwork schedule of older children waiting for the school bus — these and the greater outline of this worldly existence as beheld through new, inquisitive, and demanding eyes, all are unfolded without the benefit or need of reading. Having kids read at ever-younger ages may be high on the agenda of parents with heady images of escorting their sons and daughters off to Harvard, but given the content of most young children's reading material, learning to read is small potatoes compared with the fascination of an anthill.

I need not overstate the case. I have observed children learn to read at young ages for reasons having little to do with the discoveries to be made from content. There are children of narrow, intellectually driven parents who can gain approval only through mastery of this or some other academic skill. Woe to the natural-born gymnast or auto mechanic born into this family. There are children living in financially strapped families or with single parents who must spend virtually every waking hour making ends meet. Such children may have otherwise content-poor environments (though having lived in the Third World, I have often been awed by what a healthy child can discover with very, very little at hand), have scarce opportunity to share their daily successes and trials, and therefore may find 'book time' with a parent the only real one-on-one period they get regularly which isn't devoted to more mundane tasks. Physically challenged children may gravitate to the reading arena as one realm in which they can truly experience self-mastery and excel. Shy, emotionally sensitive, or emotionally starved or abused children may retreat to books as a domain of security in a forbidding world.

We can document the process of Ali's reading independence with some precision. Three months after her sixth birthday, we all took an extended car-camping trip to Baja California (which I reported on in the "Dog Kitties" chapter). Between taking boat trips to Guerrero del Negro — a birthplace of gray whales — and collecting of hundreds of Murex shells, every evening and over a period of two weeks Ellen sat with Ali and read through all 173 pages of Marguerite Henry's *King of the Wind*. As many previous amateur observers of child behavior have noted, young girls often have an infatuation with horses which seems to transcend race, background, or environment. Ali was no exception. Besides speaking to her fascination with horses, the book appealed to her budding interests in both history and geography, and we were all tickled by the appearance of the sober Quaker Mr. Jethro Coke who, like the good Friend he was, rescued the Godolphin Arabian from an existence marred by animal abuse and gave him to his fat dolt of a son-in-law, one Benjamin Biggle. Ali and Ellen would sometimes alternate lines, then paragraphs, and then finally whole pages.

Upon returning home, Ali proceeded to reread the entire book by herself cover to cover. I have asked her why she chose to do this rather than take on something much shorter and easier. Ali said the major factor was knowing in advance how the story would turn out. She had complete confidence that, no matter how many times she stumbled over words or how long a period she required, the ending would be there waiting for her. For at least two years following, it became her habit to read the last several chapters in a work of fiction first. The security offered by knowledge of the denouement more than offset the challenge of newness as to both content and use of the reading skill.

King of the Wind was rapidly succeeded by a whole raft of Marguerite Henry's work, first *Misty of Chincoteague* and then *Stormy, Misty's Foal*, followed by Walter Farley's *Black Stallion*. From horses, Ali moved onto wolves: Jean Craighead George's *Julie of the Wolves* and Jack London's *White Fang*. She soon discovered books could provide scientific information beyond what her parents and friends were likely to supply. Within four months of completing *King of the Wind*, she took on a college-level textbook on cetaceans. She was well-prepared for such serious work, as she had already begun her stint staffing the education table at Wolf Haven International.

Alongside this heavier reading, Ali quickly completed a comic book version of the *Tales of Hanuman*, the monkey warrior hero in the Indian epic *Ramayana*, and the *Jataka Stories*, which are ancient Buddhist folk stories similar to *Aesop's Fables*. I am sure these latter afforded the original inspiration behind Rudyard Kipling's *Just So Stories*. The Kipling tales were perhaps Ali's favorite bedtime stories between ages three and four. She adored the videos of "How the Leopard Got Its Spots" and "How the Rhinoceros Got Its Skin," and an audiotape of Jack Nicholson reading "Elephant's Child" was a long-time companion on family car trips. With a sister born in India, her own Indian name and adopted Indian grandparents, her budding fascination with South Indian music, and a child's wonder at the fluid interplay between the human and animal worlds, Ali begged me for my copy of the sublime William Buck retelling of the complete *Ramayana*, which I'd taken on our trip to Mexico. The *Ramayana* has probably been the subject of more family conversations in our household than any other single book. Crafted of exquisite vignettes that can be easily transformed into children's drama, with critical roles played by bears, monkeys, and deer, and containing poetry and exotic fantasy fused into a universal drama of good and evil and many shades in-between, *The Ramayana,* almost four years later, still occupies a favored place next to Ali's pillow.

Ali had already read children's versions of both the *Iliad* and the *Odyssey* and was progressing through the fine Robert Fitzgerald verse translation of the latter. So for her eighth birthday, I found Ali a copy of Buck's retelling of the *Mahabharata*, a sprawling Iliad-like epic of vast proportions. The *Mahabharata*, too, quickly disappeared into her room, though it often surfaced to accompany us on long automobile trips. "What's interesting," Ali informed me, "is that each of the characters — gods or humans — has at least one flaw, which leads to their downfall. And little events, even as small as a throw of the dice, can change the balance of cosmic forces in the universe." At an art class for homeschoolers, Ali showed me a new watercolor where she deliberately allowed one color to flow beyond its boundaries into the next, yet managing to keep the various shapes distinct. "It's Maya's Palace of Illusion," she said, referring to a *Mahabharata* passage in which a gift is presented to Lord Arjuna because of protection he provided to the ephemeral world from the fire god Agni.

By this time, Ali was devouring books at an astonishing rate, books with an almost unlimited range of subject matter: Shakespeare's plays; stories of the great operas and ballets; lives of scientists, artists, composers, and musicians; evolutionary biology; mythology; comparative religion; works of Mark Twain and Ursula LeGuin; philosophy; wildlife ecology, and natural history; Yiddish and Native American folktales; and astronomy. Her bed was never without at least half a dozen open volumes in various stages of consumption, one of which might be a volume of an old encyclopedia being read cover to cover. We kidded her occasionally about her voracious appetite by calling her by a well-earned nickname: "Input."

Meera's reading independence came much more erratically, virtually sneaking up on us when we weren't looking. She showed little interest in reading books, learning phonics, or even sitting on anyone's lap for more than a brief moment unless ill or extremely sleepy. A word or sentence here or there was haltingly read, letters reluctantly sounded out. Ali had more success than we in reading to Meera in an extended fashion, especially if it was part of an ongoing play activity. A spelling game in the car would bring out her competitiveness, though she rarely got beyond "dog" or "cat." Books held few secrets worth knowing, at least initially. What Meera really wanted to know about were all those pesky signs in the environment. She managed, with some initial help from us, to read every exit sign and the name of every town posted on the highway from Olympia to Seattle. Advertising billboards, junk mail flyers, supermarket inserts, food labels, restaurant menus, and event posters connected her via reading to the real stuff. Don't ask her to sound out one of these precious windows to the world; she has more important things to do, such as ascertaining where to call to obtain information about the "Amazing Formula! Lose 30 Pounds in 30 Days! Results Guaranteed!" (At six, Meera weighed all of 39 pounds.)

Given her interests, and those of untold numbers of kindergartners and first graders, Meera's indifference to phonics made perfect sense. Can you imagine going to a foreign country and asking what a word on a movie poster says, only to have your friend sound it out for you phonetically, perhaps even two or three times? It would be obvious that your friend deliberately misunderstood the question! How long would you put up with such patronizing behavior, and would you want your child to submit to the same? We quickly recognized that Meera picked up vocabulary by memorizing whole words; if she asked us to read a word for her, she trained us to give it to her straight so she could get on with meeting her owns needs for learning rather than ours for teaching. For children whose goal is simply to crack the adult written code, I can imagine phonics exercises proving useful. But what I am cautiously suggesting is that heavy emphasis on phonics *might* get *some* children to read earlier, but not necessarily better, provided 'late' readers are not stigmatized and their self-confidence damaged for not reading on someone else's time schedule. The problem with either phonics or whole language approaches to reading is that they are each all too often tied to both a timetable and a content not of the child's own devising.

Let it be remembered that the current infatuation with phonics is driven by school administrative demands for children (and schools!) to perform well on early grade standardized tests, not by appreciation of any individual child's learning aspirations. And I expect it is rare for anyone in the school system to take the trouble to explain to the so-called late reader what all the fuss is really about. After all, what would they say — "Because you are not reading up to grade level in second grade, we and the entire school

administration and even the President of the United States himself are convinced you are likely to grow up to be a drug-addicted, homeless criminal?"
This is not as much of a stretch as it may seem. The argument educators
make is that if children don't 'measure up' and read 'early,' they won't be able
to perform 'at grade level.' Since the grade level won't accommodate the kids'
own needs or timetables, they will 'fall behind.' If they fall behind, they will
miss out on future earnings potential. From there, it is only a small step to
Skid Row, a shooting gallery, or the state penitentiary. So the only way to res-
cue the five-year-olds from rack and ruin is to get them to know their vowel
sounds. We live sometimes in a very strange and wondrous world indeed.
Strange or no, I am convinced there is simply no substitute for understanding and heeding your own kids' unique needs.

  Meera's advances in literacy were often tied to her musical interests.
After spending a week teaching herself to play "Walking in a Winter
Wonderland" from sheet music, she decided she wanted to sing along. As the
words were printed in tandem with the notes, she forced her reading to keep
pace with her own brisk and fluent rhythms. One evening, I returned home
to find six-and-a-half-year-old Meera sitting on a chair next to the piano,
teaching herself the words to "My Favorite Things" from a lyrics book placed
on Ali's music stand. At seven, as a result of self-teaching, Meera can now
fluently both sing and play a range of Gershwin standards.

  Does this keen attention to the universe of words outside of books
mean there was no place for *Little Bear*? On the contrary! *Little Bear* was for
little bears! Upon going to bed every evening, after Ellen and I had said our
goodnights, Meera would read one of the wonderful *Little Bear* books by
Else Holmelund Minarik, with delightfully matched illustrations by
Maurice Sendak, to her three stuffed bears, sounding out any words *they*
might not know. The following day, she would be quite content to repeat her
triumph to us. Meera trained us so that if we insisted on helping her with
her reading, the proper time to do so was 8:30 in the evening, rather than
10:00 in the morning or 2:00 in the afternoon when she had far more
important things to do.

  We tried various "reading readiness' techniques with both Meera and
Ali along the way. Some worked well, some indifferently, some not at all; the

pattern might be quite different for other children with dissimilar predispositions. On the whole, I doubt they had any long-term effect except to demonstrate to our children and to ourselves that we cared. So, for us, phonics cards were a bust — Ali was into content, and "Sa, Fa, Me, To, Poo" wore thin pretty quickly for her, though Meera picked up some of this basic phonics stuff from *Sesame Street*; alphabet posters on the wall rapidly became part of the furniture and were ignored. At a later stage, notebooks to write down "all the big words you don't understand, so you can look them up later" were a waste of energy — "the notebook gets lost, my pencil gets lost, my place in the story gets lost, and if I'm really interested I'll shout across four rooms so you can tell me the meaning immediately; you will tell me, won't you?" A pocket dictionary might be a better idea, though Ali still prefers to query us directly, I think because she likes to hear how we — her parents — might use a particular word in a sentence. Both Ali and Meera enjoyed the silly paragraphs in Engelmann, Haddox, and Bruner's *Teach Your Child to Read in 100 Easy Lessons*, and appreciated the aid of vowel codes in breaking down the opacity of English pronunciation. Neither Ellen nor I can imagine anyone actually going through the course step by step. More useful from Meera's point of view was *The Biggest Riddle Book in the World*. Meera quickly understood that by reading the riddles aloud, she could entertain all her friends.

Neither of our kids watches much television, though not because their exposure is proscribed. We establish no advance schedule, have no hard-and-fast bans on particular shows or subjects, nor set any total-hour limits. Ellen and I both watch substantially more television than our children. Meera and Ali simply have found more compelling things to do in our home, and neither has many age-mates from daycare or school to tease their television appetites. To this day, neither Meera nor Ali know what a Mighty Morphin Power Ranger is, and might just barely recognize a Ninja Turtle or a Barney. Between ages three and five, Ali enjoyed the linear, non-animated, leisurely pace of *Reading Rainbow*. Meera picked up useful tidbits from *Sesame Street* and *Bill Nye the Science Guy*, and we share a fond place in our hearts for *Wishbone*. At eight, Ali was launched into reading a whole series of books by Robert Louis Stevenson after watching a made-for-television movie version of *Kidnapped*. But asked what her favorite TV show is, Ali will tell you she doesn't have any. Meera loves the little TV she watches and is passionate about her favorite shows, but her television desire does not seem to extend beyond these. Taken altogether, I doubt television has had a significant positive or negative impact on our children's reading prowess.

One stratagem we have managed to successfully avoid is what might be called the "gold star approach to reading." All public school students I have met and many outside have been afflicted with it, and it is now commonly utilized by libraries as well. "Read a book and get a gold star; ten stars and you get a teddy bear, an ice cream sundae, or a trip to the circus." I know of no method more likely to be effective at instilling or reinforcing a love of teddy bears, ice cream sundaes, and circuses, and at devaluing reading and books, than this scheme. An intelligent, seemingly precocious, but unfortunately shrewd seven- or nine-year-old can thus easily be trained to put aside one of the 1000-page volumes of Will Durant's *The Story of Civilization* in which she is enthralled or *The Illustrated Encyclopedia of World Mythology* or that old technical manual on flight aerodynamics she insisted you buy for her at a yard sale, for ten *Adventures of the Ketchup Sisters*. Try asking her anything about what was in these ten books after the circus is over — there is no reward for retention or for understanding! Employ this exercise two or three times and watch the volume of Will Durant gather dust, perhaps forever. I am firmly persuaded that the best reward a parent or teacher can possibly give a child for reading is neither ice cream sundae, nor gold star, nor patronizing praise, but patience as the code is being cracked, intelligent conversation about what is being read, or a chance to apply what is learned in the real world. If a child absolutely must be given a tangible reward for reading, let it be a book, one more interesting than the one she has just finished.

Meera learned to write much as she learned to read. Abstract or critical writing was not perceived as a real need. What she required was to be able to write birthday and holiday messages inside artfully constructed cards, love notes to teachers and friends, thank you communiqués for presents, and letters to grandparents. These became longer and longer as time went on, and required little prompting from us, only an occasional corrected spelling or lesson in using the apostrophe. With our encouragement, she has written to penpals on several occasions, though response has been at best spotty.

Ali's requirements were quite different, but she was able to meet them for the most part as a result of her unusually fluent reading skills. Computer word processing practice became an essential early on, as her handwriting shared the chicken-scratch quality of her father's and, as Ali puts it, "My handwriting is much too slow for my headwriting." We have intermittently required some handwriting practice at the kitchen table, using various techniques and models, but it is hard for us to take it very seriously, given the handwriting of most physicians or corporate chief executive officers, or our own. Ali, however, is committed, as she wants to be better able to take notes.

After Ali turned seven, we both read in the newspaper about a course in ecosystems being offered at the local college. I told her it was too early to be considering college course offerings, as she didn't even know how to write a research paper. I should have expected what was next. "Show me," she said with quiet insistence in her voice.

"Perhaps we should start with an essay," I suggested, "maybe like something you'd read in the newspaper." I then explained in an offhanded manner the principles of topic sentences and summations. She asked what she should write about. "The life of Schubert," I said. As she nodded excitedly, I inwardly giggled, imagining what might have happened had my first grade teacher suggested such a topic. "Alright," I said, "sit down and write me an essay, with no more than three paragraphs and nine sentences, on the life of Schubert."

Within half an hour, the computer printer spat out the following:

THE LIFE OF FRANZ PETER SCHUBERT
by Aliyah Meena Shanti

The life of Schubert was a hard one. Even though he was talented and had many friends, his talents were never recognized. So he was very poor.

In Schubert's time Beethoven was considered the best composer. Even now he is said to be one of the greatest classical composers that ever lived. Even though Schubert's favorite composer was Beethoven, and they both lived in Vienna, they only met the last year of their lives.

Today, most people would say Schubert's best compositions are his songs. Schubert's string quartets, sonatas, and his last symphonies are also very good. Schubert's life was very short, but his music made it look like he lived to be a hundred.

Ali brought me her essay, and it was clear there was little to teach per se, though much could be learned about the techniques of editing. Somewhat of a perfectionist, Ali was loathe to change a single word unless she could first be convinced such changes could better accomplish her expressive purposes. I made a pact with her which till now has stood the test of time. I said she could bring her work to me to edit whenever she wanted, and without charge. I explained that editing entailed providing a series of alternative choices. Whether to accept any of the choices would be totally up to her. I would also correct her spelling, grammar, and syntax, but only if she asks. So far, we have had nothing but an excellent relationship regarding her written work, and there have been many research papers and essays since then.

I am a professional editor. I taught critical writing at the college level for a number of years, worked with professional people with 'writer's block,' and have evaluated literally thousands of college entrance writing samples and, as former publisher, hundreds of would-be books. Most of the writing problems I have observed in my experience were created in school by mindless attention to mechanics at the expense of expression, and I have been well employed to undo the damage. Good writing should mimic speech. Both children and adults can get themselves so worked up about correct mechanics that they forget they have their own voice, the opportunity to choose their own manner of expression.

The other major cause of poor writing is imprecise and unclear *thinking*. When the thought to be expressed is unclear, one form of written expression is as good as any other. Unfortunately, schoolteachers spend precious little time with any individual child to help her develop a point of view or to encourage critical thinking generally. To write well requires an interior dialog, both with the subject matter and with oneself, that can only be modeled if but imperfectly in reasoned dialog between two thinking beings. Just as there is no reason to learn to read unless there is information or experience one seeks in the world of print, there is no use in writing, and no good reason to pay attention to the technics of writing, unless one truly has something worth committing to paper.

But to return to my main subject, reading is a tool, albeit one that is both utilitarian and pleasurable. There are artists, architects, musicians, mechanics, scientists, and policy analysts all of whom use reading to access content necessary to their employment. No one makes a living by reading itself. If there is a single lesson we have grasped through our children's reading journey, it is that the printed word is no more than a door to the many houses of wisdom. Without an animated sense of what might be found in those houses, learning to read is no more interesting, and considerably more tiresome, than other childhood chores like taking out the garbage. Support your kids in their passion for learning and give them the freedom to exercise it, and reading will take care of itself.

Alfie Kohn, *Punished by Rewards: The Trouble with Gold Stars, Incentive Plans, A's, Praise, and Other Bribes*. New York, NY: Houghton Mifflin Co., 1993. See also his excellent *No Contest: The Case Against Competition*. New York, NY: Houghton Mifflin Co., 1992.

Moore, Raymond S. and Dorothy N. et al. *School Can Wait*. Provo, UT: Brigham Young University Press, 1979. An analysis of some 7,000 early childhood education-related studies and the scientific literature, undertaken by the Hewitt Research Foundation with the aid of a substantial federal grant. One of the principal investigators was Dr. Pascal D. Forgione, currently U.S. Commissioner of Education Statistics, U.S. Department of Education. The analysis found that ever-younger out-of-home care and schooling undermine early socialization and development of values, sense of self-worth, and social competence. Evidence supports the need for later school entrance, rarely before age eight, as a wide range of ordinary life experiences in a supportive environment appears fundamental for optimal cognitive readiness. Programs designed to increase children's IQ or special early training programs have little ultimate effects on learning. The social-emotional environment plays a much greater role: "Most intensive efforts to develop academic skills in the preschool years may be dangerous and shortsighted, correlating with frustration, anxiety, and apathy in later school years." The research does suggest, however, that early childhood is the best time for preventing the effects of environmental deprivation. Studies found reading difficulties arising simply from pressured use of immature perceptual processes are often called "disabilities." Yet such difficulties may decrease or disappear completely when perceptual abilities improve, usually after the third grade. "Experiences extending and deepening understanding of the natural and social world, leaving room for creativity, exploration, and expression, are necessary for successful reading."

Mahabharata, retold by William Buck. Berkeley and Los Angeles, CA: University of California Press, 1973.

Ramayana, retold by William Buck. Berkeley and Los Angeles, CA: University of California Press, 1976. There are more than a few translations of both Indian epics available, but none will provide the kind of pleasure afforded by the William Buck retellings. Accept no substitutes!

Tolstoy, Leo, *Tolstoy on Education*, selected and edited by Alan Pinch and Michael Armstrong, translated by Alan Pinch. Rutherford, Madison, and Teaneck, NJ: Fairleigh Dickinson University Press, 1982. Tolstoy's pedagogical experiments of 1861-1862 led to his radical conclusion that "the sole method of education is experience," and that the success of any educational technique ultimately depends upon its responsiveness to an individual child's particular needs: "The only rule is the avoidance of rules."

Tolstoy's narrative account of his efforts to teach writing to peasant children remains the finest work of its kind. (Parenthetically, given other available options, why would anyone teach writing using techniques developed by someone who has never written anything more enduring than a teachers' manual?)

Cinnamon Bear

Then all must love the human form,
In heathen, turk or jew;
Where Mercy, Love & Pity dwell,
There God is dwelling too.

William Blake, "The Divine Image"
from *Songs of Innocence*

One of her fellow campers asked five-and-a-half-year-old Ali at her nature camp how she felt about having a Black sister. Ali looked at her confused for a moment, and then replied thoughtfully, "Well, I guess it's like black bears. Most black bears aren't black. They may be black, but also dark brown, light brown, and cinnamon colored. My sister is like a cinnamon bear."

———◦•◦———

Each year since 1993, I have played the veena at the annual Northwest Sri Thyagarajah Music Festival, held at the end of March. Living in South India, Thyagarajah (1767-1847) was kind of a combination Beethoven and religious ascetic and represents the pinnacle of South Indian musical achievement.

The Festival rotates locations throughout Oregon and Washington. It brings together families of South Indian extraction for a day of music,

165

prayer, food, and socializing. The day begins with a traditional worship, followed by a joint singing and playing by all able musicians of Thyagarajah's magnum opus, the *Pancharatna* or "Five Jewels." Then, starting with the children, each musician or musical group, regardless of their level of skill, offers 10-15 minutes of music continuing throughout the day. The Festival may climax with a professional concert.

Each year, much is made of my appearance, as I perform in traditional dress. Even in the South Indian community, veena players, at whatever level of attainment, are rare. Our family long had a running joke that I was the best veena player in Washington State, as well as the worst. And, for at least three years, this was actually true, as far as we could ascertain.

Meera seemed both stunned and pleased the first time she attended the event, at age four. While we belong to a loose-knit support group of parents with children adopted from India, nowhere had she imagined encountering so many children, so many people, with skin color and facial features like her own. And she was surprised to hear people, even some children, perform music like her dad's. She wasn't pleased by the spicy South Indian vegetarian cuisine.

I began seriously teaching Carnatic (the name for South Indian classical) music to Ali when she was six, the traditional age to begin learning it in India. I was not surprised that she took to it enthusiastically, fascinated as much by its intellectual complexity as by its more narrowly musical values. Carnatic music has 72 major scales (or ragas) and up to 92,000 or so minor ones, with names assigned to several thousand of them. Ali performed that year, after which I presented her with an amulet, a small, dark blue lapiz lazuli heart, a stone that is said to enhance inner hearing and inner vision. She still wears the heart around her neck whenever she performs.

At age four, Meera joined in as a singer. Now we are a musical group, "Shantiniketan" (school of peace), named after the famous learning institution of the arts established by the Bengali Nobel Prize-winning playwright and poet Rabindrinath Tagore. My own veena teacher supplies the music, complete with transliteration of the Telegu, Kannada, or Tamil texts, the original South Indian languages in which the songs, which are based on religious themes, are written. We provide our own musical arrangements for veena, violin, and

Meera, age six, prior to first performance at the Sri Thyagarajah Music Festival

voice. It has done my heart proud to have several mothers approach me to ask if I can teach their children to sing, particularly noting the purity of Ali's and Meera's diction. And now Meera, having been presented with her own amulet — an amber heart said to intensify joy and clarity — is taking her first veena lessons from me.

I don't believe there is anything more critical to teach in America, nor any subject more fraught with pitfalls, than the subject of race. And there's no question in my mind that public schools have made a hash of it up to now.

It would be easier if we knew what we were talking about. If race were purely a genetic category, then skin color would be no more important than, say, the shape of one's earlobe or the length of the second digit on the fingers of the left hand. There is more than a hint of seriousness in my jest that when people or even governments want to know about race, what they are really interested in is how closely related by blood you are to the Queen of England, the Emperor of China, or the late Haile Selassie of Ethiopia, or 'none of the above,' in which case you are to be considered either 'native' or 'aboriginal.' But skin color is no marker even for this determination. My own ancestors, as Eastern European Jews, were likely descended from North African Semites, interbred with Mongolians from the Asian steppes — I have the high cheekbones to prove it. I am for some reason classified as Caucasian. Meera, born in India, with skin of darker hue, is related by descent to the same Aryan people who spread out over Western Europe, as recent genetic research has confirmed. I would more likely be related to the Emperor of China and to Haile Selassie; she to the Queen of England. Many African-Americans, partially descended from white slaveholders or, more often than is commonly assumed, free interracial marriages, are certainly far more 'Caucasian,' more closely related to the Queen, than I could ever consider myself to be. Ali, my biological Mongol-Semitic daughter, is considered 'white'; Meera, my adopted Aryan daughter, is a 'cinnamon bear.' Of course, virtually all anthropologists now agree that if we go back far enough, we are *all* Africans.

Skin color or eye slant, at least in their more acute manifestations, are to a greater or lesser extent markers for three overlapping circles of experiences: personal, social-historical, and cultural. Ali's or my own experience of the Sri Thyagarajah Music Festival — the way we are viewed and the way we are treated — is profoundly mediated by our skin color. The fact that we have more ongoing ties to India and Indian culture than some of the third generation Indian families present does nothing to mitigate that pleased surprise at our performance, the knowing-nod recognition equivalent of "yes, it's true, Virginia, white men *can* jump." When Meera — my darker-skinned, hotdog-munching, jazz-playing, television-loving gymnast — is ready to perform Carnatic music on her own, the response will likely be quite different.

Light-skinned English-speaking Americans of European descent outside of major cities or the South rarely experience their own skin color unless they travel to what, to them, are considered exotic places or are engaged in similarly exotic activities. Where there is racial homogeneity, there can be no sense of color-based 'otherness.' The problem is that in an increasingly 'colorful' nation and world, we 'pinky grays' live in a world of denial. Our corporate culture and our media reinforce this denial. Success is achieved by people of other races to the degree that they have learned to 'pass for white.' The rare African-American Fortune 500 business executive or the even-rarer Vietnamese-American television news anchor is projected as white in every sense but skin pigmentation or facial structure.

Race in America, or anywhere else for that matter, is obviously much more than skin pigmentation or the individual personal experience that arises from it. Dark skin carries different connotations in Kenya and in South Africa, in India or Brazil, in Haiti or in Sweden. In America, it carries with it a social-historical context of violence and oppression, of opportunities denied, of promises unfulfilled. Surely we have all heard the well-meaning politician speak of, or seen the social studies textbook refer to, America as a nation of immigrants. Besides the reality that Native Americans could not be considered immigrants in anything but the most metahistorical sense, African-Americans were most assuredly *not* immigrants. Farmers and hunters, carpenters and fishermen, herbal medicine practitioners and religious leaders, weavers and storytellers, husbands and fathers, mothers and wives, with their own languages and cultures stretching back thousands of years, all were manacled neck and foot in iron clamps and chains, lashed and prodded and dragged onto ships like so many cattle. In contrast to the politicians' paean to our ancestors as hardworking families, African-Americans who survived the voyage were denied families for up to ten generations, with children yanked away from their parents for the purpose of realizing profits. When social commentators decry problems endemic to single female-headed Black families, it is conveniently forgotten that the single-parent African-American household was the historical norm created and enforced by white America. In perhaps the cruelest cut of all, African-Americans were denied ancestors. African-American history was, until scholars in this century began to help the community reclaim it, a history denied, a tale of history's obliteration.

Much the same can be said of the fate of Native Americans. What school history text sets forth the reality that the reduction in the Native population of North America from the days of Columbus to the onset of the American Revolution was the equivalent of reducing the U.S. population of today to that of Cleveland? Squanto and Pocahontas make their contribution to European settlement, but little is written of the literally dozens of attempts of the Tribes over two centuries to preserve millennia-old cultures by seeking a peaceful coexistence with their new neighbors, of their successful development of herbal medicine or of the incorporation of public health measures into tribal custom, or of details of the Iroquois' flourishing experiments in representative democracy well before the establishment of the U.S. Constitution.

When children in school open up their American history textbooks today, they may be fortunate enough to find Crispus Attucks, Frederick Douglass, Booker T. Washington, Martin Luther King, and Rosa Parks, but they are not likely to find the story of the African-American people or to learn of the value of their labors in building the nation. Even the portrayals are likely to be off-base: Rosa Parks is depicted as a poor, tired seamstress with aching feet, rather than as a seasoned, educated community organizer and activist who had attended training and strategizing sessions to search for ways to confront racial prejudice. Children will be taught the legend of George Washington chopping down the cherry tree, but will they also learn the more likely tale that the first President once traded a human being for a pig? To be fair, Washington freed his slaves in his will (though he couldn't convince Martha to do likewise). The same cannot be said of his good friend Thomas Jefferson, the author of the Declaration of Independence, who proclaimed to the entire world that "all men are created equal," but who even 50 years after committing to paper these stirring words, still had not freed his. Columbus and the gold lust of the conquistadors occupy some of the early chapters of history texts, but Hispanics — descendants of the *original* European settlers — somehow only appear much later if at all, as contemporary and inglorious additions to the melting pot.

The purpose of providing such an alternative account of our history is not to teach our children to become fixated on the sordid aspects of the past, nor to delight in the flotsam and jetsam thrown up by centuries. Rather it is tell the truth — the whole truth — about our collective pasts so that we can best build our futures. History is not just the story of oppression and victimization; it is also a vital parable of individuals, communities, and institutions being continually reborn. Just as the U.S. experiment in representative democracy comes at the end of a long period of autocratic despotism, so our future holds out the promise of moving beyond our nation's spotted racial past.

------- ◆•◆•◆ -------

> Amazing Grace! How sweet the sound
> That saved a wretch like me,
> I once was lost but now am found,
> Was blind but now I see.

Millions of American churchgoers sing this hymn regularly, but are not aware of its origins. The words to "Amazing Grace" belong to one Captain John Newton (1725-1807), a white slaveship captain. After spending half his life as a profligate seaman — during which time he actually spent a little over a year enslaved to an African woman on a Caribbean island — and then as a slave trader, Newton experienced a religious conversion, became a Christian minister, and one of England's leading abolitionists.

We have shared his story, and others like it, with Ali and Meera, but not from any "bottled" study of history. We have resisted the lure of history curricula, choosing instead to provide historical context as questions arise in the study of music, art, theater, nature, physical sciences, astronomy, religion, and society. I'm confident that our children will fill in the gaps later, and Ali has already started to do so. Rather, Ellen and I work to assure they learn that history is an account of values — moral, social, and aesthetic — in action.

Like the story of Captain Newton, history is a retelling of individuals' experiences in making choices, choices that our children — all children — will be called on to make sometime in their own lives, choices which we as parents and teachers may influence but over which ultimately we will not exercise any control. The understandings and actions of our children are but the history of generations to come.

It is easy for children to learn and retain stories like that of Captain Newton and to turn their historical favorites into heroes and saints. We, the schools, and other institutions should not have to do that for them. What is equally critical is helping children gain perspective on events, historical or contemporary, and on the reality of human ambiguity. Sadly missing in Captain Newton's story, and I have asked Ali to imagine it for herself, is how Newton's transformative conversion might have affected all those, of whatever race, with whom he came in contact. Added perspective can be incorporated into dramatic play or writing activities by suggesting children imagine historical vignettes from a multiplicity of viewpoints — in this case, those of Captain Newton, his family and friends, other slaveship captains, slave owners, religious leaders, and Africans brought to the Americas by Newton and still enslaved, but who learned of his metamorphosis.

At another level, history can be viewed as the dynamic story of people or even entire civilizations seeking to profit — economically, politically, or spiritually — by deliberately or unknowingly inflicting pain and suffering upon and at the expense of others, and of the attempts of others striving to enlighten or resist them. Utilizing this understanding as a lens can allow us to make history the centerpiece of a truly 'values-based' education.

There is a wonderful legend we have shared repeatedly with our kids. It is an Asian Indian folktale about Princess Sita's effort to pick her disguised husband Lord Rama out of a lineup of warriors. As an incarnation of the Preserver God Vishnu, Rama is always portrayed as having dark blue skin. Sita has no trouble picking out Rama, but not because he is blue. As he is the embodiment of goodness, of godliness, his feet never touch the ground.

We were unusually delighted when six-year-old Ali came home with a flyer from her ballet class announcing that the costumes for her class recital would be based on the theme "Children of the World." The poster depicting the costumes was pleasing as well. There were pictures of children dressed up as Swiss milk maidens, Austrian peasant boys in lederhosen, and Irish shamrock girls, among others. But there in the corner of the poster was a scantily clad harem dancer. We knew which costume all the little girls would covet, as it was the year of Walt Disney's *Aladdin* and Jasmine was the rage.

The Disney film seems harmless enough until one remembers that Jasmine, supposedly the daughter of a king from an unspecified Middle Eastern country, is dressed like a harem dancer. Of course, no Middle Eastern ruler would ever dress his own daughter this way, for a harem dancer is a concubine, a sex slave, somewhat below a prostitute. To dress up a six-year-old this way ... well, I'm sure you get the point. Imagine yourself going to a theater in another country and seeing the typical American child, or perhaps the President's daughter, depicted as a streetwalker. And, unfortunately, Disney's Jasmine is perhaps the only representation of a child (a 'woman-child'?) from an Islamic culture many American children may ever encounter. This is true despite the fact that there are an estimated five million Moslems in the United States, including some even in our own small community.

With some trepidation, and with the understanding that we might be perceived as unusually thin-skinned, we approached the head of the ballet school. The thought that Islamic members of the community, some of whom, for all she knew, might be attending the ballet school or the recital, might take offense had never crossed her mind. (And what country today has harem dancers anyway?) Of course she'd pull the costume.

And then she did us one better. If she simply pulled the costume, many parents might not notice, and the few who did would not know why. She invited us to write a letter to the parents of all the children in the class, which she would gladly distribute with a cover note. We eagerly took her up on her generous offer.

I have no idea whether any Islamic members of our community ever found out about the episode, and indeed that is well beside the point. From a learning perspective, the important element is that our children know about the incident, and it has become part of our family's collective memory. More than a year later, when a local Moslem leader offered an introductory lecture on Islam to an interfaith study group, Ali eagerly took up my invitation to attend, and to my pleased surprise she remembered why we didn't want to watch children dressed up as harem dancers.

I have not written the Walt Disney Company about Jasmine, or about *Snow White* — she's white and therefore she's good and therefore she's called Snow White and loved by seven little men, some of them old and some of them grumpy; what message does this send to our children? — or *Beauty and the Beast* — "I'm sure I can change him, if only I love him enough" — or the abominable racist stereotyping in *Lady and the Tramp* which makes me cringe every time I hear it is going to be rereleased. (Why isn't there a movie rating for racism?) I simply don't buy their products and tell people around me why. Most people in our community and, I think, in most communities want to do the right thing and be part of the solution, not the problem. But the lesson I want to get across to Ali and Meera is that it is not enough to 'be nice' and 'understanding' and stand back and wait for members of minority communities to bring their own injuries forward. We are all hurt by stereotyping and discrimination based on race, ethnicity, religion, handicap, age, gender, or sexual orientation, and I believe it is never too early to start the curriculum of combatting prejudice. And the only way I know how to do so effectively is by example.

———•◆•———

Ellen and I took the kids one late afternoon to see many of their friends ages seven to ten perform the medieval play *Everyman*, a project of a local youth theater workshop. The performance was reasonably good, and the children had worked hard, but there was one disturbing element. The players were mostly white girls, which would not be surprising in our predominantly white community, but there was one large-boned African-American boy, a head or more taller than the rest. Among the characters of God, angels, and humans and the personifications of various virtues and sins, the director had chosen this boy to play Death. Needless to say, he made quite an impression. I am certain more than a few younger children came away from the performance thinking God and the angels could only be white, and Death Black. It would take an explicit effort on the part of their parents, one I'm sure they were for the most part not prepared to make, even if they were aware of the potential harm done, to disabuse their children of this idea.

I called the workshop coordinator to voice my displeasure about the casting. The workshop coordinator had already shared this concern with the director, who happened to be a local schoolteacher. On being confronted, the director replied that, given that the boy had indeed performed the role well and had said he liked getting the part, what was the problem? Apparently, the director could not conceive of there being other than purely dramatic values to be considered, even in working with eight-year-olds. The damage was already done.

Most Americans who know anything about the African-American contralto Marian Anderson remember that she was denied permission to sing in Washington's Constitution Hall in 1939 by the Daughters of the American Revolution and that Eleanor Roosevelt resigned from the D.A.R. and arranged for Anderson to sing on the steps of the Lincoln Memorial. It is rarely mentioned that the D.A.R. soon changed its policy so that by 1943, she became a regular at Constitution Hall. But it is virtually entirely forgotten that 16 years were to elapse before Anderson — arguably the greatest American-born female singer of her generation — was to be invited to sing her one and only role at the Metropolitan Opera, in a 1955 production of Verdi's *Un Ballo in Maschera*. And what was that role, for which she was very grateful, though the part, according to Anderson herself, didn't even fit her voice? That of a witch.

Some public schools now make a special effort to teach about leaders and famous individuals from minority communities for the purpose of providing new role models for youth. This is generally speaking a good idea, although the truth is in the execution. Educational publishers, eyeing a new market, have rushed into the effort, sometimes with equivocal results. An account of the climax of the Marian Anderson story, written for elementary school children and used by teachers in the public schools, reads as follows:

"Marian was disappointed that she was not allowed to sing in Constitution Hall because she was Black. But that didn't stop her." Aside from the fact that major white figures in the story are never called by their first names — Eleanor Roosevelt is always "Mrs. Roosevelt," Sol Hurok (Anderson's manager) "Mr. Hurok" — the book perpetuates the myth that race, in this case, 'Blackness,' is a disability which Anderson needed to overcome. But race is not a handicap. It was ignorant and malicious white racism, not her skin color, which prevented Anderson from singing, and it is racism — a term not to be found in the overwhelming majority of school texts — that is a handicap over which we must prevail.

After she read books by the biologist E. O. Wilson and the paleontologist Stephen Jay Gould, Ali and I had some elementary conversations regarding sociobiology. "Gould says Wilson's sociobiology is not really science, because it can be used to prove anything. If animals compete and kill each other, it's because it is in their genes. If they cooperate and collaborate, it's because it is in their genes." "Well, it could be because of their environment," said Ali. "Yes," I agreed, "but the behaviors persist over generations even when the environment changes." The next day, Ali told me she had been thinking about the conversation and posed the case of the person who is mean to everyone, which certainly shouldn't help him reproduce. "Not heredity or environment," she suggested. "Perhaps," I replied, "but let's look at that a little deeper. Meanness could be an inherited mental disorder, but that would likely be an evolutionary dead end. Or meanness could be a cultural adaptation for dealing with scarcity, as some anthropologists have proposed. Or conceivably there are certain potential mates attracted to meanness. Or for a solitary adult male lion (who really isn't mean, just a lion), solo hunting and territoriality could be a more effective way of ensuring survival than cooperative behavior, so maybe it is in his genes." "So is there more than just heredity or environment?" Ali looked at me quizzically. "Perhaps," I said. "Try free will."

For when our souls have learn'd that heat to bear,
The cloud will vanish; we shall hear his voice,
Saying: 'Come out from the grove, my love & care,
And round my golden tent like lambs rejoice.'

William Blake, "The Little Black Boy"
from *Songs of Innocence*

In this country, only two groups of people are required to perform community service: convicted criminals and high school students.

The intent in both cases is reasonable enough. In the case of the criminal, community service is an alternative to incarceration. It gets him (it is usually a 'he') out into the community, giving back for the damage he has caused. The convict may also become more aware of community resources and needs, and perhaps become acquainted with positive role models.

That schools feel it is their obligation to get their kids out into the community is a telling commentary on how really isolating the contemporary experience of youth has become. Through service activities, children get out into the 'real world,' learn more about their community, work with adults outside of their own families, and may experience a sense of being valued rather than simply 'educated.'

On balance, requiring convicts and children to perform community service is probably a good thing, and for the most obvious of reasons: it gets them away from prisons and schools! The message sent to children, however, is far from clear. The convict knows he is paying his debt to society in a way that results in far less severe consequences to himself than incarceration would have. He may believe he has gotten off light, and the community knows it has saved money that would have been expended for his incarceration. Children, however, are far less likely to feel or even understand themselves as debtors. If they do, they may note that no similar obligation exists for their schoolteachers, who may or may not be active volunteer contributors to their communities and who would be justly protected from such a requirement by their union. And as it is for convicts, the students' community service sentence is circumscribed. It is counted in hours logged rather than in value of contribution or accomplishment. There is no assumption, that the service continues once the sentence is served or the semester is over — and there is certainly no incentive for this to happen. Indeed, the fact of there having been a requirement may work as a disincentive. This is one of the reasons why when students, or convicts, continue to serve beyond the period of their conscription, such a rare occurrence may be celebrated in the local newspaper.

Collectively, our children are not stupid, and they are not unaware. They know they are required to perform community service at the same time that they are being issued curfews, banned from shopping malls, forced to wear school uniforms, given citations for riding skateboards or sitting on the sidewalk, subjected to random drug tests, and, increasingly, tried, sentenced, and incarcerated as adults for criminal acts committed at ages as young as 11. Even when the motivation for the community service requirement is not mean-spirited, students understand the larger context in which it is embedded. Working in the community should enhance a child's sense of self-worth and interconnectedness; requiring her to do so, within this context, may do just the opposite.

This conscription of children has transpired at a moment when adult volunteerism is at historic lows. There are many reasons for this, too numerous to allow for elaboration here. But two trends in this regard stand out which suggest why children have recently become targets of community service requirements. Firstly, the increasing professionalization of social services, coupled with concerns about liability, has made intrinsically interesting volunteer opportunities much less common. For many agencies, unpaid labor has been relegated to envelope stuffing and the like, which has value, of course, but is not likely to remain engrossing for very long. Professionalization may or may not have had positive effects on the users of the services, but it has had a decidedly negative effect on adult volunteers, who are less likely to continue their work over the longer term. Secondly, the growing number of single-parent or two-working-parent families has decreased availability of time for volunteerism.

Ellen and I believe strongly that children, like everyone else, should contribute to their community, but conscription or the laying on of external expectations is not the way to go about it. Just as younger children first come to understand their immediate family and then slowly build up a picture of the larger social world, our children are directed to consider the needs of our community and, later, of the world, as they would those of an extended family. The chief danger inherent in the fuss now being made about school community service requirements, or even in the highlighting of service projects by religious or community organizations, lies in according volunteer and community work an aura of specialness, something to be considered beyond ordinary expectation and, hence, optional.

In the course of our children's learning, we have been guided by three principles to inform their involvement in the community:

- We look for activities in which our children are already interested or with which they can already make a real contribution, given the opportunity. We particularly seek out involvement which can give them their own sense of personal satisfaction, independent of its potential value to the community around them.

- We seek activities that can be incorporated as part of their regular schedule, whether weekly, monthly, or yearly. An activity worth doing once should be worth repeating. This isn't to say that all opportunities pan out as meriting repetition or that the kids desire to do them again, but at least we believed they had potential. We also want our children to see the fruits of their labor, which is only likely to happen through repeated involvement. The point is to inculcate in our children a sense that giving back to our community is what we do, as a matter of course, and within the normal flow of daily living.

- We try to act as role models in our own involvements. This is more complicated than it sounds. Aware kids have a sixth sense about them: they can sniff out and generally recoil from adults trying to be good for their benefit. We do not take on activities ourselves simply because we want our kids to see us performing them, or even because there is a community need; there are always more needs than we could possibly have time, energy, or other resources for. To use the Quaker terminology, we seek to heed the leadings of the spirit, to find the special niche where we may find our own well-being and that of our community conjoined. Our modeling comes in by observing the very same principles for community involvement we hope our children will follow in their own lives. With our assistance, Ali and Meera have found ways to use their music for the community's benefit. They have both played regularly at nursing homes and senior centers in the area. When our next-door neighbor Evelyn takes Meera along to visit a friend at one of the senior centers, more often than not an impromptu concert ensues. Since we don't celebrate a traditional Christmas, Ellen last year took Ali to the local hospital on Christmas Day to play carols at the bedsides of sick children.

Ali had actually taught herself the carols a week earlier. A sign had been put up at the local supermarket recruiting church choirs to sing at its entrance to raise funds for the Salvation Army. Following a suggestion from me, and with support from Ellen, Ali explained to the manager that Quakers don't have choirs (and for that matter, don't often sing Christmas carols), and so she got to play her violin, after which she took over $135 in contributions to the Salvation Army headquarters. Ali has since made a sign which she places in her violin case when playing at the local farmers' market, indicating that she is contributing 10% of her earnings to her four favorite non-profits: Wolf Haven International; Bread and Roses, the local soup kitchen; Capital Area Youth Symphony for scholarships for kids who can't afford to participate otherwise; and Olympic Wildlife Rescue, which rehabilitates injured wildlife and releases them back into the wild. Ali is now in her fourth year of work at Wolf Haven and has just begun to help with tours as well as to make presentations in area classrooms.

Ali and Meera are both familiar with the fact that there are members of our community who are homeless, and know several of them. On the first Monday of every month, the two girls and I serve dinner at the soup kitchen for homeless people. Meera insists on skipping her gymnastics class for the chance to put out pitchers of milk at each table. I make a point of us not only serving meals, but actually eating at the shelter. There is no better way to get acquainted with one's poorer neighbors than to break bread with them.

For several years, I served as a board member of the county's Associated Ministries, which brings together representatives of various faith communities to enter into adialog as well as to coordinate services for those less fortunate. To provide opportunities for congregations to share music from their various faith traditions and to make music together, as well as for fundraising, I help organize an annual Associated Ministries Festival of Music (AMFM), which takes place each spring. Both Ali and Meera participate — sometimes performing Carnatic music together or playing their respective instruments or singing in the combined choir — and enjoy the opportunity to make music with adults and to see friends from across the community. Each spring, we participate in the local CROP Walk, which is organized nationally by Church World Service to raise funds to combat hunger worldwide.

The community service activities our kids have participated in as young children fit well within their developing understandings of their physical selves and the physical world. Food, music, housing, illness, and animals are all subjects which readily engage them. As Ali has grown older, new interests related to issues of justice and fairness have also begun to exert themselves. After attending an Associated Ministries-sponsored rally on the subject, Ali volunteered to play her violin to raise funds to help rebuild burned African-American churches. Discussions and newspaper articles have occasionally provoked letter writing and petition circulating. Concerns expressed within our Quaker meeting regarding land use, logging, firearms, military spending, landmines, bigotry, and intolerance have slowly inched their way onto her radar screen.

There is no question that the size of our town contributes to the success of our efforts to encourage our children's community involvement. It is large enough that the opportunities afforded for service are rich and varied and small enough that people recognize Ali and Meera by name and the kids can actually see the fruits of their labors. Still, I am convinced that the opportunities are there regardless of where one lives. Ellen and I have shared with our children an experience we had in India before they were born. We were visiting a village in eastern India where the annual per capita income was under $100. Yet, in addition to the profusion of national, state, and religious holidays, the village held a small celebration every Thursday. Women cooked food and served it out on the street for the entire village, in what could only be described as a community-wide block party. They asked whether we had such a weekly celebration in the United States. When we explained that we didn't, their response was "Oh, you must be very poor."

To be effective over the long-term, giving must come I am persuaded, from an inner sense of abundance. Coercion comes from a feeling of scarcity. To the extent we can cultivate this sense of abundance and resourcefulness in our children, their contributions will serve to enrich not only their community and the world, but themselves as well.

———————

The majority of homeschooling families in our community are fundamentalist Christians. We're not, and our homeschooling network welcomes members regardless of religious creed. We have found areas where we can collaborate and cooperate with those with fundamentalist beliefs — on the school district's homeschool computer center, writing contests, and homeschool fairs.

It would be quite incorrect, however, to infer that our religious persuasion does not inform our approach to homeschooling. Ellen and I are both convinced Friends (Quakers) and play active roles in the local Friends community. Central to Quaker faith and practice is the testimony that there is that of God in every person which can be recognized and celebrated regardless of its social and cultural manifestations. Some Friends find special inspiration in the life and teaching of Jesus; others, including probably a majority in our Meeting community, take a more universalist approach. We all, however, share a fundamental belief that every individual can have access to the Divine which regularly reveals itself in all places and ages, that dignity and value must be accorded to every human being as a matter of birthright, and that a significant role of community is to support individuals in their spiritual search. I have also come to believe, with most Friends, that all individuals (including children, of course) are unique, created to play their own singular roles within the Divine cosmos which we are placed on earth to discover through our own personal experience.

Each of our kids has regularly attended our Meeting (Friends traditionally do not have churches) from an early age, but we subscribe to the view that people should only make decisions regarding their religious convictions as informed adults, and only after exposure to a wide array of belief systems and practices. We have drawn on resources in the community to ensure both Ali and Meera feel comfortable in a variety of religious environments. Members of our family are Jewish, our adoptive family Hindu, our next-door neighbors Catholic and Unitarian, the music teacher Episcopalian, good friends Baha'i, and we have celebrated and worshipped in as many religious settings. We have found many opportunities to explain various theologies to Ali in a broad array of contexts: music, art, the history of science, architecture, drama, and politics. Perhaps more importantly, we have had followers of various creeds explain their own beliefs to our kids, rather than relying solely on ourselves to do so. For we have learned that religious differences are not based exclusively on the existence of disparate tenets and doctrines, but also on the intensity with which they are believed and practiced. To learn the lessons of tolerance, I have come to the view that one must experience other people's beliefs in their fullness (and mutual contradiction) rather than through a bland and disinterested neutrality.

For our family, being Quakers has at least one significant drawback. Historically, Friends have an anti-music tradition, music having been considered frivolous and, being prepared in advance, not representing an authentic and spontaneous outpouring of the Divine spirit. Quaker music is truly an oxymoron. An 'unprogrammed' Friends meeting consists of people silently sitting in a circle, listening for whatever messages come forth in the course of quiet, worshipful waiting. We have turned this to our advantage by attending worship services and becoming familiar with religious musical traditions throughout our community. Ali was especially intrigued by the contrast between our silent meeting and the gospel music at our local, predominantly African-American Baptist Church. "They couldn't fit another sound in the building if they tried," was how she described it. Both of us learned 'shape note singing,' a nineteenth century four-voice musical form most commonly used in rural Baptist churches in the southern U.S., in which a specially designed hymnal, "The Sacred Harp," indicates relative pitches by means of notes of various shapes: circles, squares, diamonds, and triangles.

Ellen and I were not brought to the Religious Society of Friends by any singular process of religious conversion. We simply found that our way of looking at the world conformed to Quaker understandings. For me, the hardest lesson in Friends' discipline has been learning to listen — to inner voices and leanings and to those of others, of whatever race, creed, or nationality — and to discern those pieces of the truth which 'speak to our condition' and can inform our being and our work in the world. I trust that my own ongoing lesson in discernment can only redound to our children's benefit and is one which I hope they will themselves be equipped to take into the world, wherever their journey may carry them.

Gandhi, Mohandas, *My Religion*. Ahmedabad, India: Navajivan Trust, 1948.

Harding, Vincent, *There is a River: The Black Struggle for Freedom in America*. New York, NY: Harcourt Brace Jovanovich, 1981.

Kohl, Herbert, *Should We Burn Babar? Essays on Children's Literature and the Power of Stories*. New York, NY: The New Press, 1995.

Llewellyn, Grace (editor), *Freedom Challenge: African American Homeschoolers*. Eugene, OR: Lowry House, 1996. Llewellyn, the author of the justly acclaimed and newly republished *The Teenage Liberation Handbook: How to Quit School and Get a Real Life and Education* (Eugene, OR: Lowry House, 1998) also organizes a "Not Back to School Camp" in the summer, in northern Oregon. She also publishes an excellent newsletter and catalog. Write: Genius Tribe, PO Box 1014, Eugene, OR 97440.

Loewen, James W., *Lies My Teacher Told Me: Everything Your American History Textbook Got Wrong*. New York, NY: The New Press, 1995. A dogged, sometimes abrasive critique of 12 contemporary high school history textbooks, uncovering not only mistakes, omissions, and deliberate falsifications, but also providing a stinging analysis of why students graduate from high school historically illiterate and uninterested. Some readers will be upset, perhaps even enraged, by what they learn about school textbooks; others by the sheer relentlessness of Loewen's diatribes against them. So prepare to be challenged: Columbus Day and Thanksgiving will never look the same again! For best effect, this book should be read after or alongside (while certainly being no substitute for) Howard Zinn's masterful *A People's History of the United States, 1492 to the Present*. New York, NY: HarperPerennial, 1995.

Woolman, John, *The Journal and Major Essays of John Woolman*, edited by Phillips P. Moulton. Richmond, IN: Friends United Press, 1989. There are plenty of books about American Quakers: some of them are good, some had better been left unpublished. Woolman's *Journal*, the story of his eighteenth century spiritual journey and his work to abolish slavery and social injustice, set against the background of colonial America, is the *real* stuff: "I ... was early convinced in my mind that true religion consisted in an inward life, wherein the heart doth reverence God the Creator and learns to exercise true justice and goodness, not only toward all men but also toward the brute creatures; that as the mind was moved on an inward principle to love God as an invisible, incomprehensible being, on the same principle it was moved to love him in all his manifestations in the visible world; that as by his breath the flame of life was kindled in all animal and sensitive creatures, to say we love God as unseen and at the same time exercise cruelty toward the least creature moving by his life, or by life derived from him, was a contradiction in itself ...

There is a principle which is pure, placed in the human mind, which in different places and ages hath had different names; it is, however, pure, and proceeds from God. It is deep, and inward, confined to no forms of religion, nor excluded from any, where the heart stands in perfect sincerity. In whomsoever this takes root and grows, of what nation soever, they become brethren."

Bric-A-Brac

A Robin Red breast in a Cage
Puts all Heaven in a Rage ...
A Skylark wounded in the wing,
A Cherubim does cease to sing.

William Blake, "Auguries of Innocence"

I remember my first long look at my older daughter, only minutes after her birth. Not as small as I would have imagined (after all, she was born 11 pounds, two ounces), but self-contained, eyes peering out at a world new-created just for her, hands the size of quarters, a fuzz of dark brown hair, ears too big, cheeks as if stuffed with acorns, toes curled, but altogether more than the sum of her parts. A whole, a breathing, feeling, thinking (?) being, a bit of star-stuff gathered and newly arrived, lying next to me and I an admixture of wonder, astonishment, contentment, and more than a touch of fear, as I now began to shoulder, or to imagine shouldering, the responsibility of ancestors and of generations to come. She was beginning a new stage of life, and so was I.

We learned together. My children taught me what I needed to know about them, what their requirements were and, often enough, how to meet them. I learned to listen and to do so in new ways, vigilantly and with joy observing signs and signals and returning them with my own. Even if I had never read a book or article about parenting or children, I discovered if I was receptive to their cues and allowed what I surmise to be nature to take over, I'd do just fine. They taught me how to be a father, and they were (and are) gifted teachers.

I experienced great joy, as well as more than a little exasperation, as my daughters learned to eat and we — Ellen and I — learned to feed them. It is sometimes difficult to figure out where one ends and the other begins, and I expect we share this experience with many if not most parents. The process commenced with figuring out breastfeeding schedules and finding support when needed, and moved on to preparing bottles and formula, plotting how to cajole the kids to take their first solid food, helping them learn hand-to-mouth skills and then spoon dexterity, discovering ways to keep food out of hair (the kids' and our own) and hair out of food, and plates and bowls on the table. Later came the development of fork-and-knife skills (how does one handle those pesky peas?), basic table etiquette, and, finally, cross-cultural practices, such as learning how to use chopsticks, or advanced skills such as eating formally presented stuffed artichokes at fancy dinner parties. (We haven't gotten that far yet!) It all happens in such a seemingly natural flow that it is easy to forget how much mastery of each of these skills is dependent, firstly, upon the child's physical development, and, secondly, upon the learning which is allowed or encouraged to take place. The child of two will likely have trouble with the knife and fork even if she has witnessed their use repeatedly and been urged to try them out. But it was brought to our consciousness how important providing encouragement, assistance, and experience at the right moment is when we brought ten-month-old Meera home from the orphanage in Bombay. We quickly discovered she had no idea how to use her hands to get food from the table to her mouth. Apparently, up until that time she had never been allowed to feed herself, and, in fact, never even been permitted to put her hands anywhere near her face. She had surely never seen adults or even other children eat using their own appendages. Watching her sister wolf down a couple of chocolate chip cookies and having one placed in her hand was all that was required, and away she went, like many toddlers, trying out everything within her reach.

Of course there is more to eating than tool use and technique. There's food! I've encountered speculation that placed in an environment with healthful, nutritious foods all around and left to her own devices, a child would learn to eat a balanced diet totally on her own, without any adult assistance. While there are a few studies available suggesting this might be the case, experiments related to this hypothesis could never be fully conducted, for a child is *never* left completely to her own devices. I've heard tell of a thirteenth-century Hungarian monarch who believed that if children were kept in complete isolation from birth, they'd grow up speaking perfect Biblical Hebrew. Needless to say, none survived long enough for him to find out! What a child decides to eat, or at least decides to try, is socially and culturally mediated. This is a fancy way of saying that she eats what she's given when she's hungry, is likely to want to try what adults or siblings or friends are eating, and will develop new tastes — likes or dislikes — based on her exposure and experience. There will be physical limitations. The small-toothed toddler, like her gum-toothed grandfather, will have trouble with the artichoke leaves, and after trying them once, is likely to move on to less laborious, and perhaps more rewarding, fare. But most American children, unlike those in the highlands of Peru, will not eat grubs, mosquito eggs, or moth larvae, not because they aren't tasty (prepared well, I'm told they can be delicious), but because in the context of their culture and family they are never encouraged to try them. When American parents see their toddlers picking up bugs and putting them in their mouths, their first thought is not likely to be a sanguine "Oh, look, just like a Peruvian highlander!"

One of our favorite family adventures when Ali was a toddler was to visit the Monterey Bay Aquarium. Following our visit, we would have lunch at a nearby, reasonably priced 'all you can eat' sushi bar on Cannery Row. The proprietor was quite amused when we rolled in the stroller, and told us that Ali could eat for free. Ali was quite excited by the idea that she would get to eat "fishies" just like she had seen the larger creatures, especially the sea lions, do at the Aquarium. The sushi came around on plates mounted on trays of cute little plastic sea otters and brought to the table on motorized trestles. Ali would simply point to what she wanted next — raw tuna, shrimp, fish eggs, black cod, octopus, eel — all of them completely new to

.ne new to us, too. To the bemusement of the proprietor, Ali out-
.>th. Fortunately for us, he was not at all unhappy to see the three of
..casionally come back. Now, whenever she has to bring food along
..cause a choir rehearsal is scheduled to run late or has to fit dinner in while
traveling between two activities, Ali's inevitable first choice will be a box of
sushi. And she has even managed to entice some of her fellow choir members, all in their teens and preteens, to give it a try.

———————◆◆◆———————

"Sushi? That seems like quite a sophisticated taste, especially for one so
young." This might or might not be true, depending on one's perspective.
I'm sure one wouldn't make the same statement if my kids grew up in Japan.
However, one might be tempted to make a similar pronouncement,
metaphorically speaking, about my kids' interests in wildlife biology, theater
arts, telescope-making, or high-level piano performance. So the question to
be raised is how did Ali and Meera develop such enlightened palettes, strong
enough to impel their desire for further learning?

Well, as is often said, there's no accounting for tastes. Ali could simply have decided she didn't like raw fish, much as she doesn't like running
the videotape player. Meera could have decided she didn't like playing the
piano, much as she has no urge to read books until it is at least 8:30 in the
evening, if then. Some of these tastes, for all I am aware, might be inborn
traits and tendencies being expressed. Others might be stage-specific: what
one child doesn't like now, she might love at some future time. We've been
able to provide opportunities for some of these tastes to develop. To others,
given our own limited experience, partialities, and energy, they've never had
any exposure which might have provided the occasion for taste expression.

But what I can say with some certainty is that my kids are prepared
to encounter the new and unknown because they can do so from a supportive, safe, and secure space, free from age-appropriate expectations or messages, and we are open to what their journeys may bring. When I brought
Ali to sit next to me at choir practice, I had no inkling that within six
months she'd end up in Carnegie Hall; I didn't even expect she'd be singing

with me! When Meera disappeared over to Evelyn's house and came back with cookies, it never occurred to us that she'd be playing Bach *Inventions* fluently at age six. Ellen and I do experience our kids as 'precocious,' but only when we are forced by the surrounding culture to see them in relationship to other children. In the same context, we are also reminded how very 'normal' they seem 'for their ages,' be it in minor infatuations with Beanie Babies (though I've met more than a few 35-year-old women with greater obsessions), in fondness for bad jokes (you should hear my coworkers sometimes), or in their general unwillingness to clean their rooms (mine is not a whole lot better). But outside of the comparative framework, we simply see our kids as who they really are: interesting, unique, creative, joyful human beings who pursue their quests for knowledge in ways we never would have imagined and who invite us to join in the dance.

———•◆•———

A blight never does good to a tree & if a blight kill not a tree but it still bear fruit, let none say the fruit was in consequence of the blight.

William Blake, "Letter to William Hayley, October 7, 1803"

More than a decade ago, the late John Holt suggested in his posthumously published book *Learning All the Time* that organized education is dominated by three misleading metaphors, the first being that of the cannery. The metaphor expresses public education's late nineteenth/early twentieth-century industrial design, one that has changed little since I was in school in the 1950s and '60s. The 'empty' cans are mounted on conveyor belts where they are transported from station to station, class to class, grade to grade, and school to school. At each station, preset curricula are poured into each of the cans. For quality control purposes, each is tested for leakage at various predetermined points on the line. Significant leakage at any point is thought to affect the quality of the final product. Cans that leak repeatedly, or have been dented, are taken offline either to be repaired or remaindered. If customers become dissatisfied with the final product, different curricula can be substituted, pouring mechanisms updated or replaced, the speed of the belt adjusted, various 'spices' added or subtracted, and increased quality control procedures established, usually in the form of more standardized testing. Aggregate results of the various conveyor lines are compared against each other, but with almost no thought given to the possibility that there is something inherently inadequate with the entire design.

The point of the analogy is not to ridicule public education nor to demean the efforts of well-meaning professionals — schoolteachers and administrators alike — who have dedicated their careers to the care of children. The purpose rather is to understand the paradigm within which children's own wisdom must struggle, sometimes mightily, to express itself.

At the core of this Cannery Row lies a decision to group children according to their chronological age. This is an administrative decision rather than an educational one. It was made without regard to any individual child's interests, capacities, achievements, or desires. What matters is the rate at which various preset curricula can be poured into the child as she makes her way down the line.

This reality is so obvious it easily overlooked in the public debates about education. Future schoolteachers who attend graduate programs in education are instructed in the techniques and strategies to operate 'on the line.' The line itself is a given. They are taught to develop lesson plans and activities and strategies, to choose curricula (if they are even given a choice), and to administer standardized tests without having ever met a single child they are assigned to teach. Indeed, a certificate or degree certifying these techniques and strategies have been learned may be the only real qualification a teacher has.

But there is a problem. Schoolteachers, like so many of us who love and honor children, know too much. Deep in their hearts they know that children are not empty vessels. They witness daily the uniqueness and wisdom of individual children struggling to break free, and those who are more aware understand how this uniqueness is crushed under the pressing burdens of 'education.' Left to their own devices, many, like John Holt, would subvert the dominant paradigm. And in their own little ways, in the ways which make some of them gifted teachers, they do just that.

So along with the turn-of-the-century industrial design, a theory, really only the pretense of one, a construct, a way of thinking, is needed to reinforce belief in the necessity of this administrative approach. And this is where child development theory comes in. While we have learned much from child development experts in this century — especially from cultural anthropologists who study children — their work or, more commonly, just their language is misappropriated and misused in setting educational standards for what is to be considered 'age appropriate' within arbitrarily created classroom settings. In so doing,educators reinforce the conspiracy to suppress curiosity, information gathering, and independence and to actively curtail and control the child's capacity to learn. The *modus operandi* of the conspiracy is simple: focus as narrowly upon data retrieval and symbolic manipulation as possible, keep information away from children, and suppress their curiosity and their knowledge quests until an outside authority decides they are 'ready' for whatever the curriculum demands. In a paradoxical twist, as children approach adulthood toward the end of the line, the pouring in of curricula is calibrated down to the minute of each and every day. Children who 'leak' too much are to be punished: with extra homework, afterschool tutoring, parent-teacher conferences, and ever-present threats of being dropped from their arbitrary chronological peer group. Precociousness (which is, after all, only a social construct) must similarly be kept in check. The first and most important lesson children must learn in school is passivity. The cans on the line are not to express any of their own desires, for, as an institutional matter, it is denied that they have any. Schoolteachers use all the behavior modification resources at their disposal, up to and including mind-altering drugs, to reinforce this basic lesson, without which the line cannot operate efficiently. And make no mistake: it is a conspiracy, for it is executed without any understanding, input, or informed consent on the part of the kids themselves.

For it to be allowed to function, society too must embrace the idea behind Cannery Row, namely that chronological age can and should be the sole variable for educational and social groups to further an individual child's learning. This idea is reified through enormous expenditures on educational testing, the Holy Grail of education professionals.

Sometimes, one can even glimpse a thread of the conspiracy being executed as it winds its way through the tests themselves. I recently had occasion to peruse the California Achievement Test-5th Edition for third graders, where the following mathematics computation problem appeared:

$6 \div 5 =$

- *1 R 1*
- *11*
- *1 R 5*
- *1*
- *None of these*

The sole answer acceptable to California education authorities, who administer several million of these tests each year, is "1 R 1." But putting aside the fact that "R" (for 'remainder') is by no means a commonly accepted mathematical term and would only be known by children specifically taught using it, "None of these" is truly the only correct answer. I know more than a few nine-year-olds who would vigorously insist that the solution to the problem is either 6/5, 1 1/5, or 1.2, none of which appears among the choices. Any child choosing "None of these" on that basis would be punished by being adjudged inferior to her peers, as might her teacher, and even her school or school district once the results were published in the newspaper. The singular method by which the teacher could succeed is by conspiring to ensure the child suppresses the correct answer in favor of the only 'educationally acceptable' one.

The reason we see educational testing proliferating so quickly is that the system fails far too often, and we all know it. The emperor has no clothes. Administrators hope, against all evidence, that by micromanaging the line through testing, confidence in the enterprise can be increased. Now, not only are children compared with each other, but schools pitted against schools, and entire systems against systems. We are all taught to want to know how our kids measure up, but only against kids of exactly the same age and controlled experience, and only at skills related to data retrieval and symbolic manipulation, a bare fraction of a child's true humanity in the present moment or her human potential.

Knowing how our kids measure up is, ultimately, no substitute for knowing, really knowing, our kids, and for our kids to know themselves. We all know, deeply we know, our kids have taught us to know, that there is no substitute for mentoring, for role models, and for listening and understanding and respecting the needs and aspirations and unique wisdom of individual children, and for finding ways for children to act upon them. Inevitably, when we hear about a public education success story, it is because a teacher, somewhere along the line, took it upon herself to ignore the demands of Cannery Row so as to minister to the innate gifts, talents, or curiosity of particular children. Those of us who have had such experiences were blessed and will cherish them always. Sadly, too many of us, and our children, will never have such experiences at all.

When I was eight years old, my parents sent me away to a summer camp meant mostly for children living in New York's inner city. I remember feeling lonely and somewhat lost. Among the few items I brought with me along with my clothing was a book about stars, a gift from my father who knew absolutely nothing about, and exhibited no particular interest in, astronomy. I'd never really even looked up before. But a junior counselor, not my own either, by the name of Armand Berliner — a name I still recollect some 40 years later — noticed me with the book one afternoon. In the evening, after lights were out and campers asleep, he snuck me out of bed for a look through his telescope. But it wasn't the view through the telescope that I recall (I can't), but rather the excitement of being invited to approach the secrets of the night sky. And the stars! There were thousands and thousands of them, more than I could ever have imagined from my home on a well-lit New York street — and there they were, right there, they were there, *for me*. Until Ali reawakened it, I never did pursue an interest in astronomy, but I carry the memory of that experience around with me as a talisman, an undeviating reminder of the wonder of childhood and of my optimal and to-be-treasured role, as parent and as teacher, within it.

To see a World in a Grain of Sand
And a Heaven in a Wild Flower,
Hold Infinity in the palm of your hand
And Eternity in an hour.

William Blake, "Auguries of Innocence"

Recent debates in the media about educational paradigms focus on what we are seeking to impart to our children: process or content. My more progressive friends tend to emphasize the role of schools in imparting thinking skills. Many schoolteachers flatter themselves into believing that this is what they are doing, even if it lacks articulation in either curriculum or actual practice. The general notion is that by teachers teaching thinking skills, children will be able to apply them in a host of subject areas and be better 'prepared for life' (as if they were not already alive). This pedagogical ideology, which is clung to by schoolteachers and has been dominant in the U.S. since the 1930s, is nonetheless hampered by difficulty in evaluating either the teaching or the learning of thinking skills, and, more specifically, in tailoring such evaluation to an administrative structure of age-bound classes.

Partially in reaction to this difficulty and to the vagueness of this whole approach, some generally more politically conservative thinkers have promoted a reversion to curricula that are highly content-specific. E. D. Hirsch's books of lists of what every child needs to know at different grade levels is a crude popularization of this notion. Administrators tend to like this approach as children, as well as teachers, can more easily be held accountable to specific, quantifiable learning goals. Schoolteachers, most of whom have been trained in the more progressive approaches, may chafe at this accountability. The more critical debate, which quickly takes on highly charged and sometimes racist overtones, is over what the content should actually be and whether requirements should be set at the national, state, or local level.

We experienced the barest edge of how the scholastic content-driven approach plays itself out. When Ali turned nine, we gave her the

Metropolitan Achievement Test for students completing fifth grade, as a way of meeting a state homeschooling requirement, and also hoping, against all of our previous experience and better judgment, to perhaps find out something we could use in our education process. We didn't even consider giving her the one for her erstwhile grade level, as we expected she'd do so well we wouldn't learn anything. Ali scored extremely high — post-high school level in four of eight areas and from two to nine years higher in the others — but we already knew she'd do that well.

For us, the experience was a bust (though for the most part, Ali enjoyed the test-taking). We learned Ali knew nothing about baseball and couldn't care less (the example used for the reading comprehension section was about the national pastime). We also found out that, in 1997, national testing experts were still incredibly historically myopic. One of the few social studies questions Ali got wrong was, "The early explorers coming to the New World were looking for _____ (fill in the blank)." After looking at the multiple choice options, Ali put in "silk." The testmakers, trained at our nation's leading graduate schools, would only accept "gold." "Columbus was looking for a trade route to India and China to trade for silk and spices, right?" asked Ali after finishing the test. Of course, and, as she already knew, native Americans who came over the Bering Straits land bridge were looking for land and game. The Vikings came looking for fishing grounds. The French came to hunt for souls and beaver pelts. The English came looking to settle. And many of Columbus' own crew who stayed behind in the New World ('new' for whom?) were simply seeking to escape persecution under the Spanish Inquisition. Schoolteachers hoping to improve their students' test scores would be rewarded for conspiring to avoid the rich and diverse history of human migration. Instead, they would have to present children with mostly positive images of a rapacious Spanish king, to remain nonjudgmental about the murderous religious fanaticism of his wife, and perhaps to comment on the courage of a very small number of greedy and barbarous thrill-seeking adventurers. The children would then in turn be rewarded for parroting back this absurd historical misrepresentation. Caribbean natives, if they had survived and about whom nothing is taught, did meet some of the few gold seekers and would not have been so kind. In one well-documented episode, which always goes unmentioned in school texts, the natives poured hot molten gold down the throats of captured conquistadors. At any rate, Ali received no credit for her answer.

Having related all that, I would note that given the context of our own particular homeschooling practice, we lean toward the content-specific or, more accurately, a content-driven approach. This is less surprising than it might initially seem. For the most part, our children determine subject matter to be undertaken and are given a wide array from which to choose. Not all subjects have to be 'covered' at any particular point in time. Evaluation tools are used only to the extent that they might help our children reach their own learning goals and are never seen or presented as endpoints. Learning objectives are self-directed and do not have to conform to arbitrary administratively driven timelines. And we trust ourselves more than either national or local authorities to combat bias or prejudices which often become institutionalized in entrenched curricula.

The idea that one has to instruct a child in thinking skills is akin to the notion of teaching a fish to swim or a shark to feed. From the earliest age, she is an efficient learning animal. Like a shark, all her resources and senses are brought to bear toward a single end — in the case of children, self-mastery, mastery over the social and physical environment, and expression of an inborn curiosity. Barring severe and unresolved emotional or psychological trauma, organic problems or nutritional deficiencies, or insecure, unpredictable, or violent environments, the thinking skills develop of their own accord and on their own timetable. But a child who has to expend emotional energy on learning and practicing coping strategies directed at the world around her will have correspondingly less available for anything else. If one accounts for the development of coping strategies children cultivate to ward off the affronts to their way of being encountered within the school environment, it is little wonder that the education they receive is rarely much better than adequate. This is no less true for the so-called good student, whose classroom coping strategy may be to sacrifice curiosity and creativity in favor of memorization and regurgitation, than for the less successful student who rejects this stratagem in favor of other, less administratively acceptable ones.

The content our kids encounter is more than just a series of facts to be memorized. The content they choose to explore propels skill-building. Once fully assimilated, these skill areas become 'zones of competence,' take-off points for fresh explorations and new processes and skills to be learned. The facts or ideas themselves become a kind of bric-a-brac, like shells along the seashore, singular but serving as points of reference for other information as it is encountered along the way. Over time, the zones widen like ripples in a pond and, if successful, our children begin truly "To see a World in a Grain of Sand/And a Heaven in a Wild Flower."

Probably because of their precocity in this area, learning music has served as the paradigm for most of Ali's and Meera's education. We didn't plan it this way in advance, but over time our children revealed its wisdom. Elements of the paradigm include

- taking early expressions of interest seriously;
- providing the right tools and opportunities for exploration;
- finding adult mentors, and occasions to witness adults practicing the craft and making practical use of the knowledge to be gained;
- respecting the ebb and flow of interest and growth over time;
- avoiding arbitrary timeframes for mastery of particular skills or content unless explicitly agreed upon or contracted to by the children themselves;
- paying close attention to learning the language and vocabulary;
- offering history and context to the content under study and the skills being mastered;
- encouraging close attention to detail and technique, but without getting hung up on achievement of absolute perfection;
- keeping the educational menu varied, sometimes even purposely teaching items 'out of order,' and exposing the children to material which is likely to be beyond their current capabilities;
- providing training in multiple skill areas simultaneously; in the case of music, playing, musical interpretation, note and score reading, composition, listening, concert etiquette, music history, etc.
- recycling material over time, so they can see their own powers expanding, and rewarding mastery with more challenging material;

- being spare in evaluation, but absolutely honest when offering it;
- finding opportunities for their creativity and for sharing what they have learned;
- cultivating patience, both in our children and in ourselves.

From our kids' perspective, however, this is not so complicated. They learn to understand and play a particular piece of music (bric-a-brac); in doing so, they exercise particular talents and understandings and learn specific skills, techniques, and contexts, the stuff which makes them pianists or violinists, more broadly, musicians and artists, and, more peripherally, historians. But one doesn't teach a younger child to 'be' or 'think like' a musician; one teaches her to play Brahms. Specificity encourages depth and breadth. Mastering specific content nurtures both skill and self-confidence for taking on new learning adventures. And this is the point, and although it is a tricky one, it is not at all paradoxical: while specific content is presented for mastery, we do not delude ourselves, as school administrators and educational testing services would have us do, into thinking the content is more important than the child's experience in mastering it.

There are examples of bric-a-brac throughout this book, but an extended example might illustrate the power of this approach more thoroughly. As already noted, we have shied away from teaching history directly, as in our experience most young children have a difficult time with and little interest in understanding historical perspective. They could learn the lists of names and dates now, but these can just as well be picked up later whenever they are needed, provided the kids haven't been put off by some earlier learning experience. Even at an intellectually precocious nine and a half, Ali provided a telling indication of her lack of interest in historical perspective. Following a combined yard sale of homeschooling families, a friend's mother offered Ali four books left over from her own college days: a copy of Walt Whitman's *Leaves of Grass*, paperback editions of Shakespeare's *Julius Caesar* and *Measure for Measure*, and a copy of Darwin's *The Origin of Species*. After examining them carefully, Ali took the Whitman and Shakespeare, but left the Darwin. At first glance, I found this surprising, as evolutionary biology is her favorite subject and she is as well-versed in theories of punctuated equilibrium and sociobiology as most well-read college students. When I inquired why she left the Darwin behind, Ali asked back, rhetorically, why she would want to read a work which in so many ways had already been proven wrong? Ali's intellectual precocity does not mask the limits of her development. She is passionate about learning what is right, true, just, and proven as we conceive of it in the present, as well as what remains to be known with similar degrees of certainty. But she cannot yet fully appreciate the fumblings, missteps, dead-ends, and incomplete understandings which historically have helped us get where we are.

What did catch Ali's imagination and proved fruitful as an introduction to historical perspective were the works of Jules Verne. I recalled reading one of them as a child, which is why I suggested Verne to her. What I didn't expect is that within three months, Ali would read all the local library possessed, and a biography as well. What fascinated her was identifying, from reading the novels, what technologies existed and what scientists did and did not know in the mid-to-late nineteenth century, and Verne's degree of accuracy, or lack thereof, in predicting the future. *Around the World in Eighty Days* led to a study of geography, *Twenty Thousand Leagues Under the Sea* to reading Jacques Cousteau, *From Earth to the Moon* to a review of manned spaceflight. Verne's work, along with our discussions and related readings, facilitated the formation of a mental timeline for the history of scientific discovery and technological innovation.

Both kids started taking art classes at an early age, for which Ellen barters massage. Learning in the visual arts is another good example of the bric-a-brac principle, for individuals slowly but simultaneously evolve command of technique, medium, color, perspective, and ways of seeing, all of which are brought to bear in the creation of a single drawing, painting, or sculpture. Mastery of content is manifested in the expression of skills. Their enthusiastic art teacher Diane notes that a pleasure she now experiences, in stark contrast to her more than a decade's work within the public school system, is in being able to assist in unfolding, to gently guide, and to witness children's artistic development over the long-term, in Ali's case, now approaching six years.

At age nine, Ali informed us she wanted to study Latin. This did not come entirely out of the blue. Ali had encountered Latin in a variety of contexts over the years. She had learned about Latin names for animals, sung Latin texts in various masses and requiems, encountered Roman history through Shakespeare, and knew Latin was the language of Newton's *Principia*. Years earlier at a homeschool fair, Ellen had found a card game called "Rummy Roots," which requires one to memorize the meaning of various Greek and Latin words. Rummy Roots became a regular feature of family airplane trips. Ali also heard me joke about my own efforts to learn Latin, only partially successful and now almost entirely forgotten, some 25 years ago.

The study of foreign languages can be a challenge for monolingual homeschooling families, as living languages require constant and repeated verbal interactions to be learned well. While we likely would have found a way to facilitate the learning of another language had Ali so shown an interest, Latin is a good choice for homeschoolers. It informs learning in a host of other areas and is not spoken except in the most rarefied company. We came upon an excellent self-teaching program, *Artes Latinae*, which includes tapes, carefully designed grammar and reading workbooks, information on Roman history and culture, and tests which Ali has utilized as self-evaluation tools. There is even a compact disc of Elvis Presley songs performed in Latin. The publisher of *Artes Latinae* has created a homeschoolers' Latin network, complete with a list of Latin penpals (*amicus stylo*) ranging in ages from nine to 50. Working at it only 15 to 20 minutes every day, Ali has already made substantial progress.

By now, there must be readers of this book who are impatiently searching for our curriculum or at least the timelines we follow for introducing our children to various subjects. I am sorry to disappoint. We don't have, and we choose not to have, any. We have (and had) no preconceived plan as to what bric-a-brac is to be explored. Sometimes it arises directly from interests expressed by Ali or Meera that we are not able to trace. Meera at one point got so interested in horses' hoofs that Ellen found herself calling various horse farms to see whether Meera and she could come out to examine equine feet. Soon Ellen found herself bartering massage, for both horse and horse trainer, in exchange for a few riding lessons for Meera. Other times, it will arise from questions the kids ask or in the course of conversations. On still other occasions, though less often than one might think or we might have hoped for purposes of our own gratification, interest will be spurred by explicit suggestions from us, perhaps as a result of our recalling bric-a-brac we enjoyed exploring in our own childhoods. Where we as parents/mentors have been most useful to our kids has not been in choosing bric-a-brac for them, though exposure to potential choices is certainly a major part of our efforts. Rather it lies in providing a level-headed assessment for them, based on our experience and judgment, of what skills they are likely to need to master in order to access their chosen content effectively, and how and where they might acquire them.

Like many homeschooling families, we began the process of homeschooling being much more uptight about 'covering material' than we are today. Our own thinking has evolved with experience from a sense that we had to cover what might be expected in the school setting, 'only better,' to a much stronger commitment to allowing our kids to take the lead. They have gently prodded us toward appreciation of a witticism attributed to the eighteenth-century English historian Edward Gibbon: "The power of instruction is seldom of much efficacy except in those happy dispositions where it is almost superfluous." Much of the bric-a-brac that became the subjects of our kids' serious study, as well as the way it was introduced to them, emerged, or so it seems, almost by chance: wildlife ecology, reptile breeding, violin and piano playing, singing, opera, Shakespeare, Latin, the list goes on. Or perhaps it is more accurate to say that the kids have an inborn curriculum of childhood, the expression of an innate and all-embracing curiosity unfettered by someone else's preconceptions of age-or developmental appropriateness. And we do have timelines: it is time when they are ready, and they are remarkably adept at telling us when that is if only we trust in and cultivate our ability to listen.

Aware of our own prejudices,we try as best we can, not to screen experience and knowledge according to cultural ideas about their utility and worth. There will be plenty of time for that later. For now, the kids are building up their knowledge of the world, finding new linkages among the knowledge realms, and discovering joys in using the tools necessary to access them.

Meera is an athlete; to be more specific, a gymnast, and an awfully good one. She spends almost 12 hours a week at the gym and, given the opportunity, would spend more, if the number of times a day she walks through the kitchen on her hands is any indication. As both Ellen and I are neither athletes nor particularly sports-minded, it has taken some effort on our part to understand the athletic urge. It also initially struck us as somewhat intriguing that Meera would show such prowess and determination in two such disparate areas as gymnastics and piano-playing. I later heard a lecture by Robin McCabe, Chair of the University of Washington's Department of Music and a concert pianist in her own right, in which she indicated she took special interest in gymnasts who applied to the University to study piano. Besides the kinetic energy involved in their expression, McCabe noted the similarity in the discipline required for each, the breaking down of skills into discrete elements to be analyzed, practiced, mastered, and placed in a performance context. While the parallels are obvious enough, McCabe is contemplating the similarities from a distinctly adult perspective. There is a deeper reality going on for Meera, one which underlies her gymnastics skills, musical precocity, and what on the surface would seem like an unconnected interest in horse hoofs, disease processes, and artificial limbs. All are highly individualized expressions of an urge to explore, organize, and control bodily and sensory experience in the context of mastering a major piece of the inbuilt curriculum of early childhood, that is, to develop for herself a workable understanding and mastery of the physical world.

Gymnastics is not picked up like one gathers information and insight from bric-a-brac. It is necessarily sequential and resembles, or at least that's what it seems like to us, more the rote aspects of mathematics. More literally than figuratively, one needs to walk before one can run, to run before one can jump (or flip!). Even when working with a group, instructors must be aware at all times of an individual's physical readiness to take on a new skill and of the child's degree of comfort or fear. Not to do so is to put the gymnast at unnecessary risk of physical injury or emotional trauma. Would that schoolteachers took the same degree of care when teaching arithmetic, or anything else for that matter!

Meera's gymnastics team is organized by levels, according to individuals' abilities to perform specific skills of varying degrees of difficulty. She is by far the youngest at her level, but there is no stigma attached to children of any age competing at whatever level is appropriate. And because the competition is essentially 'pre-rigged' according to ability, the kids are actually competing against their own scores from meet to meet. Perhaps the most critical difference between the gymnastics academy and a public school class is that Meera gets to see, on a daily basis, the skills, accomplishments, and progress of those years ahead of her. She gets a very real demonstration of where her gymnastics education is leading should she apply herself. And now, every Tuesday morning, Meera has undertaken to help teach a toddler fitness class.

Ali is no athlete. But even without such a tangible daily demonstration, she has enough experience to have internalized how the learning building blocks can get her to where her innate curiosity and knowledge quests impel her. At the same time, she likes to have books and other materials around that she doesn't yet entirely understand. After watching a public television special on fractals and the Mandelbrot sets, she had me take out from the library all the books on the subject we could find, including those dealing with advanced calculus. Although she couldn't understand the vast bulk of the content, it took weeks before she would agree to surrender them from off her bed to be returned. "It shows me stuff to look forward to," she insists, "and, besides, just because people can't know everything doesn't mean they can't be interested in everything."

The weeping child could not be heard,
The weeping parents wept in vain;
They strip'd him to his little shirt,
And bound him in an iron chain;
And burn'd him in a holy place,
Where many had been burn'd before:
The weeping parents wept in vain,
Are such things done on Albion's shore?

William Blake, "A Little Boy Lost"
from *Songs of Experience*

Whenever I discuss our learning adventures with those who do not share a knowledge of, or commitment to, homeschooling, the conversation takes an almost inevitable twist. Once all are comfortable with the idea that my kids can function quite adequately academically ("at or ahead of grade level" will bring on the knowing nods), the "S" word, as if it had been skulking all along in a forbidding forest darkly draped in Spanish moss, like some huge, horrific toad, will suddenly leap out from among the stinging nettles and skunk cabbage to reveal its gnarled and grotesque, scarifying even if slightly ludicrous, visage. I'm not exactly sure why, as none of these same friends or acquaintances, once they have ever spent any time around my children, would ever ask me if the kids have been properly 'socialized.'

My kids are far from perfect. Or perhaps it is more accurate to say they are perfect in the way children are. They squabble, argue, and slam doors. They can be recalcitrant, whiny, overbearing, bossy, insensitive, selfish, rude, arrogant, and, though very rarely, cruel. In this way they remind me of our nation's political leaders, and, in my lesser moments, of myself. They each have their own quirks and idiosyncracies which, taken together, constitute their own unique personalities. Ali is intellectual, inward-looking and inner-directed, often impractical, creative, given to flights of fantasy, somewhat slow of speech though not shy, tending toward clumsy, cautious, and self-contained. She can get along in groups, especially when they have a set purpose or objective, but does better with a very small number of close friends or companions who pursue similar interests. Meera is brash, competitive, manipulative, extraordinarily energetic, voluble, athletic, practical, impatient, and aiming to please. She does fine with small numbers, but can shine in larger group settings.

The "S" word is the education juggernaut's endgame. Once it is demonstrably shown that what they profess to be their desired 'educational outcomes' can be measurably achieved without their blessing, expertise, or resources, the education establishment falls back upon the gambit of appealing to what is ultimately *immeasurable*, the future ability of your child to 'get along.' And socialization, which, it is asserted, can only be provided through the education monopoly, is postulated as a universal need. The result is that, no matter what you do, the homeschooling parent is presumed to have failed, unless the child, at some time in an inconveniently distant future, can prove otherwise. Would school administrators accept being judged by a similar standard? How ironic it is, too, that the appeal to the need for socialization directed at homeschoolers occurs even while public schools are quickly abandoning any pretense of commitment towards it, from eliminating recess and physical education to requiring more homework, stressing competition, and increasing commitments to expanded, purely academic testing.

The socialization issue is usually raised by schoolteachers or parents who have been inculcated with educational jargon without carefully examining what is behind it. The appeal to the need for socialization is an indirect way of asserting that without a government-sponsored or regulated institution engaged in training and enforcing civility, children are savages and act as such. Implicitly, they are a danger to each other and to the larger society. To use the nineteenth century rhetoric which arose at almost precisely the same historical moment as the public education movement, it is the "white man's burden" to civilize the "childlike" savages by stripping them of their natural instincts and turning them docile enough to do the white man's will. The task of civilizing is to be accomplished through specially designed efforts determined in the central command center (then called the "home office"), far from the targeted population. It is to be effected by divesting the savages of any semblance of control over their own affairs, denying them the right to negotiate about their living and working conditions. Rules may be set arbitrarily and standards of enforcement readily changed at whim, and there is no obligation that the savages be instructed regarding, and certainly no assumption that they must voluntarily agree to, the rules to which they, and they alone, are subject. The threat of brutal response to noncooperation or insubordination must always be present, but remains in the background and, if possible, is rarely if ever used. In contrast with the most basic tenets of the white man's jurisprudence, entire classes can be punished for the actions of individuals and without opportunity for people to say anything in their own defense, and certainly without a jury of their peers.

The analogy to this white man's burden can be taken a bit further. Subsets of the uncivilized population are to be separated from each other and treated as a 'class' based on a single and arbitrary characteristic — in this case, chronological age. Savages are denied the right to freely choose with whom they will associate. Individuality is to be systematically denied, while enough individual difference is to be permitted through encouraging competition meaningless in a larger societal context to help ensure individuals do not become fully aware of their commonalities. This circumscribed individuality is to be tolerated only to the extent that it helps stave off active, concerted revolt. The home office has ascertained that molding of the savage will is effectuated most successfully when those supervising the civilizing effort — among the lowest ranking and least respected civil servants — appear to care for the welfare of those savages placed under their 'protection.' Success can only be achieved through enforcement of the most rigorous social conformity and the complete colonization of the savage mind.

It is not my intent to trivialize the untold damage to colonized people that resulted from these 'civilizing' practices. On the contrary, we often observe damage on a similar scale inflicted upon children who, for whatever reason, are regarded as resistant to the socializing dynamo. We witness the same results among them as often exhibited by the colonized: alcoholism and drug dependency; interpersonal violence; personal isolation; failure to take responsibility for their own actions and for their own communities; lack of direction, and ease by which they can be misled; and resignation to their fate.

Of course, children need to be able to function appropriately in society. They need to learn to share, to respect each other and to respect differences, to cooperate freely, to make decisions democratically, to use their own gifts and special talents for community benefit, and, critically, to learn when it is appropriate, even imperative, to resist social and institutional pressures. But despite teachers' best intentions and efforts, the very structure of public schooling is set up to teach precisely the opposite — the curriculum of dependency, the mechanisms of manipulation, the techniques of social control and the role of deceit in resistance to it, and the expectation of lovelessness and alienation inherent in learning and relationships not freely chosen. And it is easy to observe how extraordinarily successful this instruction has been.

"But," I hear our local school district administrator insisting, "the typical child needs ..." Excuse me, but just as I have never met a typical 40-year-old white male, a typical housewife, a typical African-American, or a typical senior citizen, I have never met a "typical child." The whole concept of a typical child would be seen as insulting if it wasn't in such common usage and one of the many injuries children have learned to endure.

If we want to focus on the needs of typical children, we might do well to begin with those of *typical humans*, whose requirements include adequate food, clothing, shelter, medical care, loving and non-abusive homes, caring communities, unpolluted environments, peaceful nations, and opportunities to express individual talents through meaningful work and healthful recreation. We are far from assuring these needs for all adults, no less children, even though there is nearly universal agreement that these are the requisite underpinnings of any sound education. If we must talk about more narrowly educational needs, let's start with this one: children need to be listened to and to be provided the opportunities to take the lead in their own learning.

To be human means to be limited by the present. Within the compass of our physical selves, we will never grow beyond a determined height, run beyond a certain speed, see and hear beyond a circumscribed distance, occupy space without an atmosphere of a very particular gaseous composition, live beyond our round of years, planted as we are on a fragile orb circling a celestial ball of fire at 18 miles per second. These limitations are governed by our genetic makeup. But, and this too is part of our genetic birthright, we are relentless trackers and scouts of the infinite, searchers of the heavens, and seekers of the heart.

Among a certain East African tribe, when a woman believes it is time for her to conceive a child, she goes out from her village and sits under a tree. She waits, sometimes for days, until she is given a song. She returns to the village and teaches the song to her partner. At the birth of the baby, the song is sung by the midwife, later learned by the child's mentors and teachers, and thereafter repeated at every significant occasion in the child's life. The community is socialized to the needs, aspirations, and dreams — the song — of that particular child, who will grow to play an individual and distinct role in the community's life. Hence the song belongs to the child, and to the mother, and to the community. But it comes to all of them from within, and also from afar, as part of the heritage of humankind.

To educate a child well is to enable her to find her destiny as well as our own. This can only be accomplished successfully, I am persuaded, by allowing her to find the freedom to listen to and be exhilarated by the harmony of her own inner voices and that of the world around her so that, like Blake's schoolboy, she comes to know that "the skylark sings with me."

Artes Latinae, Bolchazy-Carducci Publishers, Inc., 1000 Brown Street, Wauconda, IL 60084; Tel: 1-800-392-6453; E-mail: Latin@bolc-haz.com Bolchazy-Carducci maintain an interesting website (www.bolchazy.com) and offer a free demo disc of their program. They also have a Latin professor on staff who is accessible by telephone to answer any questions that arise.

Gatto, John Taylor, *Dumbing Us Down: The Hidden Curriculum of Compulsory Schooling.* Philadelphia, PA and Gabriola Island, BC, Canada: New Society Publishers, 1992. A biting and unstinting analysis of public education, written by a highly decorated career New York City public schoolteacher. Gatto's critique of how children in school are required to become both emotionally and intellectually dependent is impossible to ignore.

Holt, John, *Learning All the Time.* New York, NY: Harper Collins, 1998. At once the culmination and best introduction to the work of the father of progressive homeschooling.

Kohl, Herbert, *"I Won't Learn From You" and Other Thoughts on Creative Maladjustment.* New York, NY: The New Press, 1994.

Rummy Roots Vocabulary Card Games. Eternal Hearts, 13021 NE 100th Street, Kirkland, WA 98033, Tel: 206 243-3236; website: members.tripod.com/~Eternal_Hearts/rummymoreroots.html

Lifton, Betty Jean, *The King of Children: A Biography of Janusz Korczak.* New York, NY: St. Martin's Press, 1997. An extraordinary biography of a most extraordinary man. Korczak was one of the world's first advocates of children's rights. A doctor, writer, and educator, Korczak started the first progressive orphanages in Poland and, with the children under his care, founded the first national children's newspaper. Korczak continued his orphanage in the Warsaw Ghetto following Hitler's invasion of Poland. Despite being offered his own personal freedom, on August 6, 1942, Korczak led his band of 192 children and ten adults, green flag flying high, on a two-mile walk to the train station, where they were all transported to the Treblinka death camp, never to be heard from again. Korczak spoke often of the need for a Declaration of Children's Rights as long as five decades before any such document was adopted by the United Nations. Drawing upon his work, Lifton has compiled a list of rights Korczak considered most essential. (Italics inside parentheses are quotations taken directly from Korczak's writings.)

Janusz Korczak's

DECLARATION OF CHILDREN'S RIGHTS

The child has a right to love.

The child has a right to respect. *(Why should dulled eyes, a wrinkled brow, untidy gray hair, or tired resignation command greater respect?)*

The child has the right to optimal conditions in which to grow and develop.

The child has the right to live in the present. *(Children are not people of tomorrow; they are people today.)*

The child has the right to be himself or herself. *(A child is not a lottery ticket, marked to win the main prize.)*

The child has a right to fail. *(We renounce the deceptive longing for perfect children.)*

The child has the right to be taken seriously.

The child has the right to be appreciated for what he or she is.

The child has the right to desire, to claim, to ask. *(As the years pass, the gap between adult demands and children's desires becomes progressively wider.)*

The child has the right to have secrets.

The child has the right to "a lie, a deception, a theft." *(He does not have the right to lie, deceive, steal.)*

The child has the right to respect for his possessions and budget.

The child has the right to education.

The child has the right to resist educational influence that conflicts with his or her own beliefs. *(It is fortunate for mankind that we are unable to force children to yield to assaults upon their common sense and humanity.)*

The child has the right to protest an injustice.

The child has the right to a Children's Court where he or she can judge and be judged by his or her peers.

The child has the right to be defended in a juvenile-justice court system.

The child has the right to respect for his grief. *(Even though it be for the loss of a pebble.)*

The child has the right to commune with God.

The child has the right to die prematurely. *(The mother's profound love for her child must give him the right to premature death, to ending his life cycle in only one or two springs.)*

The Fountain

"Piper, sit thee down and write
In a book, that all may read."
So he vanish'd from my sight,
And I pluck'd a hollow reed,

And I made a rural pen,
And I stain'd the water clear,
And I wrote my happy songs
Ever child may joy to hear.

William Blake, "Introduction"
from *Songs of Innocence*

Of all of our children's many gifts and chosen pursuits, the most challenging for us both to understand and to find ways to nurture has been Ali's interest in music composition. We don't know where Meera's gifted pianism comes from, but we can encourage her daily practice and listen to her almost daily improvement, find her new music, and seek performance outlets for her. We know when her practice is serious — we can hear the notes emanating from the living room.

Once Ali was past the most basic lessons in music theory, no such immediate feedback has been available to us from her composition work. We can't measure her daily or weekly progress by the number of notes written or make intelligent conversation about the problems caused by 'doubling thirds' or 'parallel fifths' or the best use of leading tones or various inversions, and it would be downright insulting for us to demand we be allowed to hear a composition before it is finished, especially as we know we can play no role in its editing. Even when Ali offers us an aural glimpse of a work in progress, we struggle to express anything more than awe. We are clearly far out of our depth.

And so, more than any other activity in which our kids are involved, Ali's music composition work requires us to trust. We've provided the tools: musical instruments, sketch books, music paper, and a terrific teacher. With saved-up birthday money from grandparents and her violin earnings, Ali bought herself some composition software for the computer, which she uses to get notes to paper more efficiently than her pencil. We work with her to schedule blocks of undisturbed quiet time, an absolute necessity for creativity to flourish and a difficult habit for most children, or adults for that matter, to acquire. And then it is our job to get out of the way.

We seek opportunities for Ali to receive informed feedback about her work. Ellen came upon two young composers' competitions, which provide adjudicators' comments. The competitions also proved helpful as Ali could use the annual deadlines for submission as distant target dates for completing pieces. While Ali, unlike her sister, is utterly noncompetitive by nature, we were nonetheless very proud when her first two submissions — a wedding song, and a four-movement sonata for violin and piano — were honored with awards by the Washington State Music Teachers Association and she was invited to perform at the joint Washington-Oregon Music Teachers Association Convention. She was one of only two statewide double award winners. The wedding song had actually been composed as a gift for Ali's art teacher, Diane, at whose wedding Ali performed it and presented the couple with a framed signed copy. The sonata received its world premiere in Olympia and at Seattle's Frye Art Museum Auditorium around the time of her tenth birthday.

Although her composition work may be the most difficult for us as parents, my intuition tells me that of all Ali's current learning activities, it may prove the most important for her overall development, regardless of her future educational or vocational directions. It requires a careful amalgamation of persistence, meticulousness, and creativity. Music composition perhaps best exemplifies what homeschooling can afford our children and what they could never experience in a school context, embodying the poet Shelley's maxim that we must learn to imagine that which we know. This, above all, requires time: time in solitude, time peering out the window at nothing in particular, time staring at a blank page, time daydreaming, time taking a long walk when one feels called, *wasted time*. The demands of school administrators to cover material belie the simple truth that real knowledge can only make its appearance out of a disciplined emptiness.

Music composition provides perhaps the best example of the bric-a-brac principle in action. In each new piece of work, Ali makes use of her expanding knowledge of the language of music, her increased understanding of the basic raw materials. She builds upon whatever music she has previously written as well as upon feedback she receives from her teachers. She is influenced by other music she has heard or studied or performed, even if the influence is not always conscious. And she finds inspiration in nature, or from that unnamed and unnameable fountain from whence all creativity ultimately springs. All this and more is contained in the final product which, once completed, becomes bric-a-brac for future compositional processes. Ali describes it this way: "Writing music is like incubating a bird's egg. You can stop incubating it and it won't hatch, but once it hatches you can't control it anymore. Once I'm finished composing a piece, it lives on its own."

Nathan, Ali's composition teacher, asked her to write a stanza of a poem so she could learn to set it in four-part harmony. After a week of procrastination and overtly avoiding the task, Ali sat down at the computer, and out poured the following:

> When I go down to the river,
> When I go down to the stream,
> I hear some music,
> The horns choose it,
> The horns are the water and frogs.
> Far-rar-ree-yarah,

Far-rar-ree-yarah,
Far-rar-ree-yarah-no.

When I go down to the forest,
When I go down to the wood,
I hear some music,
The singers choose it,
The singers are trees and the birds.
Fee, fal-lee-yah,
Fal-lee-yah,
Fal-la-kye-lo.

When I go down to the ocean,
When I go down to the sea,
I hear some music,
The drummers choose it,
The drummers are fish and the waves.
Tum-da-dee-dum-ta,
Tum-da-dee-dum-ta,
Tum-da-dee-dum-ta-do.

When I go down to the cavern,
When I go down to the cave,
I hear some music,
The violinists choose it,
The violinists are echoes and bats.
Ee-nar-ree,
Ee-nar-ree,
Ee-nar-rye-lee-o.

When I go down to the meadow,
When I go down to the field,
I hear some music,
The dancers choose it,
The dancers are butt'rflies and bees.

Ah-mara-lye-ah,
Ah-mara-lye-ah,
Ah-lee-ah-nahn-no.

When I go up to the mountain,
When I go up to the hill,
I hear some music,
The flutists choose it,
The flutists are stones and the wind.
Lee-mee-arah,
Lee-mee-arah,
Lee-mee-arah, lo.

When I go down to my own street,
When I go down to the road,
I hear some music,
The cellists choose it,
The cellists are cats and the dogs.
Om-ba-rah,
Om-ba-rah,
Om-bee-ar-ah, no.

When I walk around this planet,
When I walk around the earth,
I hear some music,
The musicians choose it,
The musicians are you and me.

The musicians are you and me,
Flowers and bees,
Dogs and cats, bears and bats,
A symphony of harmony:
Life is the music of the earth.

Luvmour, Josette & Sambhava, *Natural Learning Rhythms: How and When Children Learn*. Berkeley, CA: Celestial Arts, 1997. A wise and gentle book, full of insights and approaches that parents and others will find easy to apply. Readers will find themselves going "Aha!" as their own observations are confirmed from a broader, empirical, and empathetic perspective. The Luvmours run EnCompass — The Center for Natural Learning Rhythms in Nevada City, California, offering workshops in natural learning rhythms, cooperative games, and ritual rites of passage, as well as family camps and retreats. For more information, write: EnCompass, 11011 Tyler Foote Road, Nevada City, CA 95959-9309. Tel: 1-800-200-1107; E-mail: connection@encompass nlr.org or check out their website at www.encompass-nlr.org

Pearce, Joseph Chilton, *Magical Child*. New York, NY: Penguin Books USA Inc., 1992. Now two decades old, this is a profound and caring work, elucidating the wonder which is the child from the earliest age, as a learning animal and creative spirit. Recent brain research confirms much of what Pearce contended in the mid-1970s but was then only accepted as conjecture.

Youth of delight, come hither,
And see the opening morn,
Image of truth new born,
Doubt is fled, & clouds of reason,
Dark disputes & artful teazing.
Folly is an endless maze,
Tangled roots perplex her ways.
How many have fallen there!
They stumble all night over bones of the dead,
And feel they know not what but care,
And wish to lead others, when they should be led.

William Blake, "The Voice of the Ancient Bard"
from *Songs of Experience*

About the Author

David H. Albert holds degrees from Williams College, Oxford University, and the Committee on Social Thought, University of Chicago, but says the best education he has ever received he gets from his kids.

David is one of the original founders of New Society Publishers and a founding member of Co-op America and the National Association of Socially Responsible Businesses. When he is not learning with his kids, writing, playing music instruments or singing, he serves as Senior Planning and Policy Analyst for the Washington State Division of Alcohol and Substance Abuse.

David, his partner Ellen, and his daughters Aliyah (now age 12), and Meera (age 9), live in Olympia, Washington where they are active members of Olympia Friends Meeting (Quakers).

David can be reached and invites comments from readers through his website at: www.skylarksings.com

Get A FREE copy of John Holt's Bookstore!

To learn more about homeschooling
and interest-initiated learning,
request your free catalog by contacting us:

Holt Associates/*Growing Without Schooling*
2380 Massachusetts Ave. Suite 104-S
Cambridge, MA 02140-1226
(617) 864-3100

HYPERLINK "http://www.holtgws.com/" www.holtgws.com

If you have enjoyed *And the skylark sings with me* you may also enjoy our other Educational & Parenting titles, including:

▶ Boys Will Be Men: Raising Our Sons for Courage, Caring and Community, *Paul Kivel*

240 pp.   Pb US$16.95 / CAN$19.95   0-86571-395-2

▶ Daughters of the Moon, Sisters of the Sun: Young Women and Mentors on the Transition to Womanhood, *K. Wind Hughes & Linda Wolf*

240 pp.   Pb US$19.95 / CAN$24.95   0-86571-377-4

▶ Deschooling Our Lives, *Edited by Matt Hern*

160 pp.   Pb US$14.95 0-86571-165-8 / CAN$17.95   1-55092-035-9

▶ Dumbing Us Down: The Hidden Curriculum of Compulsory Schooling, *John Taylor Gatto*

128 pp.   Pb US$9.95 0-86571-231-X / CAN$11.95   1-55092-175-4

Call 800-567-6772 for a full catalog
or check out our catalog on-line: www.newsociety.com

NEW SOCIETY PUBLISHERS